新时代商务英语专业本科系列教材
New Era Business English Series

总主编/翁凤翔　郭桂杭

Principles of Marketing

市场营销原理

主　编/温　纯

参　编/程佳雪　黄宇芝

　　　陈莹婷　初　源

重庆大学出版社

图书在版编目（CIP）数据

市场营销原理 ：英文／温纯主编. --重庆: 重庆大
学出版社, 2022.8
新时代商务英语专业本科系列教材
ISBN 978-7-5689-3339-1

I. ①市⋯ II. ①温⋯ III. ①市场营销—高等学
校—教材—英文 IV. ①F713.50

中国版本图书馆CIP数据核字（2022）第095606号

市场营销原理
Principles of Marketing
主编 温 纯

责任编辑: 陈 亮　　版式设计: 牟 妮
责任校对: 刘志刚　　责任印制: 赵 晟

*

重庆大学出版社出版发行
出版人：饶帮华
社址:重庆市沙坪坝区大学城西路21号
邮编:401331
电话：（023）88617190　88617185（中小学）
传真：（023）88617186　88617166
网址：http://www.cqup.com.cn
邮箱：fxk@cqup.com.cn（营销中心）
全国新华书店经销
POD:重庆新生代彩印技术有限公司

*

开本：890mm×1240mm　1/16　印张：14　字数：530千
2022年8月第1版　2022年8月第1次印刷
ISBN 978-7-5689-3339-1　定价：57.00元

序

十二年前，温纯从广东外语外贸大学英语（国际贸易）专业毕业，来到对外经济贸易大学攻读硕士研究生学位，在本人指导下开展翻译研究和实践。两年后她顺利毕业，到号称中国翻译行业的"国家队"的中国对外翻译有限公司（简称"中译公司"）从事金融翻译。在中译公司两年的高强度专职翻译经历，不仅使她的中英双语转换能力得到极大提高，也磨练了她做枯燥的案头工作的耐心和毅力。

2013 年，她到广州城市理工学院（原华南理工大学广州学院）当起了英语教师。到目前为止，她在教师这个岗位上已经坚持了八年。在这八年期间，她坚持理论结合实践，把教学融入科研，深耕商务英语教学领域。通过不断的教课、自学和培训进修，她的教学水平与语言能力不断提高。与此同时，她继续从事财经翻译，在为各类顶级机构客户高级别文件的双语互译中，她不仅锻炼了翻译能力，也丰富了在经贸往来、市场运行、企业运营管理方面的知识。

年前获知她主编的教材 *Principles of Marketing* 即将付梓，作为她曾经的导师，我为她的不懈努力和不断成长感到高兴。本书作为面向应用型本科英语和商务英语专业的市场营销基础课程类教材，语言简洁平实，内容与时俱进，关注中国国情、市场和企业的最新情况，课后习题设置丰富多样。这本小小的教材，是她过去一年的心血，更是她多年实践积累的成果。希望该教材能够为大学专业英语教学领域添砖加瓦，锦上添花。

王恩冕

2022 年 1 月 20 日于惠园

前 言

2021年初，编者接到学院下达的编写用于市场营销课程的教材的任务。一开始编者心里慌慌不安：市面上已经那么多外国引进的英文原版教材，中国高校教师编写的英文教材也为数不少，为什么我们还要编写这样一本教材呢？我们要编写一本什么样的教材呢？如何才能更好地满足我们的目标对象——应用型本科高校商务英语专业学生的需求呢？

目前，本科院校商务英语专业的全英或双语授课的营销课程采用的教材主要有两类：一是外国引进的英文原版教材，如菲利普·科特勒（Philip Kotler）的《市场营销原理》（*Principles of Marketing*）；二是国内高校教师编写的英文/双语教材，比如对外经济贸易大学的孙宁、章爱民编写的《国际市场营销》（*International Marketing*）。外国的英文原版教材主要是为管理类专业学生编写的，优点是知识架构完整清晰、内容详细具体、编写语言生动、案例丰富。但也存在一些不足：中国学生不熟悉外国市场和行业情况，给他们的理解造成了阻碍；内容过于繁芜，旁枝末节的信息过多，导致学生在阅读过程中容易失去方向；外文教材的编写者是外国人，展现的是外国视角和外国思维，极少涉及中国市场和中国企业，不利于授课教师开展课程思政，不利于培养学生的民族自豪感和自信心。第二类国内高校教师编写的英文/双语教材，由于此前教育界还没明确提出"课程思政"的概念，此类教材普遍缺乏思政育人意识和课程思政元素。

基于上述的认识，我们明确了编写思路：这本教材应该适合应用型本科商务英语专业学生语言水平和营销知识需求。鉴于学生的英语语言水平和商务知识储备，本书的编写尽可能采用规范但简洁明了的英语，重要概念和知识点有中文译注，采用比较广为人知且新近发生的案例佐证。在课程思政的引导下，编者有意识地挖掘营销知识中的思政元素，把更多的关注点放在中国国情、民族品牌和企业上。每章课后的大案例分析题均是关于中国企业，如格兰仕、青岛啤酒、OPPO手机等。本教材在市场营销基础知识的框架下，通过把中国国情和中国企业案例融入阐述，增加关于中国企业的思考分析题，提升中国元素的显性存在，有利于授课教师在教学中成功实施隐性的思政教育。

此外，外国原版英文教材多是面向经管类专业的学生而编写，课后题一般只有问答题和案例分析题。本教材的目标对象是商务英语专业的学生，除了传授营销专业知识，还需要兼顾学生英语语言水平提高的需求。针对学生的这种需求，编者精心准备了两大类课后练习题：一类是主要以语言训练为主的题目，题型丰富，有选择题、选词填空题、翻译题等；一类是以巩固专业知识为主的题目，有简答题、判断题、案例分析题等。另外，为了锻炼学生的团队合作能力、数据收集整理能力、综合分析和创新思维能力，每章均配有综合性的大任务，教师可组织学生以小组形式开展活动。

本书由温纯主编，编写了第1、2、3、5、6、9章，编译了第5、6、7、9、10章的课后案例分析题，负责全书的整合和审校。黄宇芝编写了第4、7、8章；陈莹婷编写了第10章及该章的译注；程佳雪编写了所有章节的课后练习题目，编译了第1、2、3、4、8章的课后案例分析题；初源负责除第10章之外的所有章节的文内译注及术语表的整理。

本书在编写过程中参考了大量的著作、报刊和网络资料，我们在此向所有的作者表示诚挚的谢意。由于时间仓促，加之编者水平有限，错漏和不足之处在所难免，恳请专家、学者和广大读者批改指正。

温纯

2022年1月23日

Contents

Chapter Five Segmentation, Targeting, Positioning and Differentiation

Chapter Six Products, Services and Brands

Chapter Seven Pricing

Glossary

Chapter One
The Nature of Marketing

Objectives:

After studying this chapter, you should be able to:

- Define "marketing" and understand the three key components of the marketing concept;
- Master the core concepts related to marketing;
- Identify the key features of a market-oriented business;
- Name the elements of marketing mix;
- Know about the new marketing trends.

Framework

Chapter One The Nature of Marketing

What is marketing?

- Definition
- Key components
- Scope of marketing
- The marketing process

The core concepts on marketing

- Customer needs, wants and demands
- Marketing offerings
- Customer value and customer satisfaction
- Long-term profitable relationship with customers

Market-oriented business

Marketing mix

New marketing concepts

- Societal marketing
- Green marketing
- Relationship marketing
- Internet marketing

Businesses succeed and fail for many reasons. But a close examination on those successful businesses often reveals that marketing is central to business success. This chapter focuses on exploring what is marketing, what is important to marketing, what is a market-oriented enterprise, what can be included into the scope of marketing and what is happening in the field of marketing.

1. What is marketing?

Peter Drucker, a top management consultant, once stated: "Because the purpose of business is to create and keep customers, it has only two central functions—marketing and innovation. The basic function of marketing is to attract and retain customers at a profit."

What does the statement tell us? Marketing is central to the success of a business as its basic function is to attract and retain customers, and the importance of customers to marketing can never be overstated. As Wal-Mart founder Sam Walton once asserted: "There is only one boss. The customer. And he can fire everybody in the company from the chairman on down, simply by spending his money somewhere else."

田 市场营销是企业成功的关键，其基本功能是吸引和留住顾客，顾客对于市场营销的重要性毋庸置疑。

Business success or failure is related to various external and internal factors, but very often marketing is the key to the outcome, as marketing focuses on customers and their needs. The failure of many businesses can often be attributed to their lack of attention to customer needs.

A case in point is Nokia. Nokia used to be a worldwide market dominator of cellphones during the 1990s and the 2000s, renowned for its solidly built, good-quality feature phones. However, the brand has now completely disappeared from the market. It failed for many reasons, but the fundamental reason is that it lost track of customer needs for convenient connectivity with people, data and the outside world in this era of information.

About a decade ago, inside the backpack of many university and middle school students you could always find an e-dictionary, voice recorder or MP3 player. These used to be the necessary "tools" for language learners and were so prevalent among students, but now you just cannot see any of them. As technology advances, the needs for looking up words and for listening to English audios have been satisfied by a versatile small gadget—cellphone.

1.1 Definition

What is marketing? When marketing is mentioned, what pops up in many people's minds is often selling, advertising, business, etc. But marketing is more than selling and advertising, and marketing is not confined to business enterprises.

Philip Kotler, who is hailed as "Father of Modern Marketing", defines it as "the process by which companies create value for customers and build strong customer relationships to capture value from customers in return".

John Fahy and David Jobber express marketing as "the achievement of corporate goals through meeting and exceeding customer needs better than the competition".

The American Marketing Association defines marketing as "the activity, set of institutions and processes for creating, communicating, delivering, and exchanging offerings that have value for customers, clients, partners and society at large".

Marketing is the managing process responsible for identifying, anticipating and satisfying customer requirements profitably, according the Chartered Institute of Marketing.

Though these definitions are phrased differently with minor differences (e.g. Philip Kotler stresses the importance of "strong customer relationship" and the American Marketing Association highlights corporate responsibility for "the society at large"), they contain some common elements: creating and delivering value to customers, satisfying their needs and capturing value/profits from customers in return.

田 公司为顾客创造价值并建立牢固客户关系的过程，其目的是从顾客那里获取价值作为回报。

田 通过比竞争对手更好地满足和超越客户需求来实现企业目标。

田 为顾客、客户、合作伙伴和整个社会创造、传递、交付和交换有价值产品的活动、制度和流程。

田 营销就是管理这个识别、预测和满足客户需求以获取利润的过程。

1.2 Key components

In spite of varying definitions, the term "marketing" contains three key components: customer orientation, profit in return and integrated efforts (see Figure 1.1).

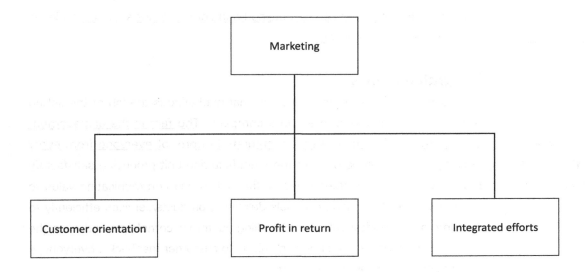

Figure 1.1 Three key components of the concept of marketing

Customer orientation

⊞ 营销的重点是通过为客户创造、沟通和提供价值来满足客户。

Marketing focuses on satisfying customers by creating, communicating and delivering value to customers. Traditional or old-fashioned businesses often have an inward look on their employees, production, products and selling. Many real-life cases have taught us if you don't take good care of customers, there is a tiny chance of long-term success.

Short video app TikTok has outstripped Youtube in terms of average watch time. Its success is by no means a coincidence, but the result of a sophisticated app tailored to the habits of today's younger generation in how they consume digital online media. Generation Z ("Gen Z") constitute the majority of TikTok users. Gen Z, typically classified as those aged between 14 and 24 (those born between the mid-to-late 1990s and the early 2010s), watch much less television than older generations, and frequently use social media, e.g. WeChat, Sina microblog, Facebook and Twitter. However, they share less personal information with such apps, but favor visual-heavy apps—TikTok is one of them. Gen Z requires instant gratification from its apps. Providing video content on demand, via bit-sized content that is less than 15 seconds long, allows the opportunity for an endless variety of content to be on display. Often unexpected and unpredictable, TikTok offers a sense of spontaneity where users can come across interesting and unique content by chance, which is enabled by sophisticated algorithms.

Profit in return

⊞ 通过满足客户，获得利润并实现企业目标。

Marketing is an exchange process. Businesses do not make all the efforts to create, communicate and deliver value to customers for nothing. It is needless to say that the existence and expansion of a business relies on profits. Where do profits come from? Of course, from customers. The management must believe that profits can be obtained and corporate goals can be achieved through satisfying customers.

Integrated efforts

⊞ 事实上，使客户满意依赖于公司各个部门的所有人的共同努力。

Many people may wrongly assume that marketing is the job of the selling or marketing team/department in a company. The fact is the achievement of customer satisfaction relies on integrated efforts of everyone from every department in a company, from the manufacturing unit producing satisfactory products that meet customer needs, the selling unit communicating value to customers, the distribution channels delivering products/services efficiently to customers to the after-sales unit handling customer complaints and even the call center receiving and responding quickly to customer feedbacks. Everyone in a company plays a part in marketing.

1.3 Scope of marketing

Marketing is everywhere. Marketing is at work from a vegetable stall at a farm produce market in your neighborhood to the world No. 1 retailer Wal-Mart. <u>Whether it is a one-person, self-employed business or a multinational with a sophisticatedly designed corporate structure, business runners have to understand the market, the customer and the competitor, produce products needed, and distribute them in a right way at the right place.</u>

People tend to assume that the application of marketing is limited to commercial settings. <u>Marketing is also applied in various fields such as non-profit, political, educational, medical institutions.</u> For example, Donald Trump's heavy use of his personal Twitter account was a big help to his surprising win at the 2016 presidential election. His campaign team clearly knew how to appeal to his "target audience" (the targeted voters) through maneuvering marketing tactics. Each year after "Gaokao" (college entrance exam in China's mainland), many institutions of higher learning host "Campus Day" and attend promotion fairs to attract perspective "customers" (students) and their parents.

⊞ 无论是个人、个体经营者还是拥有复杂企业架构的跨国公司，企业经营者都必须理解市场、顾客和竞争对手，生产迎合需求的产品，并以正确的方式将产品分销至正确的地方。

⊞ 营销还应用于非营利、政治、教育、医疗机构等各个领域。

1.4 The marketing process

Philip Kotler presents a five-step model of the marketing process (see Figure 1.2). In the first four steps, companies work to understand consumers, create customer value, and build strong customer relationships. In the final steps, companies reap the rewards of all the efforts, capturing profits from customers in return. This simple mode of the marketing process manifests customer orientation and capture of profits in return, which require integrated efforts in an institution.

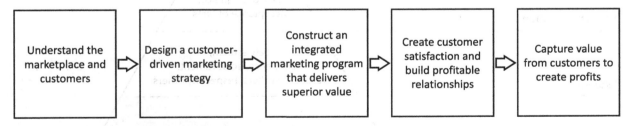

Figure 1.2 A simple model of the marketing process

2. The core concepts on marketing

This section discusses several concepts that are important to marketing. Firstly, customer needs, wants and demands must be differentiated as the distinction is of great marketing importance. Secondly, marketing offering is not limited to physical goods only, but a whole combination of products, services, experiences, people, environment and others that can deliver value to customers. Thirdly, as customer value and satisfaction are intensively referred to, it is natural to discuss how to achieve them. Lastly, organizations that regard customers as their equities strive to establish long-term profitable relationship with customers.

2.1 Customer needs, wants and demands

Needs

田 人类需要是感觉到的缺乏某种东西的状态。心理学家亚伯拉罕·马斯洛提出了五个层次的需要金字塔：生理需要、安全需要、归属感和被爱的需要、受到尊重的需要和自我实现的需要。

田 营销可以致力于满足任何层次的人类需要。

Human needs are the states of felt deprivation. Psychologist Abraham Maslow put forth a hierarchy of five levels: physiological needs, safety, love/belonging, esteem and self-actualization (see Figure 1.3). Though Maslow created the hierarchy as a way of representing different types of psychological needs and in which order he thought they should be met, our human brains are so complex that it does not say that we can only reach a higher level of needs once the lower levels are satisfied. This means that if we have not obtained one level of needs, that will be our primary motivation, but we can also aim to satisfy higher levels at the same time. Marketing can work on satisfying any level(s) of human needs.

We need foods and drinks to satisfy the physiological level, an apartment of our own to feel safe, a job or club membership to feel that we belong to certain groups, lipsticks and perfumes to feel good about ourselves, and participation in social causes for self-actualization.

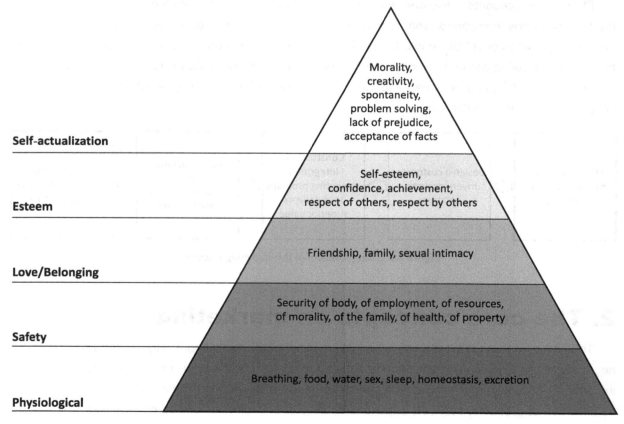

Figure 1.3 Maslow's hierarchy of needs

Wants

Wants are the form human needs take as they are shaped by culture and individual personality. Everyone needs food when he is hungry, but an American may want a hamburger, a Chinese from southern provinces may want a bowl of rice and his countryman from northern part of China probably wants noodles. As social creatures, people need to be connected with each other, most people in China rely heavily on WeChat and Sina microblog, and foreigners use Whatsapp, Facebook, Twitter and Instagram. There may not be much to do with human needs for marketers, but wants provide opportunities for them. Through studying how cultural and personal factors may influence the form of human needs, businesses can develop offerings that better satisfy consumers' needs and wants.

田 欲求是在文化和个体因素共同影响下的人类需要的表现形式。

Demands

When backed by buying power, wants become demands. With wants and resources, people demand products that provide them value and satisfaction. It is a human nature that people want nice things, like, a well-furnished villa, but not everyone can afford one. Without buying power, this part of wants cannot covert into demands.

田 有购买力支持的欲求就成为需求。

田 若无购买力的支持，这部分欲求则无法转换成需求。

2.2 Marketing offerings

Product is not the only form in which companies deliver value to customers. Instead, a marketing offering is a combination of products, services, information, experiences, environments, persons, ideas and other things that can satisfy customer needs or wants. People are willing to pay Starbucks a premium price for a cup of coffee because of not only the good taste of its coffee, but also a good environment where people can talk with friends, coworkers or business partners, or bury themselves in work. Similarly, money spent on having a meal in a Haidilao restaurant is not just for the food and drink, but also for the cordial and meticulous services provided by the staff, which may be valued even more by some customers.

田 营销提供产品、服务、信息、体验、环境、人员、想法以及其他可以满足客户需要或欲求的任何事物。

2.3 Customer value and customer satisfaction

Customer value

One of the basic functions of marketing is to create and deliver customer value. But how can a firm know if it is creating such value? After all, it is the customer, not the company that defines what represents value. Thus, value must be defined from the perspective of customers.

Customer value = Perceived benefits − Perceived sacrifices

田 客户价值 = 感知收益 − 感知成本

Table 1.1 Various forms of benefits and sacrifices

Benefits	Sacrifices
● product	● money
● service	● time
● experience	● energy
● information	● psychological cost
● idea	● emotional cost
● environment	● opportunity cost
● ...	● ...

Benefits are materialized through marketing offerings, which comprise not only products, but also services, experiences, information and other things valuable to customers. Sacrifices include not only the money customers pay for the marketing offering, but also the time, energy, psychological cost, opportunity cost and the like (see Table 1.1). That to some extent explains why instant coffee sold at a convenience store near a subway station is also good value for money, in spite of its less satisfactory taste, because the convenient location saves people time and energy to get their drink.

⊞ 当顾客感知到的价值达到或超过他们的期望时，他们就会感到满意。

⊞ 客户满意度 = 感知价值 − 期望价值

Customer satisfaction

Customer satisfaction depends on the product's perceived performance relative to a buyer's expectations—in other words, <u>customers are satisfied when their expectations are met or exceeded by perceived values</u>.

<u>Customer satisfaction = Perceived value − Expected value</u>

It is not hard to tell from this equation that it is not wise for businesses to overstate their offering in advertisements, because once customer expectations are raised to an unreasonably high level and the offering fails to meet the expectations, the predictable consequence would be customer dissatisfaction. There is little chance that dissatisfied customers will turn into regular customers.

The second inspiration from this equation is that provision of value unexpected by customers can always create customer satisfaction. For example, customers buying a high-speed railway ticket will not be delighted at the train's taking them to the destination on time, because timeliness is the basic—if not minimum— characteristic they expected when buying the ticket. On the contrary, unexpected characteristics can often surprise customers and thus lead to their satisfaction. The free manicure provided by Haidilao for waiting customers is a contributing factor of customer satisfaction.

2.4 Long-term profitable relationship with customers

Customer relationship management (CRM) is an important concept in modern marketing. CRM involves building and maintaining profitable customer relationships by delivering superior customer value and satisfaction. It deals with all aspects of acquiring, keeping and growing customers.

⊞ 客户关系管理就是通过为客户提供卓越的价值和使客户满意来建立和维持具有营利性的客户关系。

When the customer finds a good-quality product/service provider, they may be willing to stay with this provider, and as the relationship builds a high level of trust, it becomes established. It is not hard to see that in business it is more difficult and costly to capture new customers than to maintain existing ones. Thus, properly managing relationships with existing customers is a big part of CRM.

A core concept is relevant to customer relationship management, that is, customer equity. Customer equity refers to the combined customer lifetime values of all of a company's current and potential customers. Customers, existing and prospective customers, should be regarded as a company's equity, as lifetime value of a customer is recognition by the company of the potential sales, profits and endorsements that come from a repeat customer who stays with company for several years.

⊞ 客户资产是指公司所有现有顾客和潜在顾客终身所带来的价值的总和。

3. Market-oriented business

Market-oriented/Market-driven/Market-led businesses often ask themselves such questions as: What is our business? Who is the customer? What do customers want and value? How could we satisfy that want and deliver that value? Market-oriented firms are customer-oriented, in contrast to internally oriented businesses with a focus on production, products, or selling. Table 1.2 shows differences between these two types of organizations (see Table 1.2).

Table 1.2 Marketing-oriented businesses vs internally oriented businesses

Market-oriented businesses	Internally oriented businesses
Customer concern throughout business	Convenience or usual practice comes first
Know customer choice criteria and match them with desirable marketing mix	Assume that price and product are key to selling
Segment by customer differences	Segment by product
Invest in market research and track market changes	Reply on past experience
Embrace change	Cherish status quo
Try to keep up with competition	Ignore competition
Value marketing	Think little of marketing
Search for niche markets	Stick with the same segment
Strive for competitive advantage	Happy to stay where it is

Unlike traditional firms doing business from the inside out, market-oriented businesses adopt an outside-in approach. To win customers from competitors and maintain existing customers, they first start with understanding customers and the market. This is usually achieved through market research and analysis. With a good understanding of target customers, they create products/services that meet needs now and in the future, and design an integrated marketing plan (see Figure 1.4).

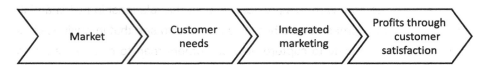

Figure 1.4 Marketing orientation

4. Marketing mix

⊞ 营销组合包括产品、价格、地点和促销。

In 1960, Jerome McCarthy put forward the concept of "marketing mix" in his book *Basic Marketing*, which comprises product, price, place and promotion (collectively referred to as "4Ps"). Product refers to choices made regarding the products/services and benefits that are going to be offered to the target customer group. Price refers to all the decisions made regarding setting prices, managing prices over time, raising or lowering prices in response to the changing competitive environment. Place refers to distribution activity, that is, the process by which products and services are delivered to customers. Promotion concerns how value is communicated to customers in the marketplace. In a word, 4Ps provides a framework for market researchers and practitioners to decide what can be included into the discipline of marketing.

⊞ 有学者争论道：4P 依旧是从企业的角度出发去考虑问题，从而提出更加以消费者为中心的 4C 来代替 4P。4C 包括商品、成本、渠道和沟通。有的学者另外加入 3 个 P（人、过程和有形展示），从而将营销组合从 4P 变成了 7P。

Though the 4Ps has been widely recognized as a package that contains issues to be studied in marketing, some scholars questioned that the 4Ps start out from the perspective of businesses instead of customers'. Robert Lauterborn thus proposed the 4Cs—commodity, cost, channel and communication, shifting the focus to customers. Some other experts argued that the 4Ps is applicable to manufacturing companies but not complete for service-oriented firms, so they included another 3Ps—people, process and physical evidence into the portfolio to make it "7Ps".

5. New marketing concepts

As marketing research and practices advance, more new marketing concepts with varying orientations have been put forward, such as societal marketing, green marketing, relationship marketing and Internet marketing. Some of these concepts are based on broader and higher-level viewpoints, and some highlights the role of new technologies in marketing.

Societal marketing

The societal marketing concept holds that the organization's task is to determine the needs, wants, and interests of target markets and to deliver the desired satisfaction more effectively and efficiently than competitors in a way that preserves or enhances the consumer's and the society's well-being. <u>Societal marketing aims to strike a balance among the society (human welfare), customers (satisfaction) and the company (profits)</u>. Societal marketing still prioritizes consumer interests through shifting the focus on short-term interests of some consumers to lifelong interests of all consumers as a whole. Upholding this belief, many successful big businesses attach great importance to the corporate social responsibility (CSR) and marketing ethics. For example, Bank of China takes "Serving Society, Delivering Excellence" as its slogan; and the slogan of Industrial and Commercial Bank of China (ICBC) is "Integrity leads to prosperity".

Since 2021, China has been tightening anti-monopoly measures for the Internet and technology sectors, signifying its strong determination in pushing businesses to give back to society for common prosperity. It has been proved worldwide that only companies that are able to create both economic and social value can thrive to the end. As income gaps continue to increase, social instability is on the rise, so it is necessary to increase the share of labor in national income distribution, appropriately curb excessive capital and take actions to promote fairness in income distribution.

In 2021, Tencent pledged RMB 50 billion to help the country's initiative for common prosperity and RMB 50 billion for sustainable social value programs. Not only industry leaders, but also tech billionaires including Meituan founder Wang Xing, Pinduoduo founder Huang Zheng and Xiaomi Corp founder Lei Jun have donated sizable amounts of their personal fortunes to social causes. These leading technology and Internet companies are expected to jump out of the battle for demographic dividends and actively seek new development, including boosting research and development capabilities. At the same time, they should take on more social responsibilities to drive sustainable social innovation.

Green marketing

<u>Investopedia defines green marketing as "the practice of developing and advertising products based on their real or perceived environmental sustainability"</u>. Environmental protection, resources conservation and sustainability issues are the concerns of green marketers. Green marketing is one component of a broader movement toward socially and environmentally conscious business practices. Increasingly, consumers have come to expect companies to demonstrate their commitment to improving their operations alongside various environmental, social, and governance (ESG)

田 社会营销力求在社会（人类福祉）、客户（满意）和公司（利润）之间取得平衡。

田 绿色营销就是基于实际或其认为的环境可持续要求而研发和广告产品。

criteria. Examples of green marketing include the use of recycled materials for a product's packaging. The fast fashion brand H&M once put up some conspicuous posters in its stores that told consumers to bring back clothes they no longer wanted to the store for recycling. Fast fashion brands have been widely criticized for the negative impact of their marketing on environmental sustainability. This is probably a posture showing their concerns for the planet.

Relationship marketing

⊞ 关系营销是指为了共同利益而与客户个人、供应商、员工、社区、政府机构和其他利益相关者建立起长期的、增值的、具有成本效益的关系。

The relationship marketing concept involves long-term, value-added, cost-effective relationships with individual customers, suppliers, employees, the community, government bodies and other stakeholders for mutual benefits. Relationship marketers believe that a business that maintains long-term success must be good at handling relationships with all the stakeholders.

Internet marketing

⊞ 营销可有效利用互联网达到病毒式营销效果，称为"病毒式营销"。

Internet marketing, also digital marketing, web marketing, online marketing, search engine marketing, or e-marketing, is the marketing of products or services over the Internet. With the wide access to the Internet, marketers rely more and more on the online network to do marketing, such as WeChat business. Effectively utilized, the Internet can achieve viral effects in marketing, which is called "Viral Marketing".

Summary

This chapter introduces the concept of marketing and discusses why and how firms become market-oriented. Despite varying definitions, marketing boils down to what John Fahy and David Jobber phrased as "the delivery of value to customers at a profit". The three key elements to the concept are: customer orientation, profit in return and integrated efforts.

Marketing is not only applicable to businesses, big and small, but also almost every other field that can benefit from application of marketing to achieve organization goals.

The marketing process can be roughly divided into five steps: understanding the marketplace and customers, designing a customer-driven marketing strategy, constructing an integrated marketing program that delivers superior value, creating customer satisfaction and building profitable relationships, and finally capturing value from customers.

This chapter also explains some core concepts on marketing: customer needs vs wants vs demands, customer offering, customer value and satisfaction, long-term profitable relationships with customers. These core concepts will thread the whole book and be revisited in the subsequent chapters.

The chapter illustrates key features of a market-oriented business by contrasting it to traditional, inward-looking businesses. The basic marketing mix 4Ps is composed of product, price, place and promotion. At the end of the chapter, some new marketing concepts, such as societal marketing, relationship marketing, Internet marketing, viral marketing, are introduced.

Key terms

marketing	customer satisfaction
customer orientation	customer relationship management (CRM)
profit in return	market-oriented business
integrated efforts	internally oriented business
needs	marketing mix
wants	societal marketing
demands	relationship marketing
marketing offering	Internet marketing
customer value	viral marketing

Exercises

Review and discussion

1. Complete the text using words from the box.

advertising	mix	price	products	promotional

Marie Curie Cancer Care is reviewing its marketing strategy in an attempt to attract a wider audience. It will stop using _____ techniques, such as mailings and events. Television _____ and face-to-face marketing are both being tested in a bid to supplement the charity's typical over-60s donor base with younger supporters. If tests prove successful, they will become part of Marie Curie Cancer Care's marketing _____.

In addition, Marie Curie Cancer Care is expanding its online shop. Stylish handbags at a _____ of $10 are attractive to younger customers. Marie Curie Cancer Care says it is responding to customers' needs and wants by selling elegant fashionwear _____.

2. Do the following words and expressions refer to product, price, place, promotion, or people?

accessibility	location	delivery	special deals	launch
customers	branding	distribution	competitors	reputation
discounts	sales force	quality	direct marketing	support

Product	
Price	
Place	
Promotion	
People	

3. Decide whether the following statements are true (T) or false (F).

_____ 1) Marketing is everywhere.

_____ 2) Marketing is the job of the selling or marketing department in a company only.

_____ 3) According to Maslow, we can only obtain sense of safety once the physiological need is satisfied.

_____ 4) Rather than assisting in the creation of value, marketing is responsible for many society's ills.

_____ 5) Market-oriented businesses rely on past experience.

4. Answer the following questions briefly.

1) You can define marketing and its functions in many ways. In your own words, explain marketing to someone who has not yet read this chapter.

2) What is the difference between a need, a want, and a demand?

3) Identify two examples of organizations that you consider provide customer value, and describe how they do it.

4) What is customer satisfaction and how to determine it?

5) Marketing is sometimes considered to be an expensive luxury. Respond to this claim by demonstrating how a marketing orientation can have a positive impact on business performance.

6) Marketing activity is used in various fields such as non-profit, political, educational, medical institutions. Give an example to support this claim.

7) What are the new global trends of marketing in the 21st century?

Projects and teamwork

1. Work with a classmate and choose a China-based company whose products you think will do well in certain markets overseas. The company can be anything from an electric appliance manufacturer to a clothing retailer—anything that interests you. Then search the company in the library or on the Internet to learn the key marketing management concepts that guide the company's business activities globally. Give examples to illustrate your judgment.

2. The advantages for a company of being socially responsible—that is, taking positive actions for the benefit of its staff and society as a whole—include enhanced brand image, and greater ease in attracting staff. There are different ways for a company to show corporate social responsibility, such as donating money to a charity, developing environmentally friendly goods, or refusing to buy materials or goods made using child labor or that have been tested on animals. Can you cite an example of Chinese company that has shown corporate social responsibility?

Case study

From Soybean Milk to Vitasoy

A bowl of soy milk and two fried dough sticks are the longstanding traditional breakfast of many Chinese people. Soybean milk, which is made of soybeans, is a by-product of tofu workshops and has a history of more than two thousand years in China. Compared with cola and milk, soy milk had an out-of-date image. In the past, most of the people who drank it were from the low class.

But now, soybean milk can be found in supermarkets in the United States, Canada, Australia and many other countries. It is placed side by side with internationally popular drinks such as cola, 7 up, and milk. Of course, the change started from the time it was renamed Vitasoy.

A 50-year-old soy company in Hong Kong successfully turned the neighborhood drink into an international drink by adapting the drink to consumers' changing values and modern lifestyles and continuously improving the product image. "Vita" comes from "Vita" in Latin and "Vitamin" in English, which means life, nutrition, vitality, etc., while "milk" is derived from the English concept of soybean milk.

Fifty years ago, Hong Kong people lived a life that was not well-off. Most people were malnourished, and diseases caused by undernutrition were quite common. At that time, the primary purpose of producing Vitasoy was to provide a cheap and nutritionally valuable milk substitute for the malnourished people, so Vitasoy was seen as poor people's milk. For the next 20 years, Vitasoy was widely regarded as a nutritious drink with a "cheap" image in the minds of the general public.

However, in the 1970s, the living standards of Hong Kong people greatly improved. Malnutrition was no longer a problem; people were faced with the problem of overnutrition instead. If soybean milk continued to be positioned as the "poor people's milk", drinking it would mean the downgrading of one's life and social status. The soy products company found that people drank soda, especially foreign sodas, with an air of proudness, while people who drank Vitasoy in public places were afraid of being seen. The business of the soy products company fell into a low ebb.

In the mid-1970s, the soybean milk producer tried to establish Vitasoy as a consumer product for young people, so that it could be closely related to the colorful lives of young people like other soft drinks. The advertisements during this period avoided such expressions as "quenching thirst, being nutritious, and allaying hunger" or "making you taller, stronger, and fitter", and were represented by "more than soda" instead. In 1983, another TV commercial was launched. With the background set in a modern city, a group of young people took Vitasoy and danced to lively music. Vitasoy was depicted as "leisure drink" during this period.

However, in the 1980s, young people in Hong Kong didn't think Vitasoy was cool and fashionable any more. Advertisements from 1988 focused on highlighting the homeliness of the drink. For many Hong Kong people, Vitasoy is an integral part of their childhood in memory. Most people have a special sense of intimacy and identification with Vitasoy. It is an integral part of Hong Kong's local culture, Hong Kong's food culture. Vitasoy is to Hong Kong people what Coca-Cola is to Americans. As a result, Vitasoy began to establish itself as a "classic drink".

During the same period, Vitasoy began to enter the international market. At that time, obesity was a major problem for citizens of the United States and other developed countries. In the United States, Vitasoy was advertised as a high-end "natural drink". The so-called natural drink had no artificial ingredients, such as coloring or additives, preventing consumers from absorbing too much fat, especially animal fat. The idea of natural drink is of course popular with Americans.

Vitasoy has realized such an interesting reversal: When Vitasoy was founded, it was advertised as the poor's milk, emphasizing its similarities with milk, and its price was lower than that of milk; in today's US market, Vitasoy emphasizes the differences (Vitasoy has all the nutrients of milk, but not as much animal fat as milk), and its price is higher than that of milk.

Questions:

1. Discuss how Vitasoy satisfied customer needs. Do you think its marketing strategy is the key to its success?

2. Do you think Vitasoy is a market-driven enterprise? What are the differences between a market-driven business and an internally oriented business?

3. Could you predict the future market prospect of Vitasoy milk based on your understanding of customer needs?

Chapter Two

The Global Marketing Environment

Objectives:

After studying this chapter, you should be able to:

- Understand the importance of scanning the market environment;
- Tell the factors and actors in the macroenvironment and the microenvironment respectively;
- Discuss the impacts of political, economic, social, technological and other macro forces on business;
- Talk about how microenvironmental actors are related to the success or failure of a business;
- Explain why it is important for organizations to scan and swiftly respond to the market environment.

Framework

```
                                            • Political factors
                                            • Economic factors
                   The macroenvironment      • Social factors
                                            • Technological factors
                                            • Other factors

Chapter Two
The Global
Marketing          The microenvironment      • Customers
Environment                                  • Intermediaries
                                             • Suppliers
                                             • Competitors
                                             • Publics

                   Scanning and responding to
                   the market environment
```

In the pandemic-plagued 2020, it is not difficult for people to see that how a public health crisis can affect the domestic and global economy, and further the business environment and performance of all businesses. Businesses were forced to shut down to prevent spread of the coronavirus for a couple of months and continued to suffer from shrinkage of customers and turnovers in the following months. In particular, catering services and entertainment industries suffered most; manufacturers, especially those export-oriented ones, struggled with shrinking market demands; other industries also had a hard time because of the falling income and buying powers of consumers.

田 以市场为导向的企业必须着眼于其经营市场的环境，分析市场环境，跟踪并迅速应对市场变化。

From Chapter One we've learned that <u>a market-oriented business must look outward to the market environment in which it operates, analyzing the marketplace and tracking and swiftly responding to market changes</u>. This chapter will examine the market environment, illustrate how macroenvironmental factors and microenvironmental actors can affect a company's ability to operate effectively in delivering value to its customers, and talk about how businesses can respond to and deal with these forces.

<u>The microenvironment consists of the actors in the firm's immediate environment or business system which affect its capability of operating effectively in its chosen market. The macroenvironment consists of a number of broader forces that affect not only the company, but also the other actors in the microenvironment</u> (see Figure 2.1).

田 微观环境由公司直接环境或业务系统中的参与者组成，这些参与者影响其在所选市场中有效运营的能力。宏观环境由多种宏观力量组成，这些力量不仅影响公司，而且影响微观环境中的其他参与者。

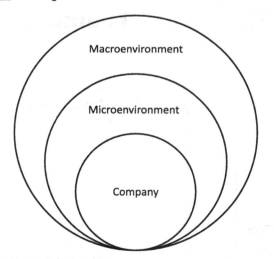

Figure 2.1 The marketing environment

1. The macroenvironment

田 PEST 代表宏观环境中四大主要力量的首字母缩写词：政治(Ｐ)、经济(Ｅ)、社 会（Ｓ）和技术（Ｔ）。

<u>PEST is the acronym that represents the four major forces in the macroenvironment: political, economic, social and technological</u> (see Figure 2.2). Apart from the major factors represented by PEST, the growing public awareness of the importance of business activities on the natural environment necessitates the discussion on physical forces.

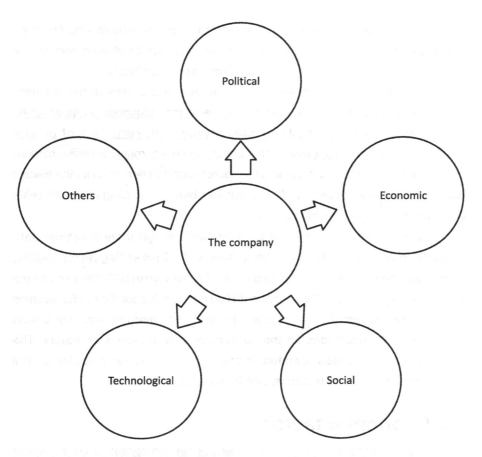

Figure 2.2 Major factors in the macroenvironment

1.1 Political factors

Marketing decisions are strongly affected by the political and legal forces. The political environment consists of laws, government agencies, and pressure groups that influence or restrict organizations and individuals in a given society. A case in point is the different treatments of Lehman Brothers and Goldman Sachs by the US government during the 2008 financial crisis. The former was allowed to fail but the latter was bailed out by the American government. In some big Chinese cities, the government adopted a lottery system for car license plates to limit the increase in car purchase and relieve traffic congestion.

Government agencies regulate business practices through promulgating laws and regulations. For instance, the 2018 amendment version of the *Advertising Law of the People's Republic of China* explicitly provides for the legal responsibility of commercial representatives, banning them from endorsing commodities they've never used or services they've never received. Regulators release regulatory policies and provisions, supervise all aspects of the industry and have the authority to penalize violators.

Apart from legislators and regulators, trade associations play a role in standardizing and guiding business through issuing codes of practice. In a recent anti-waste campaign advocated by the CPC Central Committee and the Chinese

⊞ 政治环境由影响或限制特定社会中的组织和个人的法律、政府机构及压力团体组成。

⊞ 政府机构通过颁布法律法规来规范商业行为。

⊞ 除了立法者和监管者，行业协会通过发布行为守则来规范和指导商业运作。

government, catering services are required to remind customers who are over-ordering dishes. Some fast food chains indicate the calories of each item on the menu as a reminder for consumers in an effort to reduce obesity.

In short, political and legal decisions can change the rules of the business game very quickly. <u>Marketers must be aware of the influences on its activities brought about by the political and legal environment, keep track of political variables and remain responsive to changes in the environment.</u> Sensitive market-oriented firms can often seize emerging market opportunities, such as the electric auto manufacturing industry in China that has been prospering in recent years with tremendous government supports.

2021 witnessed the Chinese government's tough stance against anti-competition behaviors. The State Administration for Market Regulation (SAMR), China's top market regulator, imposed a fine of 500,000 yuan ($78,000) each on the leading video platforms—Bilibili, Tencent Holdings and Alibaba Group for violating the *Anti-monopoly Law*. All of the cases are related to mergers and acquisitions that violate the regulations on the concentration of business operators. The concentration of business operators is that a business operator obtains control over another in the same business, which may lead to monopoly.

⊞ 营销人员必须意识到政治和法律环境对其活动的影响，跟踪各种政治因素并积极应对环境变化。

1.2 Economic factors

<u>Economic factors exert impacts on business through consumer buying power and spending patterns.</u> In a downward economic environment characterized by lower economic growth rate and higher unemployment rate, people with lower buying power tend to spend less and save more; their spending patterns change too, when they cut down spending on non-essentials and seek alternatives with good value for money. So it is not surprising to see that discount outlets outperform high-street stores in times of economic recession.

<u>Governments use fiscal and monetary policies to manage the domestic economy.</u> In the 2008 global financial crisis, the Chinese government released a package of economic stimuli worth RMB 4 trillion to spur the sluggish economy. Most of the money flowed into infrastructure construction, and a booming real estate market ensued. To encourage consumers to withdraw money out of their bank accounts for consumption and investment, the government ordered banks and other financial institutions to lower interest rates. Some consumers purchased properties in response to the low house mortgage rate.

<u>Taxation is one of the levers that governments use to adjust the income distribution pattern.</u> Income is important, but disposal income means more to marketers, because only money at the disposal of consumers can convert into purchase power.

<u>Disposable income = Income – Direct taxes (e.g. income tax, labor service tax, capital gains tax, inheritance tax, etc.)</u>

Furthermore, for some industries like luxury goods and entertainment

⊞ 经济因素通过影响消费者购买力和消费模式对商业产生影响。

⊞ 政府运用财政和货币政策来调控国内经济。

⊞ 税收是政府用来调整收入分配的工具之一。

⊞ 可支配收入＝收入－直接税收（如所得税、劳务税、资本利得税、遗产税等）

services, it is not enough to just look at the target group's disposal income, but have to examine their discretionary income—the amount of money available after paying for essentials such as food and rent.

Discretionary income = disposal income − money for essentials (e.g. food, transport, rent, etc.)

⊞ 可自由支配收入 = 可支配收入 − 必需品的支出（如食物、交通、租金等）

Taxation can change people's spending pattern as well. Taxes on a certain product affect sales of its substitute products. For instance, a heavy tax on tea may lead to a growth of the coffee market, as the tax raises the tea price and some sensitive consumers may reduce tea consumption and turn to coffee.

Though we mentioned earlier how the Chinese government saved the economy from the 2008 financial crisis with a package of economic stimuli, it is worth noting that the government's provision of liquidity can add fuel to inflation as well. Inflation is a measure of the cost of living in an economy. Rapid rises in inflation means a reduction in the future value of savings, investments and pensions.

⊞ 通货膨胀是衡量一个经济体中的生活成本的指标。高速通胀意味着储蓄、投资和养老金的未来价值的减少。

For those companies intending to enter global markets must start with a study of the international trade system. Below are some regimes related to international trades:

- **Exchange controls:** limits on the amount of foreign exchange with other countries and the exchange rate against other currencies.
- **Exchange rate:** the rates at which one currency buys another. Floating exchange rates have a significant impact on the profitability of a company's international operations.
- **Tariff:** a tax levied by a foreign government against certain imported products. The tariff may be designed either to raise revenue or to protect domestic firms. Donald Trump frequently threatened and sought to levy heavy tariffs on Chinese imports during his presidency with the excuse of "protecting American economy and American jobs".
- **Quota:** limits on the amount of goods that the importing country will accept in certain product categories. Quota is designed to keep foreign exchange and protect local industry and employment.
- **Embargo or boycott:** total bans on some kinds of imports.
- **Nontariff trade barriers:** common examples of nontariff trade barriers are anti-dumping measures and countervailing duties.

In the age of globalization, few economies can stand alone without economic or trade ties with other countries. As China is getting more and more involved into the global economy, China has become more interdependent with other economies. The world has been described by Chinese President Xi Jinping as "a community with a shared future for mankind". Traditionally China had strong economic and trade ties with developed economies like the US, the EU, but now it is shifting its focus to economic and trade relations with emerging economies such as the BRICS and ASEAN.

1.3 Social factors

Social factors are very inclusive, ranging from changes in the demographic profile or the population, cultural differences within and between nations to the increased emphasis on marketing ethics and socially responsible actions and the increased concerns with consumer protection.

Demographics is the study of human population in terms of size, density, location, age, gender, race, occupation and other population dimensions (see Figure 2.3). The demographic environment is of major interest to marketers because it involves people, and people make up markets.

⊞ 人口统计学是对人口规模、密度、位置、年龄、性别、种族、职业和其他人口维度的研究。

Rapidly growing world population

The global population has been growing rapidly, though the scenarios vary from country to country (Japan and some North European countries have long been inflicted by a low population growth rate, in contrast to India and underdeveloped countries in Africa). On the one hand, the dramatic growth in global population presents challenges about sustainability; on the other hand, it also represents opportunities for marketers in the form of growing markets and innovative solutions to the challenges.

An aging population

In the 1980s, China started to implement the one-child policy. 40 years later, the country is facing a rapidly aging population together with many consequences that ensued, one of which is the heavy burdens on the social security fund and the working population. In 2016, the Chinese government allowed each couple to have a second child. The marketing implications are the booming markets for products and services designed for the elder, babies and children. During the "two sessions" of 2021, the Chinese government has made it clear that the retirement age will be postponed, though the specific implementation plan is still being studied. This is another action to cope with the country's aging population. Marketers can keep track of this policy, anticipate what market changes it will bring about and study solutions beforehand.

Changed household patterns

Another emerging demographic trend is the growth in the number of household units and smaller household size. In the past, three or four generations lived under the same roof, but with people's increased living standards, higher income and changed views of family, more and more young people prefer living in the nuclear family. Consequently, demands for childcare, maternal care and homecare services and products will inevitably rise. Besides, as there are more and more working moms, the two-income family has more available disposal money but less time, bringing opportunities for solutions to the time-deprived wives, such as ready-to-cook or ready-to-eat foods.

Better-educated population, more white-collars, more professionals

The population is becoming better-educated throughout the world, and consequently more and more people are practicing professional occupations. In China, this trend is particularly prominent in cities, particularly the tier-1 cities of Beijing, Shanghai, Guangzhou and Shenzhen. A better-educated population has more demands for products and services of on-the-job education, health and beauty, technology, travel, financial services, lavish food and entertainment.

Increasing diversity

Countries vary in their ethnic and racial makeup. At one extreme is South Korea, where everyone is Korean. At the other extreme is the US—the so-called "melting pot". In China, there are 56 ethnic groups. With increasing population movements, both domestic and cross-border, marketers are faced with increasingly diverse markets, at home and aboard.

Geographic shifts in population

Urbanization is a trend throughout the world. In 2008, the world, for the first time, had most of its population living in towns and cities than in the rural areas. In China, the migration of workforces has resulted in a proliferation of urban residents, and subsequently rapid expansion of cities and more and more "hollow village". The trend presents both challenges and opportunities for businesses. For example, the real estate in cities benefited from a bigger urban population, but public facilities and resources are falling short of demands. In rural areas, left-behind elders and children present many big social problems. During the 13th Five-Year Plan period, the Chinese government launched a big-scale poverty alleviation program designed to develop industries in economically backward areas. Great achievements have been made in this regard. The government's efforts have to some extent solved the "hollow village" problem, and also brought development opportunities for those businesses that have actively participated in the process.

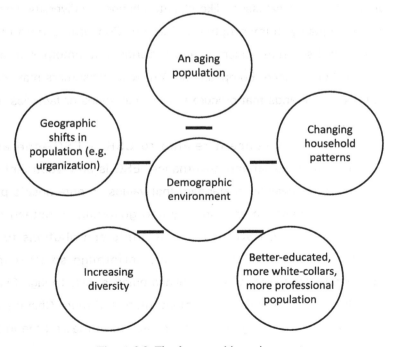

Figure 2.3 The demographic environment

CSR and marketing ethics

⊞ 企业社会责任 (CSR) 是指个人或组织应该对其行为影响自然环境和公众负责的伦理原则。

Corporate social responsibility (CSR) refers to the ethical principle that a person or an organization should be accountable for how its actions might affect the natural environment and the general public. Marketers must be aware that organizations are part of a larger society and are responsible to the society for their actions. In March 2020, Gree Electric Appliances, Inc., a Zhuhai-based manufacturer of electric appliances, donated over 2000 air conditioners and air purifiers to Wuhan, which was plagued by the coronavirus at that time. This generous act was highly praised by the authority and the public, and is rewarded by higher brand affection and brand loyalty.

Businesses fulfil social responsibility through delivering superior-quality goods and services, participating in public welfare programs, serving the neighborhood and so on. Such socially responsible actions often pay off. For instance, ERKE, a mid-range Chinese brand of sports wears, donated RMB 50 million to the flood-stricken Henan province in July 2021, without publicity about this donation. This "quiet" move was later found out by people and spread online. Consumers who are moved by its generosity given its difficult financial position flocked to its "online live-stream selling room" to buy its products. Facing consumers' zeal for shopping, its sales persons again and again called on consumers to buy with rationality.

⊞ 如今，企业社会责任不再是一个额外的选择，而是商业战略的关键部分，受到压力集团、股东、机构投资者和最终消费者的密切关注。

CSR is no longer an optional extra but a key part of business strategy that comes under close scrutiny from pressure groups, shareholders, institutional investors and ultimately consumers. Businesses are expected to take care of social and ethical issues like climate change, biodiversity, social equality, gender equality, human rights and so on. Consumers from more mature commercial societies attach greater importance to enterprises' performance of CSR. For instance, European and American consumers may refuse to buy clothes from brands that procure from sweat shops or factories using under-aged labor.

Another new concept related to CSR is ESG—the acronym of environmental, social and governance. ESG is an investment philosophy and enterprise evaluation standard that values an enterprise's performance in terms of environment, society and governance instead of financial performance only. ESG measures a firm's contributions to promoting sustainable economic development, performing social responsibility, cementing robust corporate governance practice, etc. Though China is still in the infant stage of ESG development, more and more Chinese companies, especially SOEs and high-tech enterprises, have realized the importance of the issue and started to take actions to transform.

Marketing ethics are the moral principles and values that govern the actions and decisions of an individual or group. Beyond legality and illegality there is a large grey area that involves values about right or wrong. For instance, it is not illegal to produce and sell genetically modified (GM) foods, but some food manufacturers refrain from using GM ingredients in food production, as the technology of genetic modification has not existed long enough to see its long-term effect on human health and the human genome bank.

⊞ 营销伦理是影响个人或团体行为和决定的道德原则和价值观。

Laws and administrative directives may not govern the "grey area" issues, but organizations willingly taking socially responsible actions and observing marketing ethics are often rewarded more by the masses with increasing concerns for the social issues. Consumers nowadays not only look at finished products but also show increasing interests in how the products are made, e.g. whether under-aged labors are used in the manufacturing process, whether animals are tested for cosmetic products, whether the manufacturer is a sweatshop with little care for its workers.

⊞ 由于公众越来越关注社会问题，那些愿意采取对社会负责任的行动并遵守营销伦理的机构，往往会从公众消费者处受益。

Consumer movement

Consumer movement is the set of individuals, groups and organizations whose aim is to safeguard consumer rights. Consumer movements concern product quality and safety, privacy protection, consumers' right to know, information accuracy and consumer freedom to make independent buying choices. For example, the Chinese regulators require financial institutions, when selling financial products to consumers, should disclose authentic, accurate and complete information of the products, including risks associated with buying the products, and prohibit them from over-exaggerating investment returns.

⊞ 消费者运动涉及维护消费者权益的个人、团体和组织。

Consumer protection is realized not only through regulatory requirements but also through voluntary acts of socially responsible organizations. Nowadays, the heavy use of smartphones and the unprecedented access to the Internet pose problems with privacy issues. Apps can access information of their users, but how to use the information is an ethical issue.

⊞ 消费者保护不仅通过监管机构颁布要求来实现，还需通过企业负责任的自愿行为来实现。

March 15 is known as annual World Consumer Rights Day. Every year, China's national TV channel—CCTV launches an annual program exposing fake or low-quality goods and malpractices that hurt consumers' interests or rights. The program is liked by the public and daunts profiteers.

1.4 Technological factors

<u>Technological environment consists of forces that create new technologies, creating new product and market opportunities</u>. After personal computers, the Internet and smartphones have become common articles of daily use. High-tech enterprises are now concentrated on the application of new technologies such as 5G, big data, quantum mechanics, the Internet of Things, block chain and so on. Huawei, a Shenzhen-based high-tech enterprise that formerly focused on providing information and communications technology (ICT) infrastructure, has become the world's top 3 smartphone maker and is likely to outperform a very powerful competitor—Apple, soon. The reason? Its world-leading 5G technology.

> 田 技术环境包括创造新技术的力量、创造新的产品和市场机会。

1.5 Other factors

In the business world there are many other influences than the PEST factors, one of which is referred to as "physical forces"—natural and environmental issues of particular concern, e.g. climate change, pollution, scarce resource conservation, recycling, environmentally friendly ingredients and animal testing. Hybrid and electric cars are receiving increasing popularity not only because they are fuel-efficient and cost-saving over time, but also because they appeal to those environment-conscious buyers. Carpooling services (e.g. Uber) are born of consumers' increasing concerns for environmental protection and resources conservation.

On September 22, 2020, Chinese President Xi Jinping announced at the General Debate of the United Nations General Assembly that China would strive to reach carbon emissions peak by 2030 and achieve carbon neutrality by 2060 ("30-60" Decarbonization Goal). Subsequently, China will launch many initiatives to realize its "30-60" Decarbonization Goal. This brings opportunities for green industries, such as green finance, renewable energy, waste recycling, green technology R&D and so on.

2. The microenvironment

Microenvironmental variables also have impacts on the opportunities and threats facing the organization. A company's microenvironment consists of customers, intermediaries, suppliers, competitors and publics (see Figure 2.4).

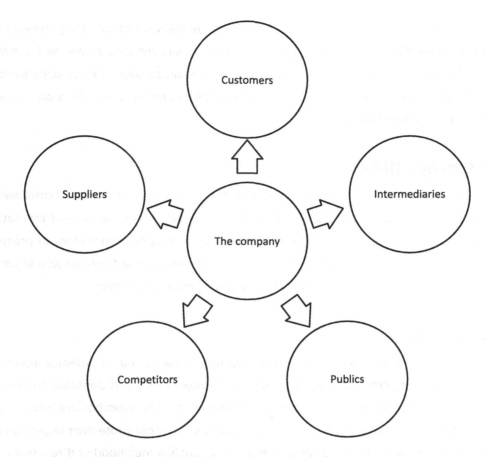

Figure 2.4 Major actors in the microenvironment

2.1 Customers

Customers are at the center of marketing, and ultimately it is the customers that determine the success or failure of a business. Companies need to identify customer needs and wants, try to obtain customer satisfaction, build and maintain long-term relationships with customers.

2.2 Intermediaries

Few companies can create and directly deliver value to end users without using services of others. Instead, most businesses rely on services of independent market intermediaries that help companies to promote, sell and distribute goods to final users, such as wholesalers, retailers, physical distribution firms, marketing service agencies and financial intermediaries. For example, JD.com is a big online intermediary platform that provides selling and door-to-door distribution services; Taobao is not a manufacturer either but plays an intermediary role in connecting businesses with customers.

2.3 Suppliers

Businesses are influenced by not only intermediaries, but also suppliers. Suppliers constitute an important link of the customer value delivery chain. They provide the resources needed by the company to produce its goods and services, as well as finished or half-finished products. Just as powerful distributors can press down the company's profits (e.g. Wal-Mart is infamous for its harshness on suppliers), powerful suppliers can force up prices and thus affect profitability.

2.4 Competitors

To be successful, a business must provide greater customer value and better satisfy customers than its competitors do. Though competition is not the core of marketing, marketers often have to carefully examine and closely track competitors in practice. Especially in a fierce competitive environment, companies must not only be able to satisfy customer needs, but also gain a differential advantage over competitors.

2.5 Publics

Philip Kotler defined "public" as "any group that has an actual or potential interest in or impact on an organization's ability to achieve its objectives", and classified publics into seven categories: financial publics (banks, investment houses, stockholders, etc.), media publics, government publics, citizen-action publics (consumer protection organizations, environmental groups, minority groups, etc.), local publics (neighborhood residents and community organizations), general publics, and internal publics (employees, managers, volunteers, etc.). All these publics are closely related to business operation.

3. Scanning and responding to the market environment

⊞ 营销人员需要监控和分析宏观环境和微观环境中的所有因素和行动，这个过程被称为"环境评析"。

In face of a constantly changing marketing environment, <u>marketers must monitor and analyze all factors and actions in the macroenvironment and microenvironment. This process is known as "environmental scanning".</u> The first task is to define a feasible range of forces that require monitoring, and the second is to design a system that provide predictions of and fast responses to changes.

No doubt macroenvironmental forces are often out of control of a company. But by taking action, companies can often overcome seemingly uncontrollable environmental events, or at least, minimize the impacts of various factors in the marketing environment.

Summary

Business operations are inevitably affected by various factors and forces in the marketing environment. This chapter has extensively discussed macroenvironmental and microenvironmental influences on business by giving real-life examples. Forces in the macroenvironment are put under the framework of PEST for scrutiny, namely, political, economic, social and technological. New trends in these four environments are discussed as well as business opportunities, challenges and marketing implications. Apart from macroenvironmental influences, the microenvironment, which consists of customers, intermediaries, suppliers, competitors and publics, also affects business operations and marketing decisions. Those organizations that can monitor, analyze and track environmental forces and changes stand a larger chance of success. This chapter also introduces the concepts of corporate social responsibility (CSR) and marketing ethics, though the topics will be referred to throughout the whole book. With consumers' increasing concerns for the physical environment, public welfare and the society as a whole, businesses have increasingly realized the importance of performing CSR and upholding high standards of marketing ethics. Many real-life cases have proved that socially responsible moves often pay off.

Key terms

microenvironment	demographics
macroenvironment	CSR
PEST	marketing ethics
disposable income	consumer movement
discretionary income	consumer protection
essentials/daily necessities	environmental scanning

Exercises

Review and discussion

1. Decide whether the following market environment characteristics are micro factors or macro factors.

	Micro	Macro
High unemployment in a region reduces spending on leisure activities.		
The Internet has opened up new distribution and marketing channels.		
Good relations between a supplier and a company mean that goods are always delivered on time.		

Continued

	Micro	Macro
Legislation in European countries is restricting the right to smoke in public places.		
Positive reports in the national press about a brand.		
The staff for the telephone hotline of an Internet bank are trained to be polite and friendly.		
During the FIFA World Cup, more snack food is consumed in front of the TV set.		

2. Complete the action plans (1–6) and then match them with the micro factors (a–f). The first one has been done for you.

a. competitors	c. employees	e. shareholders
b. consumers	d. media	f. suppliers

___e___ 1) Convince shareholders that the best way to _satisfy_ their needs in the long term is to invest in research and development.

_____ 2) Carry out market research to better _____ needs and desires.

_____ 3) Prepare a press release for a _____ magazine about the launch of a new product.

_____ 4) Build and maintain good _____ by always paying on time.

_____ 5) Do a SWOT analysis to assess how to _____ your brand from your competitors'.

_____ 6) Implement a training and _____ plan to motivate and keep good members.

3. Complete the PEST analysis of France. Consult the "Reference" to help you.

Reference

Below is a PEST analysis for an online supermarket in Britain.

Sociological factors

Dominant religions: Mainly Christian, with significant minorities in some regions.

Special diets in some areas.

Leisure activities: Watching TV, cooking, socializing.

Gender roles: Now that younger men shop as much as women, we need to target both sexes equally.

Birth rates: Birth rates are continuing to decline, with fewer babies born every year.

Average life expectancy: This is increasing so we should think about products for older customers.

Attitudes to foreign products: Consumers like to experiment with foreign food and drink.

Opinions on environmental issues: We should use only recyclable packaging and hybrid-fuel delivery vans.

Technological factors

Innovation and technological advances:

Production: New product lines and product types are continually coming onto the market.

Offer: We now offer a new service—ordering by mobile phone.

Distribution: Online ordering has changed the way supermarkets operate. We no longer need actual shops.

Communication with consumers: Broadband Internet connections make it possible to include more product photos on our site. We could even think about adding video.

Economic factors

The economic forecast is good:

Interest rates: Stable at 5%.

Unemployment rate: Less than 9% of people are out work.

GDP (gross domestic product): Growing steadily.

Political factors

Political stability: Very good. Consumers feel relaxed about the political situation and ready to use consumer credit.

New tax/ business legislation: No changes to the law for our business sector in the near future.

International trade agreements: We can import products from the EU without paying extra import duties.

France is a member of the European Union and as such has trade _____ with the other members. It has one of the worst unemployment _____ in Europe and the government is keen to bring this down.

France has one of the highest _____ rates in Europe (1.9 children per woman) and a large proportion of French mothers go back to work, reflecting changes in _____ roles. Men are almost as likely as women to do the shopping for the family and take care of the children.

The dominant _____ is Catholicism, but there is a large Muslim community. The religious beliefs do not significantly affect the marketplace, except at Christmas and Easter time when the demand for Christmas trees and chocolate increases dramatically.

Internet penetration is high: Most households own a computer and have high speed Internet access. This has opened up new channels of _____ and there are now several Internet grocery stores.

Nearly all teenagers own a mobile phone and they are increasingly using SMS messages to keep in touch with their peers. Marketing campaigns are beginning to exploit this line of _____ by sending SMS messages to their audience.

4. Translate the following sentences into English.

1) 根据营销环境对企业市场营销活动发生影响的方式和程度，可将市场营销环境分成两大类：微观营销环境和宏观营销环境。

   _____

   _____

2) 正所谓"知己知彼，百战百胜"，一个企业想要在竞争中取胜，必须能够比竞争者更好地满足目标市场消费者的需求。

   _____

   _____

3) 营销者要对政治法律环境有明确的了解，并且要知道它们对企业营销活动的影响，否则将招致不可逆转的损失。

   _____

   _____

4) 市场营销学中所说的社会文化因素，一般指在一个社会长期发展过程中形成的价值观念、生活方式、宗教信仰、道德规范、审美观念以及风俗习惯等。

   _____

   _____

5) 个人可支配收入指在个人总收入中扣除税金后，消费者真正可用于消费的部分，它是影响消费者购买力水平的决定性因素。

   _____

   _____

5. Answer the following questions briefly.

1) Assume you are a marketing manager for an automobile company. Your job is to reposition an SUV model that was once identified as a "fuel guzzler". The model now comes with a superefficient, nonpolluting hybrid engine. Which of the seven types of publics discussed in the chapter would have the greatest impact on your plans to the more fuel-efficient model?

2) What can a mobile phones marketer do to take a more proactive approach to the changes in the marketing environment? Discuss specific forces, including macroenvironmental and microenvironmental forces.

3) Visit www.trendwatching.com. Select five key trends that you feel marketers need to monitor closely and discuss their likely impact on marketing activity.

4) Discuss the alternative ways in which companies might respond to changes in the macroenvironment.

5) Discuss five business opportunities arising from the growth in concern for the physical environment.

6) With all the problems facing companies that "go global", why are so many companies still choosing to expand internationally? What are the advantages of expanding beyond the domestic market?

7) When exporting goods to a foreign country, a marketer may be faced with various trade restrictions. Discuss the effects that these restrictions have on an exporter's marketing mix:

- Tariffs;
- Quota;
- Nontariff trade barriers.

Projects and teamwork

1. Explore the development of Alipay, Weibo, WeChat, and JD.com. How do they respond to the changing marketing environment?

2. Visit a large electronics and appliance store that sells products such as televisions, stereos, and microwaves. Pick one or two product categories to examine.

   Make a list of brand names in the category, and classify each name as being either Chinese or foreign. How did you decide whether a brand was Chinese or foreign?

   Look at where these different brands were produced. Are any of the brands you labeled foreign actually manufactured in China? Are any of the brands assumed to be America made or Italy made actually made in developing countries? What does this tell you about international marketing? Is global a better word to describe some of these brands?

Case study

Galanz Battles in Microwave Oven War

More than 20 years ago, the spring breeze of reform and opening-up swept over the Pearl River Delta, including the barren land of Guizhou, Shunde. At that time, Liang Qingde, who was then the director of the town's labor transfer office, resolutely took over the important task assigned by the town government and set up a rudimentary feather products factory (the predecessor of Galanz Group) and started a difficult business venture.

This small factory developed and expanded step by step, and gradually got rid of the original predicament. In 1985, Guizhou Animal Products Industry Co., Ltd. announced its establishment. In 1986, the company had established a joint venture named Huali Garment, and in 1987, another joint venture named Huamei Industrial Co... Today Galanz Group is already a large-scale enterprise that integrates household appliances, down feature, clothing, woolen, industry and trade, etc. with 10 subordinate companies. The head office covers an area of 120,000 square meters. The total number of employees is more than 2,000. The fixed assets are worth 400 million yuan. The annual foreign exchange earnings are 35 million US dollars.

After two years of market investigation and feasibility demonstration, Galanz's senior leaders made an amazing decision in 1993: starting to produce microwave ovens. Since the first Galanz microwave oven was launched in 1993, this "dark horse" has developed at an extraordinary speed and has turned the tide in the microwave oven industry at a rapid pace. In just three years, Galanz has developed into a large microwave oven producer with an annual production capacity of 1.5 million ovens. Galanz is now a "microwave oven kingdom". Galanz has also been known as "the top brand of microwave ovens in China".

The prosperity of China's microwave oven market has attracted the attention of overseas companies. Companies such as Panasonic, Sharp, Hitachi, Sanyo and Mitsubishi in Japan, Samsung and Daewoo in South Korea, Luxi, Hewlett-Packard and General Electric in the United States, Magnum in France and other companies began to invest in China and started to devour the market shares of domestic brands. They used joint ventures, mergers, holdings, etc., relied on capital advantages and domestic preferential policies, and leveraged on the original Chinese sales channels and networks to march aggressively and seize market share.

In 1996, with the unprecedented development of the market, market competition became increasingly fierce. Many well-known foreign brands were unwilling to lose to Galanz. One Japanese consortium once bragged at its high-level business meeting that it must regain the Chinese microwave oven market even at the risk of loss for three consecutive years. Big companies such as South Korea's Samsung started a fierce sales campaign with huge investments into advertising.

Facing the large-scale invasion of overseas consortia, the rush of domestic enterprises, and the disorder of the microwave oven market, Galanz resolutely shut down its feature product factory with annual outputs worth 80 million yuan and profits and taxes of nearly 8 million yuan, so as to get fully engaged in the production of microwave ovens. In August 1999, Galanz microwave ovens reduced their prices by 40%. This move aroused widespread concerns in the microwave oven industry.

Liang Qingde believed that the significance of Galanz's price reduction lay in the following three reasons: First, it could greatly beef up potential market vitality, increase market share, and consolidate market position. Second, it could enable enterprises to achieve intensive production and form economies of scale. Third, it could squeeze some uncompetitive companies out of the microwave oven market.

Like other home appliances, the reason why foreign goods could take the lead in the Chinese market lay in its capital advantage, in addition to its technology, quality and brand advantages. Galanz was obviously powerless in front of these multinational rivals. It is like a small boat contending with a combined fleet, with a huge gap in strength.

In the first few months of 1999, Galanz's market share in certain regions declined slightly. Panasonic occupied the Beijing market, Samsung occupied the Tianjin market, while Galanz had no more material and financial resources to fight the war, and could only concentrate on maintaining its advantageous position in East China and Northwest China.

Liang Qingde said: "Our battle is really difficult. Those foreign companies have a history of decades or even hundreds of years. Their annual advertising investment is big enough to buy a domestic medium-sized company. They have advantages in brand establishment as well as in the supply of components. However, we only have a short history of development. They have a preferential financing environment with an annual interest rate of 5% to 8%, while for us getting a 12% annual interest rate is lucky enough. They enjoy preferential policies for tax reduction and exemption. Our products are taxed before they leave the factory. How can we not struggle with such unfair competition?"

With the popularity of Galanz microwave ovens, the brand of Galanz has gradually established. Galanz clearly realized that if they did not have their own brand, they could only become "workers" of foreign brands. In order to create its own brand, Galanz introduced international advanced technology and management, created its unique style, and finally entered the international top ranks.

In order to produce internationally leading products, Galanz used all resources it had accumulated in the 14 years since the establishment of the factory to introduce a full set of internationally advanced microwave oven production technology and equipment from Japan and the United States, and used the best-quality components in the world. It strictly followed the international quality system standards and regulations in production and strengthened the staff's awareness of quality products through rigorous procedural norms. For this reason, Galanz has set the quality goal of "100% excellent product rate" and successfully passed the ISO9000 international quality system certification, signifying that the quality of Galanz microwave ovens has reached the world's first-class level.

In addition to good products, good marketing is also necessary. Therefore, Galanz formulated the corporate slogan of "Work hard to move customers", developed a full range of quality marketing strategies, and continuously introduced measures to serve customers, which really moved customers. For example, it compiled and published the "Use of Microwave Ovens and 900 Dishes Prepared with Microwave Ovens" on 150 newspapers and magazines, and distributed hundreds of thousands of free books on "How to Buy Microwave Ovens", costing nearly one million yuan. With all these efforts, it is inevitable that Galanz products sold well.

Questions:

1. Discuss under what macroenvironmental background Glanz entered the microwave oven market.

2. What marketing strategies did Glanz adopt to cope with the fierce market competition?

Chapter Three

Understanding Customer Behavior

Objectives:

After studying this chapter, you should be able to:

- Understand that external stimuli and consumers' internal cognition process work together on the buying behavior;
- Identify the five roles participating in the buying decision process;
- Define the four types of buying decision behavior and give typical examples for each type;
- Identify the four factors affecting the consumer's level of involvement;
- Identify the five stages of the typical consumer buying decision process;
- Discuss how psychological, personal, social and cultural factors can affect consumer buying behavior;
- Evaluate consumers' choice criteria for a purchase.

Framework

Chapter Three Understanding Customer Behavior

Model of consumer behavior

Who buys?

- Initator
- Influencer
- Decider
- Buyer
- User

How they buy?

- Four types of buying decision behavior
- Four factors affecting consumer involvement
- The consumer buying decision process

What affects buying behavior?

- Psychological factors
- Personal factors
- Social factors
- Cultural factors

What are consumers' choice criteria?

- Technical criteria
- Economic criteria
- Social criteria
- Personal criteria

After analyzing the marketing environment, the next step to successful marketing is to examine the customer, as we learn from Chapter One that an in-depth knowledge of customers is a prerequisite of marketing success. This chapter first introduces a stimulus-response model of consumer behavior and focuses on answering such questions as who buys, how they buy, what influences buying behavior and what are consumers' choice criteria.

1. Model of consumer behavior

Philip Kotler introduced a stimulus-response model of buyer behavior (see Figure 3.1). Under this model, <u>external stimuli and consumers' internal cognition process jointly work on the buying behavior</u>. External stimuli comprise the marketing stimulus 4Ps—the core of marketing efforts, and other environmental stimuli—economic, technological, political and cultural factors. All these inputs enter the buyer's minds, "the black box", where they are turned into a set of observable buying responses: product choice, brand choice, dealer choice, purchase timing, purchase amount and so on.

田 外部刺激和消费者的内部认知过程共同作用于购买行为。

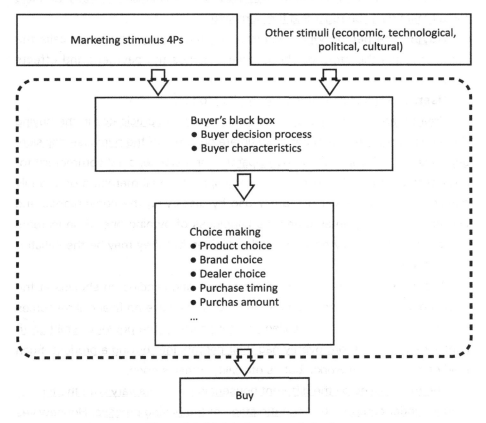

Figure 3.1 Model of consumer behavior

2. Who buys?

Blackwell, Miniard and Engel identified five roles in the buying decision-making process (see Figure 3.2): initiator, influencer, decider, buyer and user.

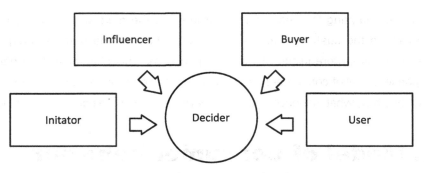

Figure 3.2 Five roles in the buying decision process

田 发起者：发起购买决策过程的人。

田 影响者：试图就购买决策结果说服他人的人。

田 决策者：拥有权力和／或经济能力就购买做出最终决定的人。

田 购买者：进行交易的人。

田 使用者：产品的实际消费者或使用者。

Initiator: The person who starts the process of considering a purchase. Information may be gathered by this person to help the decision.

Influencer: The person who attempts to persuade others concerning the outcome of the buying decision. Influencers typically collect information and attempt to impose their choice criteria and personal opinions on the decision.

Decider: The individual with the power and/or financial authority to make the ultimate decision regarding the purchase.

Buyer: The person who conducts the transaction. The buyer calls the supplier, visits the store or shops online, makes the payment and effects delivery.

User: The actual consumer/user of the product.

Smart marketers realize that more than one role participates in the buying decision process and may alter the ultimate outcome of the purchase decision, and thus try to involve all the participants. For instance, a TV commercial for a Chinese auto brand—Chang'an cleverly appeals to all members of a family considering buying a car for family use by displaying the convenience and comfort of a Chang'an auto and the happiness of owning one. Grandparents and children in a family may not be the decider, but they may be the initiator, influencer and user.

田 聪明的营销人员意识到参与购买决策过程的角色不止一个，并且每一个角色都可能会改变购买决策的最终结果，因此他们试图让所有参与者都参与进来。

Another example is the placement of toys and candies on shelves at the same height of children's in supermarket. Children have no financial resources to buy, but they have the so-called "pester power"—the power of children to subtly influence or more overtly nag their parents into buying a product. Such marketing trick often works, but its ethicality remains open.

田 "纠缠力"是指孩子们能够隐蔽地影响或公开地纠缠父母使其购买他们想要的产品的能力。

The roles played by the different household members vary with the type of product under consideration and the stage of the buying process. Housewives often act as initiator, decider, buyer and user of foods and daily fast moving consumer goods such as shampoo, body wash and detergent, while men have a bigger say in purchase of more valuable articles like property, car, insurance scheme and household electric appliances. However, as more and more women now work and earn money, joint-decision making is common in most two-income families.

田 不同家庭成员所扮演的角色，会因考虑购买的产品类型和购买过程阶段的不同，而不尽相同。

The marketing implications of understanding the roles in the buying decision process lie in marketing communications. For initiators, we need to arouse their awareness of a need or a problem; for influencers, we provide information they need to persuade the decider; on deciders, we concentrate most of our marketing efforts as they make ultimate choice; for buyers, we make the purchase, payment and delivery convenient; from users we collect information about consumer needs, wants and demands, requirements, buying choice criteria and post-purchase feedback.

> 田 理解购买决策过程
> 中的角色，对于营销
> 的意义在于与消费者
> 进行营销沟通。

TikTok's success is inseparable from a large influencer industry that is emerging in China. Young people of Generation Z—those born between the mid-to-late 1990s and the early 2010s and the main users of TikTok—in particular are much more likely to buy items recommended to them by influencers they follow who have included a purchase link to their social commerce post, rather than through official channels. As 35 percent of influencers have started to utilize TikTok more heavily as part of their brand strategy, ever more intelligent algorithms match users with content specifically tailored to them, maximizing the incentive for companies to heavily incorporate the platform as part of their marketing strategy.

3. How they buy?

Attempting to understand influences on the buyer's perceptions of and responses to the stimuli and the buyer's decision process have always been the core questions in the field of consumer behavior.

3.1 Four types of buying decision behavior

Buying behavior differs greatly for a toothbrush, a dress, an iPhone, financial services and a new car. By the degree of consumer involvement and the amount of difference between different alternatives under consideration, buying behaviors can be classified into four types (see Table 3.1).

Table 3.1 Types of consumer decisions

	High customer involvement	Low customer involvement
Significant difference between alternatives	Complex buying behavior/ Extended problem solving	Variety-seeking behavior
Few difference between alternatives	Dissonance-reducing buying behavior/Limited problem solving	Habitual buying behavior

田 复杂型购买行为:
当消费者高度参与购
买决策过程并感知到
不同选择之间的巨大
差异时，他们会产生
复杂的购买行为。

田 和谐型购买行为:
当消费者高度参与购
买决策过程，这种购
买通常是昂贵的、不
常发生的或有风险
的，他们几乎看不出
不同选择之间的差异
时，就会产生这种购
买行为。

田 多变型购买行为:
其特点是消费者参与
程度低，但消费者能
够感知到不同选择之
间的显著差异。

田 习惯型购买行为:
消费者习惯性地购买
东西，参与度低，且
不同选择之间几乎没
有差异。

Complex buying behavior/Extended problem solving: Consumers have complex buying behavior when they are highly involved in a purchase and perceive big differences among alternatives. In this buying situation, consumers do a lot of information search and closely evaluate and compare alterative solutions using their choice criteria. It is commonly seen in the purchase of expensive articles like properties, cars, luxuries.

Dissonance-reducing buying behavior/Limited problem solving: It occurs when consumers are highly involved with an expensive, infrequent or risky purchase, but see few differences among alternatives. For instance, consumers have dissonance-reducing buying behavior for common household appliances such as microwave oven, rice cooker and even larger pieces falling into the same price range like TV set and washing machine, as the production technology and craftsmanship of these household appliances show a trend of convergence among different brands.

Variety-seeking behavior: It is characterized by a low degree of consumer involvement but perceived significant differences among alternatives. For example, consumers may swift from one brand of soft drinks or shampoos to another, simply to try something new, as products like soft drinks and shampoos of different producers have differences in product features and benefits. Variety-seeking behaviors can be encouraged by providing small trial samples.

Habitual buying behavior: Consumers buy things habitually with low involvement and few differences among alternatives. Purchases of inexpensive and frequently bought daily necessities fall into this category, such as salt and bottled drinking water. However, marketers should be aware that repeated buying is the result of brand familiarity, instead of brand conviction. Consumers do not hold strong preference toward a brand, but choose the brand just because it is familiar. For new market entrants, it is an effective option to launch big sale promotions to win over habitual buyers from competitors.

3.2 Four factors affecting consumer involvement

Consumers' level of involvement refers to the extent to which they participate in the buying decision process. What may affect the level of involvement? Laurent and Kapferer identified four factors: self-image, perceived risk, social factors and hedonistic influence (see Figure 3.3).

田 消费者的参与程度
是指他们参与购买决
策过程的程度。

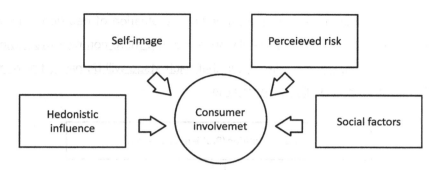

Figure 3.3 Four factors affecting the degree of consumer involvement

Self-image: Consumer involvement is likely to be high when a purchase potentially affects one's self–image, as in the case of buying jewelry, clothing, cosmetics and outfits for a job interview.

Perceived risk: Involvement is likely to be high when the perceived risk of making a mistake is high. Perceived risk is closely related to the price, as often evidenced in large purchases such as a house or a new car. Perceived risk is also linked to the consumer's buying power—consumers with higher purchasing power are more likely to shorten the buying decision process.

Social factors: Involvement is likely to be high when social acceptance is dependent upon making a correct choice. Social factors constitute a very inclusive category—many external factors influencing consumer involvement can be put under this category. For instance, peer pressure is a significant social influence on some purchases. In recent years, many luxury car brands have launched entry-level models priced between RMB 200,000 to RMB 350,000 targeting the enlarging "new middle class" in the Chinese market, because the car makers have perceived the needs of this customer group for a car that represents their self-identity and rising social status.

Hedonistic influence: Involvement is usually high when the purchase provides a high degree of pleasures or a guarantee for future happiness. For instance, you will be highly involved in choosing a restaurant for a dinner with your future mother-in-law or in deciding the holiday resort for a long-expected family trip.

田 自我形象：当购买可能影响一个人的自我形象时，消费者的参与度相对较高。

田 感知风险：当感知到购买犯错所带来的风险较高时，消费者的参与度相对较高。

田 社会因素：当个人是否被社会接受取决于其做出正确的购买选择时，消费者的参与度相对较高。

田 享乐影响：当购买带来高度的快乐或保证未来的幸福时，消费者参与度通常较高。

3.3 The consumer buying decision process

The typical consumer buying decision process comprises five stages (see Figure 3.4), but in some buying situations, one or more than one stage may be skipped, and some stages may be repeated, depending on the specific buying situation. In habitual buying, for example, the stages of information search,

⊞ 购买决策的情况越复杂，消费者就越有可能经历购买决策过程的所有阶段，这个过程将花费更多的时间。

evaluation of alternatives and post–purchase evaluation of decision may be very brief or even omitted. Generally speaking, <u>the more complex the buying decision situation, the more likely it is that each stage will be passed through and that the process will take more time.</u>

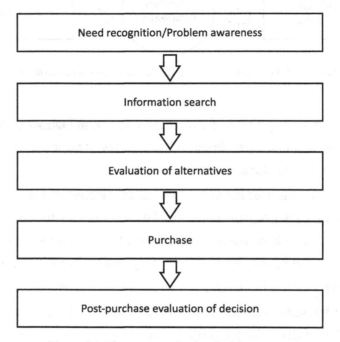

Figure 3.4 The consumer buying decision process

Stage 1: Need recognition/Problem awareness

⊞ 需要受内部刺激：日常消耗（例如食物、燃料、沐浴露）或外部刺激（例如广告、促销）而触发。

The buying process starts with need recognition—the buyer recognizes a need or a problem. <u>The need can be triggered by internal stimuli as routine depletion (e.g. food, fuel, body wash) or external stimuli (e.g. advertisement, sales promotion)</u>. In this stage, marketers should find out the need of customers and the problem they face. For instance, Family Mart has realized that more and more Chinese white-collars are developing a habit of drinking coffee for refreshment at work, so it offers instant coffee at premises near subway stations or on the ground floor of office blocks. Office workers can conveniently grab one cup of coffee in their way to work.

⊞ 需要抑制因素：阻止消费者从意识到需要进入购买决策过程下一个阶段的事物。

Besides, marketers should be aware of <u>need inhibitors—things that prevent consumers from moving from need recognition to the next stage of the buying process</u>. Alipay, an independent third-party payment platform, is a solution to the need inhibitor holding back B2C online transactions. Alibaba originally developed this platform to solve the problem of lack of trust between buyers and sellers on Taobao resulting from the asynchrony between payment and delivery.

Marketers should also know that some needs arise from external stimuli. In supermarket, a conspicuous shelve place and a big discount are effective stimuli for fast moving consumer products. For non-essentials, particularly luxurious goods, marketers can appeal to target consumers' emotion by displaying a desirable self-image or lifestyle. Xiaohongshu, a thriving lifestyle community platform established in 2013, gathers many beauty bloggers, who frequently update videos about use instructions or comments on cosmetics or personal care products. These videos, on the one hand, provide information for prospective buyers, and on the other hand, serve as external stimuli upon "online window shoppers".

Stage 2: Information search

Information research will begin when the need/problem recognition is strong enough for people to take action. However, an interested consumer may or may not search for more information. The amount of information search depends on the strength of your drive, the amount of information you already have, the ease of obtaining more information, the value you place on additional information and the satisfaction you get from searching.

Consumers usually start with internal search—retrieving information from their memory which is built upon personal experiences and marketing communications. If internal search fails to produce a satisfactory outcome, external search begins. Consumers can obtain information from various external sources: personal sources (e.g. family, friends, neighbors, acquaintances), commercial sources (e.g. advertising, salespeople, websites, dealers), public sources (e.g. mass media, consumer-rating organizations, Internet searches) and experiential sources (personal tryout).

> 田 内部搜寻：消费者从记忆中检索基于个人经验和营销传播所获得的信息。

The Internet is now playing an increasingly bigger role in consumers' information search. In addition to an organization's official website, B2C platforms such as JD.com, Taobao and Dangdang allow buyers and users to post comments online. Needless to say properly managing customer comments is an important job for marketers as they may affect the decision process of people considering buying the product and even alter the decision outcome.

Stage 3: Evaluation of alternatives

The result of information search is an awareness set—the array of brands and products that come into your awareness. Often unconsciously affected by various factors, people use their choice criteria to narrow the awareness set down to an evoked set—a shortlist of options for serious consideration and careful evaluation.

> 田 认知集：一系列进入消费者认知的品牌和产品。
>
> 田 诱发集：供消费者认真考虑和仔细评估的候选品牌和产品清单。

In some cases, consumers use careful calculations and logical thinking. At other times, the same consumers do little or no evaluation; instead they buy on impulse or rely on intuition. Sometimes consumers make buying decisions on their own; sometimes they discuss with family, friends, consumer guides or salespersons for advice. It depends on the kind of product, the buyer's perceived risk, the buyer's personality, the buying situation and so on.

Consumers easily fall victim to the so-called "Herd mentality", a phenomenon wherein individual members of a crowd subvert their will to the perceived unified will of the mass. Crowdedness is seen as an evaluative indicator of good quality and good value for money in commercial contexts. A crowded setting can often excite potential buyers and spur them to shorten the evaluation stage and move into the next stage of purchase. Some B2C platforms attach a label "hot" to products that are being promoted in the hope of tapping into consumers' herd mentality.

田 "从众心态"，是指人群中的个体成员放弃他们的个人意志，与感知到的大众统一意愿趋同的现象。

Stage 4: Purchase

Generally, consumers will buy the most preferred alternative after the evaluation of alternatives, but two factors may come between the intention and the action. The first is attitudes of others. The second is unexpected situational factors. For example, after extensive information search and careful evaluation, you finally go to the store to buy a luxurious bag of the chosen style, but you find that a big discount is offered for bags of another style that were originally priced higher than your choice. The unexpected situation may change your purchase decision.

Stage 5: Post-purchase evaluation of decision

Customer satisfaction arises when perceived product performance meets or exceeds customer expectation. It is predictable that satisfied customers will repeat purchase, spread favorable word of mouth, pay less attention to the offerings of your competitors and buy products from you, while dissatisfied customers may do the opposite. Satisfied customers have higher lifetime value, and are thus higher customer equity (see Figure 3.5).

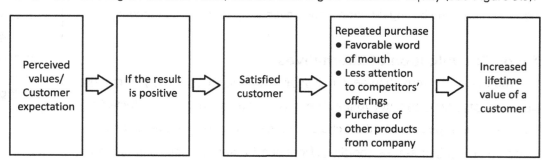

Figure 3.5 Importance of customer satisfaction

However, it is quite common for customers to experience "cognitive dissonance" in this post-purchase stage, which refers to discomfort buyers experience after buying something when they are concerned or feel uneasy about drawbacks of the chosen brand and about losing the benefits of other alternatives not purchased. There are things that marketers can do to reduce cognitive dissonance. For example, many online stores on Taobao offer the policy of no-reason return and refund within seven days. When the decision is irrevocable, the purchaser is more likely to experience anxiety, so this policy is designed to give consumers more assurance and reduce their anxiety about placing an order. Another policy adopted by big online shops to reduce cognitive dissonance is the price guarantee policy—consumers can get a refund of the gap between the price they pay and a discounted price for the same product in case a sales promotion should be launched later.

> 田 顾客在购买后通常会经历"认知失调"，即购买者在购买某样商品后对所选品牌的缺点，及其他被放弃的选择的好处而感到担忧或不安。

4. What affects buying behavior?

Consumer buying is influenced by psychological, personal, social and cultural factors, as shown in Figure 3.6. In most cases, marketers are unable to control these factors, but they must take them into consideration and try to mitigate or maneuver the influences.

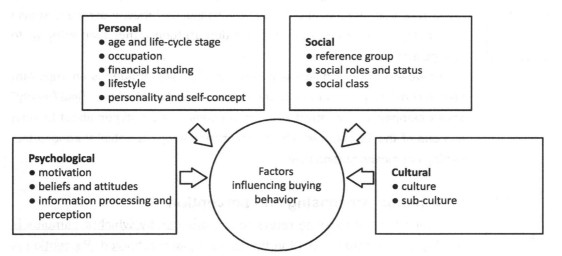

Figure 3.6 Factors influencing consumers' buying behavior

4.1 Psychological factors

Motivation

A person has many needs at the same time. Some are physiological, arising from hunger, thirst or physical discomfort, to name a few; some are psychological, arising from the need for feelings of safety, belonging, esteem and self-actualization (based on Maslow's hierarchy of needs). A need becomes a motive when it is raised to a sufficient level of intensity. A key issue here is the distinction between needs and wants. Wants are the needs

> 田 当需要有足够的强度时就变成了动机。

shaped by culture and individual personality.

From a marketing point of view, businesses can cater to different levels of needs with different offerings. Chinese people used to regard commercial insurance as gimmicks or tricks, because with a low level of economic development and low income, people naturally focused on satisfying physiological needs while neglecting higher levels of psychological needs. However, as the living standards are on the rise, more and more people now buy commercial insurance to satisfy the need of feeling safe.

Beliefs and attitudes

田 信仰是个人对某事所持的描述性想法。

A belief is a descriptive thought that a person has about something. Beliefs about oneself are known as "self-concept". Marketers are interested in the beliefs that people hold about specific products and services, because these beliefs make up product and brand images in consumer minds that affect buying behavior. That also explains the importance of building a good brand and corporate image.

田 态度是个人对某个事物或观点的相对稳定的评价、感觉和倾向。

Attitude is a person's relatively consistent evaluations, feelings and tendencies towards an object or idea. Attitudes put people into a frame of mind of liking or disliking things, of moving toward or away from them. Philip Kotler held that attitudes are difficult to change, and thus, a company should usually try to fit its products into existing attitude rather than attempt to change attitudes.

However, some scholars believed that changing attitude is an important step in convincing consumers to try a brand. Dove launched the "Real Beauty" series campaign in an effort to change people's stereotypes about beauty, and one of the TV commercials aim to change people's established idea that getting old means getting ugly.

Information processing and perception

田 信息处理是指人们接收、解读刺激，并将刺激存储在记忆中，随后进行检索的过程。感知是人们选择、组织和解释信息以赋予这个世界意义的过程。

田 选择性注意是指人们筛选掉他们所接触到的大部分信息的倾向。

Information processing refers to the process by which a stimulus is received, interpreted, stored in memory and later retrieved. Perception is the process by which people select, organize and interpret information to form a meaningful picture of the world. Research on consumers' information processing and perception is meaningful to understand their buying behavior.

People develop different perceptions from the same stimulus. There are three perceptual processes: selective attention, selective distortion and selective retention. Selective attention is the tendency for people to screen out most of the information to which they are exposed. Especially in the era of information explosion, everyone is exposed to abundant information every day. It is naturally that we pay attention to only a smart fragment of information that comes to us. That to some extent explains the importance of launching creative commercials and of competing for eye-level positions on supermarket shelves.

Selective distortion describes the tendency of people to interpret information in a way that will support what they always believe. It means marketers must try to understand the mindset of consumers and how they will affect interpretations of advertising and sales information, and ensure that information is clearly delivered and correctly received in marketing communication.

Selective retention means that consumers are likely to remember good points made about a brand they favor and to forget good points made about competing brands.

Because of selective attention, selective distortion and selective retention, it is hard for marketers to get their messages through. That explains why drama and repetition are used so much in sending messages to the market. For example, people stay in the elevator for a very brief time, and it is difficult to arouse their attention and impress them with a small screen hung on the wall, so marketers often resort to the repetition technique (consecutively repeating the slogan or name of the product/brand for five or six times) or use songs adapted from popular melodies that are so familiar to people's ears.

4.2 Personal factors

A buyer's decision can be influenced by personal characteristics such as age and life-cycle stage, occupation, financial standing, lifestyle, personality, family background, to name a few.

Age and life-cycle stage

People's buying behaviors change over their lifetime. Tastes in food, clothes, furniture and recreation are often age-related. Buying is also shaped by the stage of family life cycle. Compared with people in their 20s who spend most money on products for self-image and entertainment, people in their 30s may reduce spending on themselves as expenditures on children and elder family members are on the rise.

The "grey market" often attracts attention of marketers for health care, recreational services, tourism, high-end financial services and so on, because people in their late 40s and 50s have more discretionary income to spend on these fancy stuffs, as most of them have paid off the house mortgage, reached the peak of career/income and finished resource inputs into their adult offspring.

Apart from buying power, different stages of life cycle mean different priorities in buying and consuming the same thing. For example, unlike young people who consider more about the variety of dishes, tastes and styles of the dishes, middle-aged people may care more about the cleanness, crowdedness, comfort and atmosphere of the dining environment.

⊞ 选择性失真指人们倾向于用自己一贯的思维来解释信息。

⊞ 选择性保留意味着消费者很可能会记住他们喜欢的品牌的优点，而忘记竞争品牌的优点。

⊞ 食物、衣服、家具和娱乐的品位通常与年龄有关，这些东西的购买受到家庭生命周期阶段的影响。

⊞ 人处于生命周期的不同阶段意味着购买和消费相同物品的优先级不同。

Occupation

Some purchases are occupation-related. For example, business suits are bought by white-collars working in office, and teachers are the target buyers of stationaries and teaching aids.

Financial standing

A person's financial standing will affect product choice. Marketers of income-sensitive goods should track trends in personal income, savings and interest rates. Financial service offerings are often segmented based on the financial standing of customers. For instance, credit cards are classified into diamond, platinum, golden and general cards that give cardholders different credit limits, and which type of card is to be issued to a specific applicant is determined based on his or her financial standing.

Lifestyle

Lifestyle is a person's pattern of living as expressed in his or her psychographics. It involves measuring consumers' major AIO dimensions—activities (work, hobbies, shopping, sports and social events), interests (food, fashion, family, recreation), and opinions (about themselves, social issues, business, products). Marketers can appeal to customers sharing a certain lifestyle. For example, IKEA's "Kitchen Party" campaign appeals to young people who live an energetic, modern and urban lifestyle. The thriving food delivery platforms such as Meituan are also closely connected to people's changed lifestyle. Many office workers live on the so-called 996 work schedule, which refers to employees working from 9 am to 9 pm six days a week. They have neither time nor energy to prepare meals for themselves and the loved ones, so foods delivered door-to-door are really what they need.

Personality

Personality is the sum of inner psychological characteristics of individuals, which lead to consistent responses to their environment. Personality is usually described in terms of traits such as self-confidence, dominance, sociability, autonomy, defensiveness, adaptability and aggressiveness. Personality will be reflected in buying behaviors and consumption choice. Though personality is difficult to measure, in practice marketers may combine personality with other influences such as lifestyle and life cycle stage to study buying behaviors of the target group.

Brands also have personality, and consumers are likely to choose brands with personalities with which they can resonate. "Brand personality" is the characterization of brands as perceived by consumers. For example, targeting the flamboyant, high-key, aspiring young people, Converse, an American sports and casual shoe brand, is best known for the canvas "All Star" shoe, subtly indicating that wearing a pair of Converse shoes you are a star.

⊞ 虽然个性难以衡量，但在实践中，营销人员可以将个性与生活方式、生命周期阶段等其他影响因素结合起来，研究目标群体的购买行为。

4.3 Social factors

There are various social influences on consumers' buying behavior. Here we focus on the following three: reference group, social roles and status, social class.

Reference group

Reference group refers to a group of people that influences an individual's attitude or behavior. Reference groups can be your family, friends, colleagues, or members of a social club or society, or celebrities, sport starts, key opinion leaders (KOL). Reference groups have access to product information and influence the purchase behavior and choices of others. Xiaohongshu fully taps into the influence of reference groups—opinion leaders who have experienced the product or service, allowing prospective buyers to access their comments or interact with them.

⊞ 参照群体是指影响个人态度或行为的一群人。

Here introduced is the diffusion of innovation model (see Figure 3.7). Consumers are classified into five categories according to the time they adopt an innovation: innovators, early adopters, early majority, late majority and laggards. Opinion leaders are often innovators and early adopters. They are the early nuts to crack for marketers of a new product. Provision of sufficient product information and a chance of tryout can help develop these two groups, which in turn spread the product by word of mouth to the majority.

⊞ 根据消费者采纳新事物的时间先后，可将他们分为五类：创新者、早期采用者、早期大众、晚期大众和落伍者。意见领袖通常是创新者和早期采用者。

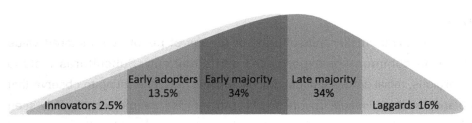

Figure 3.7 Diffusion of innovation model

Social roles and status

A person belongs to many groups—family, clubs and organizations. The person's position in each group can be defined in terms of role and status. People usually choose products appropriate to their roles and status. For example, teachers are less likely to be fans of miniskirts, and stay-at-home moms are heavy buyers of groceries and baby stuffs.

Social class

Social class is measured as a combination of income, occupation, education, wealth and other variables. Marketers are interested in social class because people within a given social class tend to exhibit similar buying behaviors. The distinct product and brand preferences in areas of clothing, home furnishings, leisure activity and automobiles are the resulting

⊞ 在服装、家居、休闲活动和汽车领域，特定产品和品牌偏好能够体现社会阶层。

demonstration of social class. For example, in the UK, tabloids, a newspaper with short articles and a lot of pictures and stories about famous people, are thought of as less serious than other newspapers and mostly read by the working class, while the middle-class elites favor *Financial Times* and other serious publications.

4.4 Cultural factors

Cultural factors are a very inclusive group. Consumer wants are shaped by their cultural background and personality. Apart from wants, consumer buying behaviors are also affected by the culture where they live in.

Culture

Growing up in a society, a child learns basic values, perceptions, wants and behaviors from the given culture. For westerners and people from some parts of Asia, wearing perfume is customary; for Chinese people, perfume is not a necessity. The difference may originate from physical difference, but as time goes on, wearing perfume or not has become a consumption pattern shaped by culture.

But culture is not constant, but changing all the time. For example, the cultural shift toward greater concerns about health and fitness in the Chinese society has created huge business opportunities for health-and-fitness services, exercise equipment and clothing, natural and organic foods.

Sub-culture

Each culture contains smaller subcultures, or groups of people with shared value systems based on common life experiences and situations. Subcultures include nationalities, religions, racial groups and geographic regions. It is interesting to observe that economical brands such as Honda, Toyota and Nissan vehicles are more commonly seen on roads in Guangzhou than in Beijing. The fact can be partially explained by the subcultural difference—Guangdong people are known for their pragmatic orientation.

⊞ 消费者大多数时候在不知不觉中受上述心理、个人、社会和文化因素的影响，他们自己本身也持有和使用一套标准来评估可供选择的产品。

5. What are consumers' choice criteria?

The standards a consumer uses to evaluate products and services under consideration are known as "choice criteria". When unconsciously, most of the time, influenced by the psychological, personal, social and cultural factors discussed above, consumers also uphold and use a set of criteria to evaluate the alternatives. These criteria can be broadly categorized into four types (see Table 3.2).

Table 3.2 Choice criteria used when making purchase decisions

Type of choice criteria	Examples
Technical	<ul><li>Reliability</li><li>Durability</li><li>Performance</li><li>Style</li><li>Comfort</li><li>Delivery</li><li>Convenience</li><li>Taste</li></ul>
Economic	<ul><li>Price</li><li>Value for money</li><li>Running cost</li><li>Residual value</li><li>Life cycle cost</li></ul>
Social	<ul><li>Status</li><li>Social belonging</li><li>Convention</li><li>Fashion</li></ul>
Personal	<ul><li>Self-image</li><li>Risk reduction</li><li>Morals</li><li>Emotions</li></ul>

5.1 Technical criteria

Technical criteria are related to the performance of the product or service, such as reliability, durability, performance, style, comfort, delivery, convenience and taste. Individual and household consumers often think a lot over technical aspects in large purchases such as a family car, a house, a smartphone or a laptop. Delivery is also a technical criterion. In the past, people shopped in supermarket from time to time to buy groceries, but now people tend to buy heavy things such as rice, flour, edible oil, detergent, shampoo, etc. online or in those supermarkets that provide door-to-door service so as to save their trouble and strength to carry these things home.

田 技术标准与产品或服务的性能表现有关，例如可靠性、耐用性、性能、风格、舒适度、交付、便利性和品位。

5.2 Economic criteria

Economic criteria concern price, running cost and residual values (e.g. the trade-in-value of a car). Honda's Fit, an economical compact car, is not

田 经济标准涉及价格、运营成本和残值（例如汽车的以旧换新抵价）。

expensive, but has a high trade-in-value. For buyers of a new Fit, the car depreciates less compared with other models during the same length of service time. Japanese auto brands, the three most famous ones—Toyota, Honda and Nissan, may not produce the solidest built vehicles, but are highly favored by consumers because of high fuel efficiency, low maintenance cost, absence of small problems and good value for money.

5.3 Social criteria

⊞ 社会标准关于某项购买对个人感知到的与他人关系的影响，以及社会规范对个人的影响。

Social criteria concern the impact that the purchase makes on the person's perceived relationships with other people, and the influence of social norms on the person. In the past, technical and economic criteria play a big role in Chinese people's purchases of household appliances, but recently more and more buyers will check the energy-saving performance before purchase, because increasing attention to environmental issues has become a social trend.

5.4 Personal criteria

⊞ 个人标准关于产品或服务与个人心理的关联。

Personal criteria concern how the product or service relates to the individual psychologically. Emotions are an important element of buying decision-making. Some marketers cleverly appealed to consumers' emotions, such as the slogan of IBM—"No one ever got fired for buying IBM" that is intended to highlight IBM as a "safe" brand for organizational procurement personnel.

We should know that in reality it is very difficult, if not impossible at all, for consumers to find a product or service that lives up to all of these standards, so consumers make decisions based on balanced considerations and personal preference. For marketers, it is also impossible to cover all the criteria, and the best solution possibly could be offerings with differential advantages that cater to target customers. For instance, the Chinese smartphone brands Vivo and OPPO may not have the same state-of-the-art technology as powerful competitors Apple and Huawei, but they focus on the camera function to appeal to the 20-year-old, who takes selfies a lot in daily life.

Summary

Market-oriented companies start business with understanding the market and the customer. Customer behavior research is a big branch of the marketing discipline. This chapter focuses on answering four major questions: who buys, how they buy, what affects consumer buying behavior and what are consumers' choice criteria.

For the question "who buys", five roles have been identified: initiator, influencer, decider, buyer and user. Each of the roles in the buying decision process and its marketing implications are discussed.

The major part of this chapter deals with "how they buy". By the degree of consumer involvement and the amount of differences between alternatives, buying decision behaviors can be classified into four types: complex buying behavior/extended problem solving, dissonance-reducing buying behavior/limited problem solving, variety-seeking behavior and habitual buying behavior. Some scholars broadly identified four factors working upon the level of consumer involvement: self-image, perceived risk, social factors and hedonistic influence. The typical buying decision process for individual and household consumers comprises five stages: need recognition/problem awareness, information search, evaluation of alternatives, purchase and post-purchase evaluation of decision.

Another topic concerning how consumers buy is the influences on buying behavior. Various factors come into play in a consumer's purchase decision process. These factors can be generally put into four categories: psychological, personal, social and cultural. For each category, abundant examples are given to illustrate how these factors can work on consumers' buying behavior.

Even facing the same array of options, different consumers adopt different criteria to help with their decision making. Consumers' choice criteria can be classified into four types: technical, economic, social and personal. Each consumer may attach more importance to some criteria than to others. The important task for marketers is to design and launch a differential offering that appeals to the target group.

Key terms

model of consumer behavior	belief
initiator	attitude
influencer	information processing
decider	selective attention
buyer	selective retention
user	selective distortion
complex buying behavior	life-cycle stage
dissonance-reducing buying behavior	grey market
variety-seeking behavior	grey buying power
habitual buying behavior	pester power
the consumer buying decision process	liftstyle
need stimuli	personality
need inhibitor	reference group
awareness set	the diffusion of innovation model
evoked set	social status
herd mentality	social class
cognitive dissonance	consumers' choice criteria
motivation	

Exercises

── Review and Discussion ──

1. **Match the needs from Maslow's pyramid (1–5) with the reasons for buying certain products (a–e).**

_____ 1) Physiological needs

_____ 2) Safety needs

_____ 3) Social needs

_____ 4) Esteem needs

_____ 5) Self-fulfilment needs

---

a. A consumer buys a smoke alarm for her house because she wants to be warned if there is a fire.

b. A consumer buys a yearly subscription to a swimming pool because she would like to train and win a gold medal at the next Olympic Games.

c. A consumer buys popcorn and drinks because he has invited his friends round to watch important football match on the television.

d. A consumer buys a chocolate bar because he is hungry.

e. A consumer buys the latest fashion accessory so that she can look and feel good.

---

2. **A marketing specialist is talking about purchasing behavior. Replace the underlined expressions with alternative expressions from the "Reference" below. One question has two possible answers.**

Reference

Purchasing behavior or **purchasing patterns** refer to what a consumer buys, and when and how they make their **final purchasing decision**. The first step is usually awareness of the brand. The consumer forms **purchase intentions**—plans to buy things—which they may or may not act on. **Routine purchases** of the same products on a repetitive basis (for example, coffee from the coffee machine at the office) have low levels of **personal involvement**. Some consumers have very high levels of **loyalty** to a brand or product and they will always buy the same brand.

The 1) <u>actual decision to buy a product</u> depends on the type of product or service. With yoghurt, for example, many customers wait until they are in the supermarket, in front of the row of yoghurts, before they decide. On the other hand, for a more expensive product with higher 2) <u>thought and psychological investment from the consumer</u>, it may take place a long time before the purchase. Our research shows that some customers spend three years thinking about the next type of car they will buy. Obviously, over these three years 3) <u>the plans to buy</u> may change a lot. Then there are those 4) <u>purchases without any thought because they are a habit</u> that we all make without thinking. I always get pasta, eggs and milk at the supermarket so I never write them on the list and I always look out for special offers and promotions. This kind of 5) <u>shopping habit</u> is very difficult for a marketing team to change. However, 6) <u>buying something you like when you see it</u> is created by different customer needs, and here we can really make a difference.

1)	4)
2)	5)
3)	6)

3. The chapter defines "alternative evaluation" as "how the consumer processes information to arrive at brand choices". Suppose that, as discussed in the chapter, you have narrowed your choice of new cars to brand A, B, or C. You have finalized the four most important new car attributes and their weights and have created the evaluation matrix. Which new car brand will you likely to select?

New car alternatives				
Attributes	Importance weight	Brand A	Brand B	Brand C
Styling	0.5	3	7	4
Operating economy	0.2	6	5	7
Warranty	0.1	5	5	6
Price	0.2	8	7	8

4. Translate the following sentences into English.

1) 营销研究者建立了一个购买决策过程的 "阶段模型"。消费者会经历五个阶段：认知需求、信息收集、评价方案、购买决策和购后过程。

2) 消费者的购买决策是从意识到某个需求解决的问题开始的。

_____

_____

3) 复杂的购买行为是指消费者高度介入，在众多具有明显差异的品牌中进行反复选择的购买行为。

_____

_____

4) 文化在消费者行为中起着最广泛和最深刻的影响。营销者需要研究文化、亚文化及社会阶层对消费者购买所起的作用。

_____

_____

5) 处于不同年龄的消费者对产品的需求偏好和消费行为有很大的差异。

_____

_____

5. Decide whether the following statements are true (T) or false (F).

_____ 1) Smart marketers should try to involve all the participants in the buying decision process.

_____ 2) A buying decision process always comprises five stages.

_____ 3) People form the same perceptions from the same stimulus.

_____ 4) Consumers do not always use careful calculations and logical thinking.

_____ 5) The need to buy something can be triggered by internal stimuli or external stimuli.

6. Answer the following questions briefly.

1) Choose a recent purchase that included not only yourself but also other people in making the decision. What role(s) did you play in the buying center? What roles did these other people play and how did they influence your choice?

2) Review your decision to choose the educational establishment you are attending in terms of need recognition, information search, evaluation of alternatives and post-selection evaluation.

3) Explain the cultural, social, and personal characteristics that affect people when they choose a restaurant at which to celebrate their birthdays.

4) The marketing manager for a sushi chain says, "We believe our customers exhibit high involvement buying behaviors." Do you agree? Why or why not?

5) Review the choice criteria influencing some recent purchases such as a hairstyle, a meal, etc.

6) Why must international companies understand consumer behavior in different market segments?

7) Why do cultural factors serve as the basic factors in influencing consumer buying behavior?

8) How do you identify subcultures in a society? Set China as an example to list the possible subcultures.

9) What is the first stage in the buying decision process? What should marketers do to influence buyers at this stage?

10) Why is the post-purchase behavior stage included in the process? What relevance does this stage have for marketers?

Projects and teamwork

1. Different types of products can fulfill different functional and psychological needs. Work with your partners on the following tasks.

   List five luxury products that are very interesting or important to you. Some possibilities might be cars, clothing, sports equipment, music, or cosmetics. List five other necessities that you use which have little interest to you, such as pencils, laundry detergent, or gasoline.

   Make a list of words that describe how you feel about each of the products that you listed. Are there differences between the types of words you used for luxuries and necessities? What does this tell you about the different psychological needs that these products fulfill?

2. Examine our own purchases can reveal ways in which buying decisions really occur. Work in a group to complete the following tasks.

   Describe the five stages of your own buying decision process for a major purchase such as a camera, cellphone, or PC.

   Next, describe your decision process for a minor purchase such as a candy bar or a soda.

   Are the decision processes the same for major and minor purchases? In which stages do they differ, and why?

Case study

Big Data Helps Taobao with Precision Marketing

In today's market, it is not the most powerful companies that can survive, but companies that can quickly adapt to changes in the environment.

Many people have this experience: One day they tried to choose a razor in a B2C mall but couldn't find a suitable one. The next day, when they browsed other news websites, they saw pop-up advertisements recommending razors, and couldn't help but click to browse the advert or even buy one.

This visitor tracking & recommendation technology is developed by marketing companies. With the aid of this technology, remarketing to target users is much more accurate than other targeting techniques. And behind this is data analysis at work. The use of data in marketing is changing the traditional way of communication and consumer insight.

2013 is the year that witnessed the explosion of big data. The big data technology is applied to Internet marketing, helping companies do better at advertising and marketing.

Whether it is Baidu, Tencent, Taobao or Sina, there is a huge amount of data on each platform. Even the data on a single media platform can reflect behaviors of netizens. For example, Baidu accumulates data about search-related behaviors of netizens, while Taobao has data about buying decision making behaviors of netizens, and the reading behaviors of netizens can be reflected by data on Sina.

In terms of business nature, marketing process is the process of satisfying demand, providing value, completing transactions, and finally realizing profits. The rapid development of the Internet has changed the consumption patterns and behavioral habits of consumers, as well as the traditional business model. "This is the best time; this is the worst time." Dickens's words can't be more appropriate to describe what is happening today. "Huge changes" feature this era, and the most important thing for companies is to adjust their mode of thinking.

Before the era of big data, which platforms did companies extract data from, and what marketing data did they extract? Generally, it was structured data such as customer information, market promotions, advertising activities, exhibitions, etc. in the CRM or BI system, as well as data from the company's official website. But information from these traditional channels could only satisfy 10% of the enterprise's regular marketing management needs. It was not enough to enlighten an important insight or find a pattern.

The other 85% of the data comes from social media, email, geographic positioning, audio and video, as well as from the gradually widely-used sensor-based IoT, and mobile 5G, the Internet, etc. These unstructured or multi-structured data produced by the big data technology are more frequently presented in the form of pictures and videos. A few years ago, they may be left out in data collection. But today they can further enhance the function of algorithms and machine analysis. This type of data is becoming increasingly valuable in today's fiercely competitive market, and with a more prominent role, it can be fully tapped into and applied to practice by big data technology.

Questions:

1. What customer behavior insights can be gained through the use of the big data technology on Taobao?

2. Analyze the level of consumer involvement in the purchase of clothes online.

3. Discuss the influences on consumer buying behavior during the November 11 shopping spree based on your personal experience.

Chapter Four

Marketing Information and Marketing Research

Objectives:

After studying this chapter, you should be able to:

- Define the marketing information system and the steps involved in the system;
- Identify the three major sources of marketing information;
- Distinguish primary and secondary data;
- Distinguish qualitative and quantitative research and identify the marketing occasions on which they can be applied;
- Understand the three major market research approaches: observation, personal interview and survey, their applicable occasions, use, data expected, advantages and disadvantages;
- Develop some rough ideas about designing questionnaires and try to design questions on your own;
- Think critically on marketing ethics issues related to the acquisition and use of marketing information.

Framework

Chapter Four Marketing Information and Marketing Research

Assessing marketing information needs

Analyzing marketing information

Distributing and using marketing information

Ethics in marketing research

Developing marketing information

- Internal database
- Marketing intelligence
- Marketing research

- Step 1: Defining the problem and research objectives
- Step 2: Developing the research plan
- Step 3: Implementing the research plan
- Step 4: Interpreting and reporting the findings

Marketers need information to help make decisions concerning market segmentation, target marketing, positioning, and marketing mix, etc. There are various types of information in the market, which can be obtained internally by sorting out internal database, or externally from marketing intelligence. On other occasions marketers go beyond the border of information readily available and embark on developing their own specific market information from marketing research. Information collected is then analyzed to form customer insights which assist in marketing decision making. Obtaining information from internal database, marketing intelligence, marketing research and information analysis are the four big issues related to developing marketing information, which forms a crucial part of marketing information system.

⊞ 营销信息系统 (MIS) 涵盖能够及时准确地收集、整理、分析、评估和分发所需信息给营销决策者的人员、设备和程序。

Kotler defines <u>marketing information system (MIS) as people, equipment, and procedures needed to gather, sort out, analyze, evaluate, and distribute the needed information to marketing decision makers timely and accurately</u>.

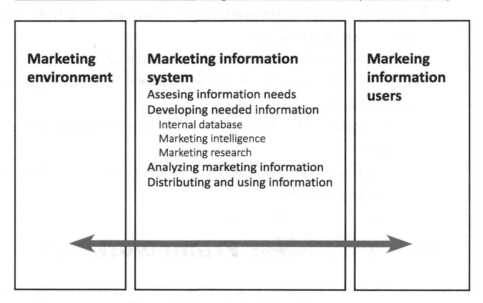

Figure 4.1 The marketing information system

1. Assessing marketing information needs

Developing marketing information starts from defining the information needs. It's often prompted by a problem or situation faced by the company. Sometimes marketers also need to balance between the information they want to get and the information they really need, or information that can be obtained within the resources available.

2. Developing marketing information

The second step is to develop marketing information. There are mainly three ways, e.g., by obtaining it from internal database, marketing intelligence, or marketing research.

2.1 Internal database

Departments in the company collect or develop information about products, markets or consumers for different purposes, some of which can be used in making marketing decisions. For example, accounting department collects information of transactions, products and customers when preparing financial statements. The customer service center may have data about customer complaints and after-sales service needs. Information collected internally can help marketers develop marketing ideas from different aspects. Internal database is a convenient and economical way to obtain marketing information. For instance, supermarkets and many other businesses nowadays are keen to issue loyalty cards to their buyers, because in this way they can accumulate data about customers' purchases and develop ideas about customer preference, buying behaviors and so on.

However, there are drawbacks of using data from internal database. One major problem is that information stored in various departments is always fragmented. But this can be solved to some extent by some <u>customer relationship management (CRM) system—a system integrating information from all departments to inform all staff who deal with customers</u>. Nowadays, the big data technology also makes it possible and easier to pool all internal data together and then develop a bigger picture. The limitation is that it only forms internal perspectives about the company itself, but is incapable of revealing external environment and competition situations.

> ⊞ 客户关系管理
> （CRM）系统：整
> 合各部门信息，并提
> 供给所有与客户打交
> 道的员工。

2.2 Marketing intelligence

Apart from information obtained from internal departments in the company, there are also different types of information readily available out there in the market. Among them, what marketers care most may be the information about competitors and developments in the marketplace. <u>The systematic collection and analysis of such type of publicly available information about competitors and developments in the marketplace is called marketing intelligence</u>.

> ⊞ 营销情报涉及系统
> 地收集和分析关于竞
> 争对手和市场变化的
> 公开信息。

In an imperfectly competitive market, the profit of a company depends not only on its own decision, but also on the decision of competitors. For example, when competitors lower the price or develop new features of the product while the company does not, it may lose some customers. That's why companies need to act strategically by analyzing the decision of competitors. Market intelligence can be obtained from suppliers, resellers, and key customers through many practices, from chatting with clients of competitors on a trade show, hiring former employees of the competitors, to analyzing the advertisement or products of the competitive companies. Some companies even dig into the trash bin of competitors to find out important intelligence. Such behavior is legal since the documents and materials are no longer considered as the property of the competitor once it leaves that company. Yet it may not be that ethical.

2.3 Marketing research

田 营销调研是指一家组织对其所面对的市场环境的相关数据进行系统的设计、收集、分析和汇报。

Publicly available information may not completely suit the needs of marketers. For instance, when they need to find out how customers respond to a new marketing initiative like the launch of a new product, there's no such public information available. In such case, marketers develop their own information through marketing research. Marketing research is the systematic design, collection, analysis, and reporting of data relevant to a specific marketing situation facing an organization.

There are four steps in marketing research.

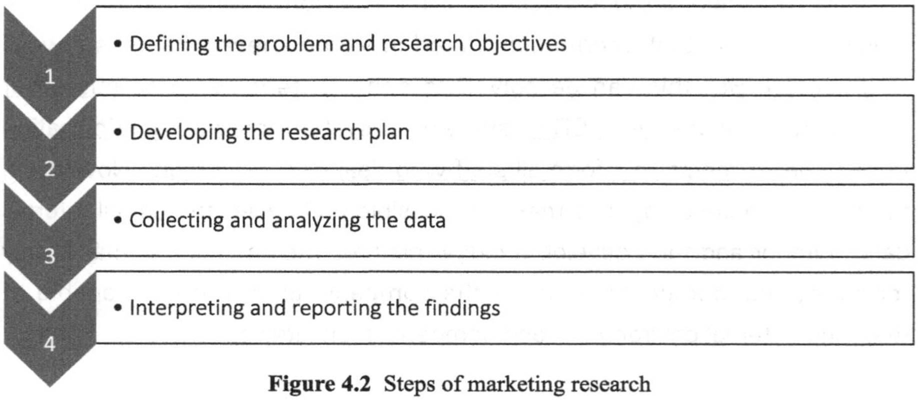

1 • Defining the problem and research objectives

2 • Developing the research plan

3 • Collecting and analyzing the data

4 • Interpreting and reporting the findings

Figure 4.2 Steps of marketing research

Step 1: Defining the problem and research objectives

Each research plan starts with a question to answer, and a clearly and specifically defined question is the first step into success. Researchers need to discuss with information users like the marketing manager to pinpoint the problem, which then helps to specify the objectives of the market research. The company either asks employees within the company such as the marketing department or marketing research team to do the research, or hires an independent marketing research agency to do the work, which is considered more experienced and professional.

There are different types of research. For exploratory research, the objective is to gather preliminary information that will help gain some initial ideas and suggest hypotheses. For descriptive research, the objective is to describe the market, including the market potential for a product, competitiveness of rivals and the demographics of consumers, etc. For causal research, the objective is to test hypotheses about cause-and-effect relationships. Normally, researchers start with exploratory research and later follow with descriptive or causal research.

Step 2: Developing the research plan

After specifying the research objectives and the specific information needed, the researcher designs a plan to collect it, and then present the plan to the marketing manager. The most important part of the plan is the description of the method to collect the data— obtaining secondary data available or developing the company's own primary data or combining both.

Secondary research

Marketing research may start from gathering secondary data readily available. The company can buy secondary data from data suppliers or use commercial online databases. Secondary data refers to readily available information that has been developed by others for another purpose and comes to the marketers second-hand. (Information obtained from marketing intelligence and internal database is also called secondary data.)

The advantages of using secondary data include the following. Firstly, they can be obtained at a lower cost. Suppliers of secondary data can achieve economies of scale by specializing in providing a large sum of data so that the unit cost is reduced. Secondly, since the data is readily available, it saves time in collecting them. Thirdly, some of the data cannot be developed by the company itself either because they are beyond the reach or they would be too costly to obtain, so it is advisable for the company to rely on external suppliers. However, the information needed may not exist or the available information may not be usable, i.e., it's not relevant, accurate or up-to-date.

> ⊞ 二手数据是指现成的信息，该信息是他人为其他目的而开发的，作为二手信息为营销人员所获得。

Primary research

Given the limitations of secondary data, companies usually need to develop their own data which are tailored to their specific need. Such process is called primary data collection, or primary research. Primary data refers to information proactively collected by researchers for the current specific situation or purpose. The first step in collecting primary data is to determine the subject to be researched on. Researchers normally select a sample to represent the population since it's not possible or too costly to study the whole population, and it's unnecessary. A sample is a segment of the population selected to represent the whole population in marketing research. By studying the sample researchers get reasonable estimate of the behavior or attitude of the large population.

> ⊞ 一手数据是指研究人员为了当前具体情况或目的而主动收集的信息。

> ⊞ 样本是指在营销研究中被选中代表整个群体的一部分人群。

A. Research approaches

Researchers make a distinction between drawing quantitative results by studying a large sample, and obtaining qualitative results by studying a small sample. Qualitative research refers to the in-depth study of a small sample in order to gain deep insights into customer behavior, attitudes and feelings, etc. Research approaches to gaining qualitative results include observation, in-depth personal interview, focus-group interview and ethnographic research. Quantitative research focuses on systematically collecting a large number of

> ⊞ 定性研究是指对小样本的深入研究，目的是深入了解客户行为、态度和感受等。

田 通过研究或大或小的样本，定量研究侧重于系统地收集大量可量化的数据，并得出统计结论。

田 观察法是指不干预过程地观察人们、人们的行动和情况来收集一手数据。

田 人种学研究，包括派遣训练有素的观察员在消费者的自然生活环境中观察他们并与他们互动。

田 深度访谈，也称为单独访谈，就单一主题深入面谈单个客户，面谈可在他们的家中或办公室、街道或商场中进行。小组访谈是由主持人（研究人员）对一组客户进行非结构化或半结构化面谈。由于主持人通常将小组讨论聚焦在某些主题上，因此也称为焦点小组访谈。

quantifiable data and drawing statistical conclusions by studying large or small samples. Quantitative research techniques include surveys and experiments. Here three major research approaches—observation, personal interview and survey will be elaborated upon.

a. Observation

Observation means gathering primary data by observing people, their actions and situations without interfering in the process. The researcher can design observation forms to record respondents' actions. Observation studies are applied by marketers in retail business when they want to observe the behavior of shoppers in supermarkets, clothing shops or other retail shops. Observation has two major advantages. First, it helps researchers obtain information that respondents are unwilling or unable to provide. Second, some types of information can only be collected through observation such as the traffic in a certain neighborhood. However, there are things that cannot be observed, such as feelings, attitudes and motives, or private behavior.

One particular observational study is field study conducted by anthropologists, who spend a certain period living with local people and observing how they lead their daily lives. Some marketers learn from anthropologists and conduct ethnographic research, which involves sending trained observers to watch and interact with consumers in their natural living environment. It includes on-site and in-home ethnographic research, in which the researcher observes when consumers are using the product in restaurant, store, or office, etc.; or researcher observes consumers behaviors in their home environment.

b. Personal interview

As feelings, attitudes and motives cannot be observed directly, personal interview is indispensable. Personal interview takes two forms, i.e., individual in-depth interview and focus group interview. In-depth interview, also called individual interview, involves interviewing individual customers about a single topic in depth, in their homes or offices, on the street, or in shopping malls. Group interview is an unstructured or semi-structured interview conducted by a moderator (the researcher) on a group of customers. Since the moderator normally focuses the group discussion on certain topics, it's also called focus group interview.

In-depth interview is effective in obtaining qualitative data since it allows the researcher to have detailed discussion with the customer. It's often conducted on important individuals such as opinion leaders, experts, key customers (e.g. regular buyers, loyal customers) or other individuals that play an important role in the targeted market segment. It's also applied when the topic requires individual treatment or when the presence of other interviewee inhibits the honest expression of opinions. Yet it takes time and is costly.

In group interview, the moderator includes a number of areas within the topic to discuss with the group of around six to twelve customers, but allows the group considerable freedom to discuss issues that are important to them. By observing and participating in the discussion, the moderator gains insights into the customers' behaviors, attitudes, or even feelings and motives. Focus group discussion can take place face-to-face or through the Internet, with the help of online chat rooms. Questions can be posted online and respondents are not under time pressure to respond. This encourages more detailed responses since respondents can take their time to think carefully. However, the lack of direct personal contact reduces interpersonal quality achieved through interaction and the chance to observe body language among group members.

c. Survey

<u>Survey is a quantitative method for collecting information from a pool of respondents by asking survey questions.</u> It is the most widely adopted method for gathering descriptive primary data since it's most effective and trustworthy. Questionnaire is an important research tool used in survey.

田 调研是指通过向一组受访者询问调查问题来收集信息的定量方法。

Advantages of survey methods include: (1) standardization, (2) ease of administration, (3) ability to explore the invisible, and (4) suitability to statistical analysis. Firstly, since the questions are preset and standardized, all respondents are asked the same questions and given the same response options. Secondly, administering the questionnaire is simpler and less costly than conducting focus group or in-depth interview, especially when the questionnaire is sent through mail. Thirdly, as compared with observation, questionnaire enables the researcher to ask about the attitude, perception and feelings of the respondents. For example, the researcher can ask the parents to rate the importance of location of a school when they choose the child's school. Finally, as the questionnaire is normally distributed to a large number of respondents and most of the answers are computable, it's convenient for researchers to compute the results and reach statistical conclusions.

However, the survey method also has some limitations. Sometimes people are either unable to answer survey questions, or unwilling to respond to unknown researchers or on matters related to privacy. Respondents may try to help the researcher by giving pleasing answers, answer the question even when they don't know the answer to appear more informed, or they may understate or overstate the results so as to create a favorable image of themselves. For example, respondents may decline answering question on income since they consider it private, or conservative respondents tend to understate their income to keep a low profile.

Design of questionnaire

The design of questionnaire involves three decisions. Firstly, the types and ordering of the topics need to be determined. A questionnaire normally begins with easy-to-answer questions then followed by complicated or sensitive

> 田 问卷问题主要分为三类，即正误判断题、选择题和开放性题目。

questions. Secondly, the type of question needs to be decided. <u>There are mainly three types of questions, namely, dichotomous questions ("Yes"/"No" questions), multiple-choice questions, and open questions</u>. Answers to close questions (dichotomous and multiple-choice questions) are computable while open questions allow researchers to explore in detail and in depth as respondents can provide their personalized answers. The use of "scale" is also popular. Respondents are asked to choose a position in a scale in deciding their attitude or frequency of certain behavior. For example, respondents are provided with a statement "Families should be encouraged to have a second baby" and a scale ranging from "strongly agree" to "strongly disagree".

Contact methods

There are three ways to distribute the questionnaire: (1) have a person ask the question, (2) have a computer assist or direct the questioning, or (3) let the respondents fill in the questionnaire themselves. To be specific, there are 10 contact methods, i.e., in-home interview, mall-intercept interview, in-office interview, traditional telephone interview, central location telephone interview, computer-assisted telephone interview (CATI), fully computerized interview, group-self-administered survey, drop-off survey and mail survey.[1]

These 10 specific contact methods can be grouped into three categories: face-to-face interview, telephone interview, mail and online survey.

Using face-to-face interview encourages higher response rate, and allows greater control of who is in the sample. It's also efficient and flexible in obtaining data. The trained interviewer can guide the interview and explain difficult questions. However, face-to-face interview costs three to four times as much as telephone interview. The presence of an interviewer also causes bias partly because the way the interviewer asks questions may influence the response, and partly because respondents may be unwilling or embarrassed to provide sensitive information in the presence of the interviewer.

Telephone interview lies between personal interview and mail survey in

---

[1] In-home interview: The interviewer conducts the interview in the respondent's home.

Mall-intercept interview: Shoppers in a mall are approached and asked to take part in the survey.

In-office interview: The interviewer makes an appointment with managers or executives to have the interview in the respondent's office.

Traditional telephone interview: The interviewer phones the household or business representatives to conduct the interview.

Central location telephone interview: Interviewers work in a data collection company's office using cubicles or work areas for each interviewer.

Computer-assisted telephone interview (CATI): With a central location telephone interview, the questions are programmed for a computer screen and the interviewer then reads them off. Responses are entered directly into the computer program by the interviewer.

Fully computerized interview: A computer is programmed to administer the questions. Respondents interact with the computer and enters their own answers.

Group self-administered survey: Respondents take the survey in a group context.

Drop-off survey: Questionnaires are left with the respondents to fill in.

Mail survey: Questionnaires are mailed to and returned through mail by prospective respondents.

terms of response rate and survey cost. Response rate is lower than that of face-to-face interview, while it saves cost. It also guarantees a certain degree of flexibility. However, there's a limit to the number of questions that can be asked before the respondent on the phone gets exhausted or impatient. Similar to face-to-face interview, telephone interview is also limited in terms of the use of sensitive questions.

Mail survey is an economical way of collecting quantitative data, yet the response rate and the quality of answers obtained cannot be guaranteed. When response rate is low, the sample may not be representative. In a similar vein, the low quality of answers reduces the credibility of the survey result. Nowadays the Internet has become an important way of conducting surveys, and online research is probably the most popular form of survey research. The Internet questionnaire is usually administered by email or is presented on a website. The major advantages of online research include its low cost, high speed and wide coverage. However, when a questionnaire is distributed online, it's difficult to control who answer the questions. Besides, researcher cannot reach people with restricted Internet access. Perhaps the most challenging issue faced by online researchers is consumer privacy. Respondents may be unwilling to provide sensitive information for fear that unethical researchers unduly use the information.

Table 4.1 Comparison of various contact methods in survey

	Personal	**Telephone**	**Mail**	**Online**
Quantity of data that can be collected	Excellent	Fair	Good	Good
Control of interviewer bias	Poor	Fair	Excellent	Fair
Control of sample	Good	Excellent	Fair	Excellent
Use of sensitive questions	Fair	Poor	Good	Poor
Speed of data collection	Good	Excellent	Poor	Excellent
Flexibility	Excellent	Good	Poor	Good
Response rate	Good	Good	Fair	Good
Cost	Poor	Fair	Good	Excellent

B. Sampling plan

Another decision involved in marketing research is sampling plan. Determining the sample involves three steps. First, define the population, which is about who is to be researched on. For example, in order to study the popularity of video games on campus, college students are the research subjects. Second, determine the sample size, which refers to the number of people included in the sample. In the previous example, researchers select a number of college students to represent the whole population. The larger the sample size, the more representative of the sample. Yet the cost is higher. Researchers thus need to balance the representativeness and cost. Third, specify the sample method, i.e., how the sample is to be selected. There're three approaches. In simple random sampling, the sample is chosen at random and each individual has an equal chance of being selected. In stratified random sampling, the population is first divided

⊞ 在简单随机抽样
中，样本是随机选择
的，每个个体被选中
的机会均等。 在分
层随机抽样中，首先
将总体划分为若干组
别或类别，然后从每
个组别中随机抽取样
本。在配额抽样中，
首先将总体划分为类
别，然后研究人员从
每个类别中选取配额
内的个体。

into groups or categories and then from each group a random sample is drawn. In quota sampling, the population is first divided into categories and the researcher selects a number of individuals from each category within the quota, so that, for example, the sample is composed of a set percentage of students from Grade 1, 2, and 3.

Step 3: Implementing the research plan

After careful design of the research plan, researchers then put it into action. This involves collecting, processing, and analyzing the information. Data collection can either be done by the company's marketing department or by external third parties. The data collection phase is normally most expensive and most subject to error. Researchers need to guard against the problems related to different research approaches, contact methods, as well as challenges from respondents who refuse to cooperate.

Step 4: Interpreting and reporting the findings

Researchers then interpret and report the findings to marketing managers. Basic interpretation involves describing the phenomenon or comparing the results using means, frequency, standard deviation or t-test. More sophisticated interpretation is to find out relationships. One common mistake is to misinterpret association as cause-and-effect relation. For example, when sales go up and advertising expenditure increases at the same time, researchers cannot rush to the conclusion that greater advertising effort leads to better sales. There might be association only. Besides, researchers need to pay attention to representativeness of samples and the resulting sampling error when inferring the population using sample variables.

⊞ 例如，销售额上
升和广告支出同时
增加，研究人员不
能急于得出结论：
更多的广告投入会
带来更好的销售额。
这两者之间可能只
是相关关系。

When reporting results, researchers need to transform the statistical figures into findings that are relevant to marketing decision making. They need to work with marketing managers to interpret the results. Marketing managers know better about the problems and decisions that need to be made, while they may tend to accept pleasing results. Discussion between researchers and managers is thus very important.

3. Analyzing marketing information

After gathering information from internal database, marketing intelligence and marketing research, marketing managers need to analyze the data to gain customer insights. Making best use of a large number of individual customer data can be a challenge. Smart companies catch information at every possible customer touch point. Such touch point refers to every contact between the customer and the company, including Website or store visits, customer

⊞ 接触点是指客户
与公司之间的每一
次接触。

purchases, sales staff contacts, after-sales service calls, satisfaction surveys, market research studies, payment interactions, etc. However, those data are scattered in separate databases in the company. Effective customer relationship management (CRM) helps to solve the problem. <u>CRM is defined as managing detailed information about individual customers and carefully managing customer "touch points" so as to maximize customer loyalty.</u>

⊞ 客户关系管理（CRM）是指管理详细的客户信息并细致管理客户的"接触点"，以最大限度地提高客户的忠诚度。

CRM consists of sophisticated software and analytical tools that integrate customer information from all sources, analyze it in depth, and apply the results to build stronger customer relationships. Using CRM enables companies to understand customers better, so that they can tailor their services to each category of customers, pinpoint high-value customers, and provide high-quality services to retain high-value customers.

4. Distributing and using marketing information

The marketing information and the analysis are then distributed to relevant decision makers in the form of regular performance reports, intelligence updates, and reports on the research results. Apart from regular reports, marketing managers also need non-routine information for special occasions. Company intranet enables the access to relevant marketing information readily available. For example, when receiving customer calls for enquiries or complaints, some company staffs can get access to up-to-date information about the customer background and past purchases. Website analysis is essential to e-commerce platforms. Customer behaviors on shopping websites, e.g. the commodities they've browsed, the linking point to the website, the length of time they spend on each page, etc., can be analyzed to gain customer insights.

5. Ethics in marketing research

Some respondents to marketing research are resistant or even hostile, because either they consider the information enquired about as privacy or they are uncertain about how the information will be used. Therefore, marketing research staff need to be aware of not intruding on customer privacy or misusing the information in an unethical way. Apart from customers' concerns for individual privacy and the use of research findings, there are other ethical issues related to the process of marketing research, such as the customer's right to know the real purpose of the research, background information and other information that they need to know, accuracy, authenticity and completeness of research reports and so on.

Summary

A market-oriented organization always starts operations with knowing their customers and the external environment. To this end, they rely on abundant marketing information. The marketing information system (MIS) consists of the following steps: assessing information needs, developing needed information, analyzing marketing information, distributing and using information.

Developing needed information is no doubt the most important part of this chapter. Marketing information has three major sources: internal database, marketing intelligence and market research. Internal database is a convenient and economical way to obtain marketing information, but the limitation is that it only produces data that forms internal perspectives about the company itself. If the company wants to know about the business environment and competitors, for example, it may need marketing intelligence. Marketing intelligence refers to publicly available information about competitors and developments in the marketplace. However, neither data from the internal database nor marketing intelligence can suit all the needs of marketers. In this case, marketing research can play a role.

Marketing research is the systematic design, collection, analysis, and reporting of data relevant to a specific marketing situation facing an organization. There are four steps in a marketing research: defining the problem and research objectives, developing the research plan, collecting and analyzing the data, interpreting and reporting the findings.

The first distinction that market researchers need to make is probably primary and secondary data. Primary data refers to information proactively collected by researchers for the current specific situation or purpose. Secondary data refers to readily available information that has been developed by others for another purpose and comes to the marketers second-hand. Primary and secondary data have their respective pros and cons. The important thing is researchers need to decide which type of data is needed on a specific occasion.

The second distinction is qualitative research and quantitative research. Qualitative research refers to the in-depth study of a small sample in order to gain deep insights into customer behavior, attitudes and feelings, etc. Quantitative research focuses on systematically collecting a large number of quantifiable data and drawing statistical conclusions by studying large or small samples. Qualitative data and quantitative data satisfy different information needs.

This chapter details three major research approaches: observation, personal interview and survey. In marketing research, observation is employed, often in retail context, to gather primary data about customer behaviors without interference. Personal interview takes two forms: individual in-depth interview and focus group interview. The distinction lies in the number of subjects involved in the interview. Survey is a quantitative method for collecting information from a pool of respondents by asking survey questions. The design of questionnaire and sampling are two pivotal links in the survey process.

At the end of this chapter, the readers' attention is drawn to some ethical issues related to the process of market research, such as the protection of customer privacy, the misuse of research findings, customers' right to know and so on.

Key terms

marketing information system (MIS)	interview
marketing intelligence	in-depth interview
marketing research	focus group interview
primary data	survey
secondary data	questionnaire
qualitative research	touch point
quantitative research	sample
observation	sampling process

Exercises

Review and discussion

1. Match the types of research (1–4) with the research problems below (a–d).

_____ 1) desktop + secondary

_____ 2) qualitative + field

_____ 3) motivation + primary

_____ 4) quantitative + primary

a. The R&D department want to know why people buy mobile phones so that they can develop a new model that answers all the major needs.

b. The design team want to know how consumers feel about the new layout of the company website before they finalize and launch the new homepage.

c. A manger wants to have financial data on her company, her competitors and the economy in general.

d. The marketing team want to have a lot of data on their consumers: age, shopping habits, email address, etc.

2. Complete the sentences. Consult the "Reference" to help you.

Reference

Focus groups: Small groups from the **target group** plus one **moderator** to **mediate** or **run** the session. The moderator prepares questions for the session.

Package test: Used to test ideas for new packaging; could be in a focus group.

Taste test: Used to test what consumers think about new flavors.

Home test: Consumers try to the products at home, in a real situation.

A **self-administered questionnaire** is **completed** or **filled in** by the respondent, and an **interviewer-administered** questionnaire is filled in on behalf of the respondent by an interviewer.

Telephone surveys are carried out by telephoning the respondent and asking questions.

A **mail survey** is mailed to the respondent, who completes it and posts it back.

Online surveys are administered on the Internet.

Mystery shopping: A person poses as a consumer and checks the level of service and hygiene in a restaurant, hotel or shop.

Omnibus surveys: A market research institute **carries out** or **conducts research** for several companies at the same time. A long survey is given to respondents; some institutes have a **panel** of existing respondents who are accustomed to answering the surveys.

1) A lot of marketing research institutes carry out _____ surveys. They ring people at home and ask them questions.

2) A _____ _____ is a small discussion group, led by a _____ who asks questions to get detailed and qualitative information.

3) A marketing research institute may prepare a lengthy _____ survey which it posts to consumers at their homes. These _____ surveys have questions from several different companies on them.

4) Some questionnaires are completed by the _____ (self-administered questionnaires) and some are completed by the interviewer (_____-_____ questionnaires).

5) _____ _____ surveys are usually carried out in-store to assess the levels of service quality and cleanliness.

6) A _____ test is designed to find out what consumers think about packaging, and a _____ test is to find out what they think about the flavor of a product.

3. Cross out the incorrect sentence in each group.

1) a. We carried out the research last week.

   b. We conducted the research last week.

   c. We collected the research last week.

2) a. It can take a long time to mine data.

   b. It can take a long time to carry out data.

   c. It can take a long time to analyze data.

3) a. The respondents completed a questionnaire.

   b. The respondents analyzed a questionnaire.

   c. The respondents filled in a questionnaire.

4) a. We are filling in three focus groups.

   b. We are mediating three focus groups.

   c. We are running three focus groups.

5) a. We must run the data quickly.

    b. We must collect the data quickly.

    c. We must gather the data quickly.

4. Translate the following sentences into English.

1) 探测性调查是指当市场情况不十分明了时，为了发现问题，找出问题的症结，明确进一步深入调查的具体内容和重点而进行的非正式调查。

_____

_____

2) 描述性调查是指对需要调查的客观现象的有关方面而进行的正式调查。

_____

_____

3) 定性研究主要是判别事物发展变化的性质、方向、好处、趋向等。

_____

_____

4) 定量研究主要是运用数据来认识事物的发展变化的规模、水平、结构、速度和数量特征与规律。

_____

_____

5) 焦点访谈使用类似头脑风暴的方法，比一对一的面谈更容易发现新概念、新思路。

_____

_____

5. Answer the following questions briefly.

1) What are the differences between qualitative and quantitative research? Explained the roles played by each.

2) Many firms are now investing heavily in analyzing their own customers through CRM and websites analysis. What are the advantages and disadvantages of this trend for both firms and consumers?

3) What is the major difference between primary data and secondary data?

4) Compare the advantages and disadvantages between primary and secondary data.

5) What are the research approaches used by researchers to collect primary data?

6) Why does an effective questionnaire need both closed-ended and open-ended questions? What are the purposed of each kind of the questions?

── **Projects and teamwork** ──

1. It has been argued that research data can be manipulated to support any conclusion. Assume you are attending a meeting where a research project for a new product in a new market is being presented. List five questions that you would ask to test the interpretation and objectivity of the findings being presented.

2. Assume you are responsible for launching a new category of skincare products for young people between 18–26, with separate product lines for males and females. Design a questionnaire to collect primary data among university students. You can send the questionnaire either by mail or electronically. There should be close-ended questions and open-ended ones, and they should be arranged logically.

── **Case study** ──

An Effective Tool for Customer Behavior Analysis: Eye Tracker

Which product packaging can attract customers more? Which part of the shelf catches most eyeballs of customers? Which area of a website page is the most noticeable? These are the questions that marketers often encounter. With the development of modern technology, we can solve these problems with the help of an eye tracker through experiments. An eye tracker is an instrument that specifically measures the focus of the user's line of sight. Its principle is similar to that of measuring myopia. It can test where the focus of the line of sight stays so as to help marketers determine the focus of customers' attention.

Online Questionnaire System: WJX

As a professional online platform for questionnaire, evaluation, and voting, WJX (Wenjuanxing) is specialized in providing users with powerful and user-friendly online questionnaire design, data collection, custom reports, and survey results analysis services. Compared with traditional survey methods and other survey websites or systems, WJX has evident advantages: fast, easy-to-use, and low-cost. It has been widely used by a large number of enterprises and individuals. It has the following functions:

(1) Design online questionnaire. WJX provides a WYSIWYG (what you see is what you get) interface for questionnaire design, supports a variety of question types, information columns and page columns, and allows users to set scores for options (for scale questions or test questionnaires). In addition, dozens of professional questionnaire templates are available.

(2) Release questionnaire and set attributes of questionnaire. After a questionnaire is designed, you can directly release it and set its attributes, such as questionnaire classification, description, scope of disclosure, access password, etc.

(3) Send questionnaire. Send an invitation email or embed the questionnaire on the website of the company to be investigated, or send the questionnaire link to friends via QQ, Weibo, email, etc.

(4) Check survey results. You can view the statistical results in graphs automatically generated, or check the details of answers in card form, and access details of respondents such as time, region and platform used to fill in the questionnaire.

(5) Create custom reports. A series of filter conditions can be set in custom reports, which can not only do cross-analysis and classified statistics based on the answers, but also filter out eligible answer sheets based on the length of time used to complete the questionnaire, the respondent's region and the platform they use to answer the questionnaire, etc.

(6) Download survey data. After the investigation is completed, the investigator can download the statistical chart to save in computer and print in Word, or download the original data in Excel, and import the survey analysis software such as SPSS for further analysis.

Questions:

1. Discuss commercial contexts where the eye tracking technology can be used to collect marketing data.

2. Identity a set of research questions which can be answered by means of the eye tracking technology.

3. Suppose you are a marketer of a personal care company, which is about to launch a new shampoo. Use WJX to design a questionnaire to collect data about target customers.

Chapter Five

Segmentation, Targeting, Positioning and Differentiation

Objectives:

After studying this chapter, you should be able to:

- Truly understand market segmentation, targeting, positioning and differentiation and their importance;
- List benefits of segmentation;
- Discuss the major variables for segmenting consumer markets;
- Explain the criteria for successful marketing;
- Identify the four major types of targeting and explain how companies can choose an appropriate targeting strategy;
- Discuss how companies position and reposition their offerings in the minds of target customers;
- Explain the keys to successful positioning;
- Discuss how businesses can design market offerings that differentiate themselves from competitors.

Framework

Chapter Five Segmentation, Targeting, Positioning and Differentiation

Segmenting consumer market

- Definition
- Benefits of segmentation
- Major segmentation variables for consumer markets
- Criteria for successful segmentation

Target marketing

- Undifferentiated marketing
- Differentiated marketing
- Focused marketing
- Customized marketing
- Mass customization
- Choosing a targeting strategy

Positioning and repositioning

- Definition of positioning
- Keys to successful positioning
- Repositioning alternatives

Differentiation

- Product differentiation
- Service differentiation
- Channel differentiation
- Price differentiation
- People differentiation

So far, we have learned what marketing is and about the importance of analyzing the marketplace environment and understanding customer behaviors. This chapter looks further into some key marketing strategy decisions—how to divide up markets into meaningful segments (segmentation), choose which segments to serve (targeting), create what marketing offerings that best serve target customers (differentiation) and position the offering in the minds of customers (positioning).

1. Segmenting consumer market

As we know from Chapter Three, customer behaviors are subject to various personal, psychological, social and cultural influences. Because customers' needs, wants, buying behaviors and choice criteria vary, no matter how good your product or service is, it is almost impossible that you can satisfy all customers in the market, at least not in the same way. That is why businesses need to design different offerings for diverse customer groups. The process of dividing up the market into small groups for marketing purposes is referred to as "segmentation".

1.1 Definition

Philip Kotler defined segmentation as <u>"dividing a market into smaller groups with distinct needs, characteristics, or behaviors who might require separate products or marketing mixes"</u>, while John Fahy and David Jobber referred to market segmentation as <u>"the identification of individuals or organizations with similar characteristics that have significant implications for the determination of marketing strategy"</u>.

> 田 将市场划分为具有特定需要、特征或行为的较小客户群体，不同的群体需要单独的产品或营销组合"。
>
> ············
>
> 田 识别具有相似特征的个人或组织，这些特征对确定营销策略具有重要的影响。

Two things can be known from the above definitions of segmentation. First, customers in a smaller submarket—a segmented market must share common needs, characteristics and behaviors. It is the homogeneity that increases marketing effectiveness through segmentation. A segment should be neither too large nor too small. If it is too large, segmentation does little help to effectiveness enhancement. If it is too small, efficiency will be compromised. Second, segments should be distinctive enough from one another, allowing segmentation to provide a commercially viable method of serving customer needs.

1.2 Benefits of segmentation

There are many reasons why it is sensible for companies to segment the market (see Figure 5.1). First and foremost, <u>segmentation enhances a company's profitability</u>. Airline companies divide a civil plane into economy cabin, business cabin and first-class cabin. During the same flight, a business seat or a first-class seat only takes a little more costs than an economy seat, e.g. extra space, fancy drinks and meals, more meticulous and attentive services, but brings much more profit margins, because business executives

> 田 细分可提高一间公司的盈利能力。

⊞ 对于较小的公司而言，市场细分为寻找利基市场和发展业务创造了机会。

⊞ 市场细分提高了公司在细分市场获得优势的机会。
通过服务好目标群体，公司可提高顾客保留率，从而有助于保持长期客户关系。

and less budget-concerned passengers are more than happy to pay a premium price in exchange of comforts during the journey.

For smaller companies, segmentation creates opportunities for finding a niche market and growing the business. In its infancy, Apple found its personal computers hard to compete head to head with powerful PC market dominants like IBM, Dell and HP. However, Apple smartly identified a niche market—art students, fashion designers and other PC users with high demands for high-fidelity color display, and developed computers with distinctive features for the target group. Apple's PCs are known for high fidelity and authentic display of colors. Segmentation is the basis of more effective targeting.

Moreover, if a small company is able to keep growing in the niche market and a big company focuses on expanding a segmented market, the possible result would be segment dominance. Segmentation enhances opportunities for segment dominance. At the same time, by serving target groups well, companies can improve the rate of customer retention, thus helping maintaining long-term relationships with customers.

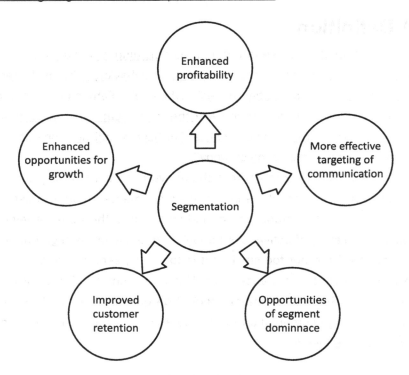

Figure 5.1 The benefits of market segmentation

1.3 Major segmentation variables for consumer markets

Segmentation should be meaningful. By meaningful, it means segmentation should be able to help enhance the effectiveness and efficiency of marketing. For instance, segmentation by gender is meaningful for garments, footwear, skincare products, cosmetics, perfume and magazines. But gender is not an effective variable for segmenting most foods, instant noodles, for example.

There is no single way to segment a market. <u>Marketers can try different segmentation variables, alone or in combination, to find the best way to view the market structure.</u> The table below lists the major variables for segmenting the consumer market as well as corresponding examples (see Table 5.1). But please note that even using one same segmentation variable, the segmentation results vary from product to product and from business to business.

> 田 营销人员可以尝试使用不同的独个或组合的细分标准，以找到观察市场结构的最佳方式。

Table 5.1 Major variables for segmentation of consumer markets

Behavioral	
• Occasions	Regular purchase, one-off purchase, special purpose
• Benefits sought	Convenience, performance, low price, quality
• Usage	
-Use status	Nonuser, ex-user, potential user, first-time user, regular user
-Use rate	Light user, medium user, heavy user
• Readiness stage	Unaware, aware, informed, interested, desirous, intending to buy
• Perceptions, beliefs and attitudes	Enthusiastic, positive, indifferent, negative, hostile
• ...	...
Psychographic	
• Lifestyle	Achievers, strivers, survivors
• Personality	Compulsive, filial, ambitious, cautious, generous
• ...	...
Profile	
• Demographic	
-Age	Under 6, 6–11, 12–19, 20–34, 35–49, 50–64, 65+
-Gender	Male, female
-Family size	1–2, 3–4, 5+
-Family life cycle	Single, married, no child, married with children, retired, old
-Income	Under RMB 5,000, RMB 5,000–10,000, RMB 10,000–20,000...
-Occupation	Professional and technical, managers, officials, clerical, sales...
-Education	Grade school or less, high school graduate, college graduate...
-Religion	Buddhist, Catholic, Hindu, Muslim, Protestant, other
-Race	Chinese, Indian, Malay, Korean, other
-Generation	Millennials, Generation Z, the Post-80s Generation...
-Nationality	Chinese, British, French, German, Japanese...
• Geographic	
-World region or country	Southeast Asian, Central Asia, North America, Middle East, Pacific Rim...
-Country region	Northeast China, South China, Central China...
-City size	Under 5,000, 5,001–20,000, 20,001–50,000, 50,001–100,000...
-Density	Urban, suburban, rural
• Social class	Lower class, working class, middle class, upper class

Behavioral

• Occasions

Buyers can be grouped according to occasions when they get the idea to buy, make their purchase or use the purchased goods. Some holidays, such as Chinese Lunar New Year, the Valentine's Day, Mother's Day and Father's Day, were promoted by businesses to boost sales of candy, flowers, chocolates, cards and other gifts. Marketers smartly use special occasions to launch big promotional activities. Taobao succeeded in building an originally ordinary day November 11 into an annual shopping spree festival. After years of marketing operations, the B2C platform was finally rewarded, as it reaped sales revenues of hundreds of billions of renminbi around each year's "November 11 Day". During the 2021 Chinese Luna New Year, some mask manufacturers launched specially designed masks for the occasion, which are red in color and printed with some auspicious patterns. The masks designed for the occasion of Chinese New Year caught on quickly.

⊞ 利益细分需找到消费者在某个产品类别中寻求的主要利益以及寻求每种利益的人群。

• Benefits sought

<u>Benefit segmentation requires finding the major benefits consumers look for in the product class and the kinds of people who look for each benefit.</u> P&G is a segmentation master. It boasts several well-known shampoo brands, one differentiating from another in terms of benefits offered, e.g. Head & Shoulders for addressing the dandruff problem, Rejoice for people wanting silky hair and Sassoon for repairing damaged hair. Focusing on benefits helps companies to spot business development opportunities. For instance, Yunnan Baiyao, a pharmaceutical enterprise in China, has a toothpaste brand widely acclaimed for treating bleeding gums.

• Usage

By usage status, consumers can be grouped into non-users, ex-users, potential users, first-time users and regular users. <u>Marketers need to find out why ex-users stop buying from them and what prevent non-users from trying their products or services, and come up with ideas about how to convert potential users into first-time users and first-time users into regular users and how to retain regular users.</u> In the obstetrical department of a hospital, sometimes we may see salespersons of baby products hand out free samples of formula milk power or diapers to pregnant women, because apparently these expecting parents are their potential customers. In a similar vein, photographic studios distribute their leaflets/brochures or even give one or two snapshots for free to newly wedded couples who have just stepped out of the municipal bureau of civil affairs, in an effort to promote their wedding photo business.

⊞ 营销人员需要搞清楚前用户为何停止购买，什么因素阻止非用户尝试他们的产品或服务；想出如何将潜在用户转化为首次使用者，将首次使用者转化为老顾客以及如何留住老顾客。

By usage frequency, consumers can be divided into heavy users, light users or non-users. Marketers should bear in mind that the 80:20 rule often applies in the business circle, that is, 80% of a business' revenue is brought by 20% of its customers, so we need to identify who are those 20% and focus more resources and efforts on them. It is not a difficult thing nowadays with the wide application of the big data technology.

- Readiness stage

Different marketing efforts and strategies are required for consumers who are unaware, aware, informed, interested, desirous and intending to buy. Mass communication techniques such as TV commercial, newspaper advertisement, etc. may work to bring a product or a brand to the awareness of unaware customers. But for those informed, interested, even desirous or intending-to-buy customers, they just need a little nudge to make a purchase, e.g. providing more detailed information, giving free samples, offering a big discount.

⊞ 针对不了解、了解、知情、感兴趣、渴望和有购买意愿的消费者，我们需要不同的营销努力和策略。

Psychographic

- Lifestyle

Lifestyle segmentation aims to categorize people in terms of their way of life, which is reflected in their activities, interests and opinions. For example, indoorsy people (also called "homebody") who enjoy spending time at home are heavy users of takeout delivery service, online shopping service and social media. By attitude towards cooking, people can be generally categorized into "live-to-cook" and "cook-to-live". The former has a passion for cooking, for discovering new recipes and for preparing exquisite meals for themselves and loved ones. The latter often prefer quick and easy preparation of foods, so instant frozen foods target at this group. Lifestyle segmentation helps marketers choose particular communication media and communication vehicle. With insights into the lifestyle of a particular group, marketers can reasonably infer their favored channels to access information, thus helping with marketing communications.

⊞ 生活方式细分旨在根据人们的生活方式对消费者进行分类；生活方式反映在人们的日常活动、兴趣和看法中。

⊞ 生活方式细分有助于营销人员选择特定的传播媒体和传播媒介。

- Personality

Personality is a variable that is hard to define and measure, so segmentation based on personality alone may not be a valid practice. But if this variable is combined with other variables like lifestyle, the segmentation may still work.

Profile

- Demographic

Demographic segmentation divides the market into groups based on variables such as age, gender, family size, family life cycle, income, occupation, education, religion, race, generation, nationality and so on. Demographic factors are the most popular bases for segmenting customer groups.

It is a common sense that consumer needs and wants change with age. Clothes, cosmetics, personal care products, household articles often rely on age-based segmentation. Besides, people in different stages of family

⊞ 按人口统计细分是根据诸如年龄、性别、家庭规模、家庭所处生命周期阶段、收入、职业、教育、宗教、种族、世代、国籍等标准将市场划分为多个群体。

life cycle apparently have different needs and wants. A young couple with a newborn will spend quite a proportion of their income on baby products, such as formula milk power, diapers, etc., while an older couple in their 50s will spend more money on personal entertainment and enjoyment. It is worth pointing out that a person's age is not necessarily linked with his life-cycle stage. In marketing practice, sometimes it is necessary to distinguish these two variables.

Income segmentation usually applies to automobiles, clothing, cosmetics, financial services and so on. For instances, bank's private banking services target at high-net-worth persons with abundant assets and high incomes. Factory outlets are shopped by budget-conscious, price-sensitive buyers.

Gender is a segmentation variable for clothing, cosmetics, perfume and magazines. For instance, Nike has the sideline brands—Nike Women and Nike Kids. Unilever's shampoo brand CLEAR has products specially designed for men.

● Geographic

Markets can be segmented based on country or regions within a country or city size. In recent years, more and more marketers combine geographic variables and demographic variables into what we call "geodemographics" in segmentation. For example, Coca-Cola developed four ready-to-drink canned coffees for the Japanese market, each targeting a specific geographic region. It also found that Japanese young people were always on the go, and they did not like to have coffee cans left open when they are walking. Ring-pull cans, the frequently used container for instant coffee, are not a good solution for this group of consumers. Hence, Coca-Cola introduced bottles with a twisted cap, which allows a bottle to be sealed up again after it is opened.

Another example of geodemographic segmentation is New Oriental, an established foreign language training institution in China. Most of New Oriental schools are opened in the tier-1 and tier-2 Chinese cities with a big population, more parents who are able to afford and care enough to pay for their children's extracurricular training tuitions and more adults who have plans to go abroad for business or for further study.

● Social class

Social class is a profile factor that may be used in segmentation. Though the concept of social class is quite blurred in China, it still works in one way or another in some countries like the UK. In the UK, tabloids are more read by the working class, while traditional broadsheets such as *Financial Times* take the middle and upper classes as their target readers.

Using multiple segmentation variables

In practice, marketers are increasingly using multiple variables to identify smaller, better defined target groups. An asset management company may

⊞ 近年来，越来越多的营销人员将地理变量和人口统计变量结合起来，变成所谓的"地理人口统计细分"。

⊞ 在实践中，营销人员越来越多地使用多个标准来识别更细小、更明确的目标群体。

identify its target customers based on not only income and assets, but also occupation, risk preference and risk tolerance and lifestyle. Using these variables, the asset management company can develop different product series with varying risks and returns for different segments. Segmentation based on multiple variables provides a powerful tool for marketers. <u>It helps companies identity and better understand the key segments, target them more effectively and efficiently, and tailor marketing offerings and communication messages to their specific needs.</u>

> 田 基于多种标准的市场细分可帮助公司识别和更好地了解关键的细分市场，更有效和高效地针对他们，根据其特定需求定制营销产品和营销传播信息。

1.4 Criteria for successful segmentation

We have discussed various ways to segment the consumer market. But how do we know our segmentation is successful? Does it help with marketing strategies? There are five measurement gauges that can help answer the questions (see Figure 5.2).

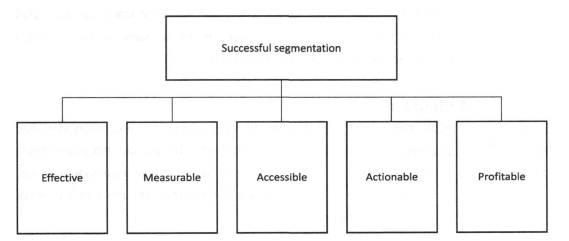

Figure 5.2 Criteria for successful segmentation

Effective

Effective segmentation divides a whole market into segments that are neither too large nor too small. If a defined segment is too large, the segmentation is not effective; if it is too small, the segmentation is not efficient. <u>A segment should be composed of customers whose needs, characteristics and behaviors are relatively homogeneous within a segment but significantly different from those in other segments.</u> Failure to identify customers with similar needs, characteristics, or behaviors for a segment is ineffective segmentation.

> 田 在一个细分市场内部，顾客具有相对同质的需要、特征和行为，但他们与其他细分市场的顾客在这些方面又具有显著的差异。

Measurable

Marketers should pay heed to the measurability of variables used for market segmentation. For instance, personality traits like "extrovert vs introvert" or "conscientious" are unmeasurable variables that are difficult to pin down, whereas variables like income, age, occupation and family size can be reliably measured. Segmentation on personality alone, most of the time, is invalid practice, but segmentation based on a combination of several variables including personality may still be effective.

Accessible

田 公司必须能够为确定的细分市场设计有效的营销方案，包括如何接触细分市场的目标顾客以进行营销传播。

A company must be able to design effective marketing programs for the segments it identifies, including how to approach target customers in a segment for marketing communications. For instance, a perfume maker intended to launch a new product targeting at "single men and women who hang out and socialize a lot". The problem is how marketers can access and deliver messages to such a group? The marital status "single" is easy to pin down, but people who like socializing can appear in many places around the city, coffee shops, restaurants, bars, parks, to name a few. How can marketers hunt these people down around the city?

Actionable

田 公司必须具有足够的资源来利用通过市场细分所获得的机会。

Companies must have the resources to exploit the opportunities identified through segmentation. Some market segments, those in international markets or high-tech segments, for example, may be lucratively attractive but small and medium-sized enterprises may not have the resources or expertise necessary to serve them.

Profitable

The goal of marketing is profits in return. Theoretically speaking, the smaller a segment is, the better customers in the segment can be served. For some industries like advertising, advertising agencies often adopt a one-to-one marketing mode, tailoring a marketing program that suits each of its potential clients. But the customized marketing is not suitable for most industries, because it is not profitable.

2. Target marketing

田 目标市场确定是指评估每个细分市场的吸引力并选择一个或多个细分市场进行服务的过程。

Targeting refers to the process of evaluating each market segment's attractiveness and selecting one or more segments to serve. In evaluating different market segments, companies should consider three factors: segment size and growth, segment structural attractiveness, as well as the company's objectives and resources available.

After evaluating the segments, the company must decide which segment(s) it will target. A target market consists of a set of buyers who share similar needs, behaviors or characteristics that the company has decided to serve. Targeting strategies can be divided into undifferentiated marketing (mass marketing), differentiated marketing (segmented marketing), focused/concentrated marketing (niche marketing) and customized marketing (individual marketing).

2.1 Undifferentiated marketing (mass marketing)

Undifferentiated marketing (also "mass marketing") is market-coverage strategy in which a firm decides to ignore market segment differences and go after the whole market with one marketing mix (see Figure 5.3). This mass-marketing strategy focuses on what is common with all customers instead of what is different. Sometimes, this strategy makes sense in markets which have no apparent differences in customer characteristics that have implications for marketers, for instance, postal services of the post office that target everyone in the market. The risk is that the standard offering may be supplanted by an entirely new technology. Moreover, attempts to satisfy everyone in the market with one standard offering often result in low customer satisfaction. Marketers must not use mass marketing as an excuse to get away from the troubles of segmenting markets and designing differential offerings for different segments. The strategy of undifferentiated marketing is relatively vulnerable as compared with the other alternatives.

⊞ 无差异营销策略（也称为"大众营销策略"）是指公司决定忽略细分市场之间的差异，以一种营销组合来应对整个市场的策略。

⊞ 这种营销策略的风险在于标准化产品可能会被全新的技术所取代。此外，试图用一种标准产品来满足市场上的所有人往往会导致顾客满意度低。

| Marketing mix | ⇨ | The whole market |

Figure 5.3 Undifferentiated marketing

2.2 Differentiated marketing (segmented marketing)

Companies adopting differentiated marketing (also "segmented marketing") decide to target several market segments and design separate offerings for each (see Figure 5.4). A good example of segmented marketing is Toyota's targeting strategy: Yaris & Vios are subcompact vehicles for first-time car buyers with tight budgets; Corolla featuring relatively larger space inside is designed for family use; Camry, a higher-level sub-brand of midsize sedan, is intended for business purposes; the top-end brand Lexus is for high-end buyers. Other car manufacturers such as Honda, Nissan and Volkswagen

⊞ 采用差异化的营销策略（也称为"细分营销策略"）的公司针对多个目标市场并为每个细分市场设计单独的产品。

田 差异化的营销策
略可更好地满足具
有不同需要、欲求和
特征的顾客,从而获
得更高的顾客满意
度、更高的利润和更
多的增长机会。

also adopt the differentiated marketing strategy, so do many smartphone makers and computer manufacturers.

The advantage of differentiated marketing is obvious. <u>Customers with different needs, wants and characteristics can be better satisfied, resulting in higher customer satisfaction, higher profitability and more opportunities for growth</u>. But we can plainly see that this targeting strategy increases the cost of doing business. Thus, the strategy is often adopted by powerful established businesses instead of small and medium-sized enterprises.

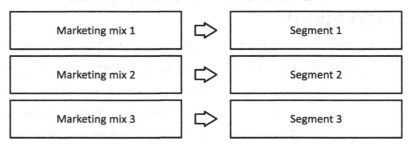

Figure 5.4 Differentiated marketing

2.3 Focused/Concentrated marketing (niche marketing)

田 集中化营销策略
(也称为"利基营
销策略")是指公
司追求单独的细分
市场或利基市场的
大部分市场份额。

⋯⋯⋯⋯⋯⋯⋯⋯⋯

田 利基营销为小企
业提供了参与竞争
的机会,使得它们能
够把有限的资源集
中于服务被竞争力
较强的市场主导者
所忽视的利基市场。

<u>Focused/Concentrated marketing (also "niche marketing") is a market-coverage strategy in which a firm goes after a large share of one segment or niche</u> (see Figure 5.5). This strategy is particularly appealing to companies with limited resources. <u>Niching offers smaller companies an opportunity to compete by focusing their limited resources on serving niches that are overlooked by competitive market dominants</u>. For example, the private tutoring market is a fast-growing market with huge growth potential in the Chinese society, as parents are attaching greater importance to their children's academic performance nowadays. Xueersi is no doubt a market leader with an established reputation and competitive strength, in big Chinese cities in particular. But still, a startup Zuoyebang (literally meaning "help with your homework") was able to find a niche market to enter the education industry by offering online helps with students' homework and test papers.

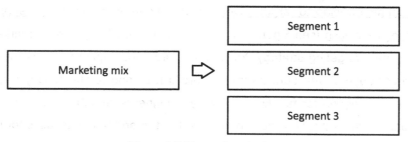

Figure 5.5 Focused marketing

2.4 Customized marketing (individual marketing)

Customized marketing (also "individual marketing" and "one-to-one marketing") refers to the process through which firms interact one-to-one with masses of customers to design products and services tailored to individual needs and preferences (see Figure 5.6). Customized marketing makes sense when the requirements of individual customers in some markets are unique, and their purchasing power is sufficient enough to make commercially viable the customization of marketing mix for each customer. Customized marketing is often adopted by service providers, such as advertising and marketing research agencies, private banking, architects and solicitors, matchmaking services (e.g. Zhenai.com, an online matchmaking service provider), which vary offerings on a customer-by-customer basis.

田 定制营销策略（也称为"个体营销策略"或"一对一营销"）是指企业与广大顾客一对一地互动，以设计出满足个人需要和偏好的产品和服务。

田 服务提供商通常采用定制营销策略，例如广告公司和营销调研机构、私人银行、建筑师和律师事务所、婚介服务商等。

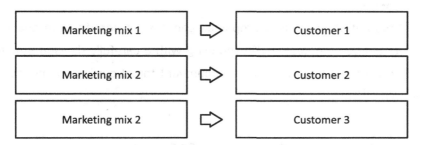

Figure 5.6 Customized marketing

2.5 Mass customization

Mass customization in consumer markets is a variation on customized marketing. The development of the Internet and big data technology has rendered it possible for companies to deliver customized products and services to private consumers on a massive scale. But mass customization does not mean customizing everything in a product; a more viable way is to add some customized elements to a standard base (see Figure 5.7), e.g. NikeiD, iGoogle, Dell. Many cellphone apps offer various modules or sections for subscribers to choose from. Information feeds on apps vary from person to person, for the apps use the big data technology to infer topics that may interest each customer based on his or her past views.

田 大众定制并非定制产品中所有的内容，更可行的方法是在标准化产品/服务的基础上添加一些定制元素。

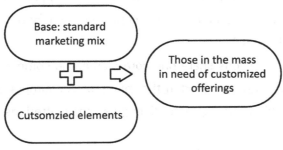

Figure 5.7 Mass customization

2.6 Choosing a targeting strategy

Companies must consider the following factors when choosing a targeting strategy.

- Company resources: When a firm has limited resources, it is sensible to choose the focused marketing strategy.
- Product variability: Undifferentiated marketing is suitable for uniform, standardized products and services, while products that vary in features, performance, design, etc. are more suitable for differentiation or concentration.
- Product's life-cycle stage: At the initial stage of launch a new product, it would be more practical to start with only one version, where undifferentiated or focused marketing is more appropriate.
- Market variability: In a market where customers show few differences in tastes, buying behaviors and responses to the same marketing stimuli, undifferentiated marketing may work.
- Competitors' marketing strategy: Companies can always benefit from analyzing competitors' targeting strategies and responding with a carefully devised strategy, whether it is to compete head to head or circumvent throat-cutting competition by choosing niche marketing.

3. Positioning and repositioning

Positioning and repositioning are essential marketing strategies. Positioning enables companies to occupy a meaningful position for their products or brands in the minds of consumers.

3.1 Definition of positioning

Philip Kotler defined, "A product's position is the complex set of perceptions, impressions, and feelings that consumers have for the product compared with competing products". John Fahy and David Jobber defined positioning as "the act of designing the company's offering so that it occupies a meaningful and distinct position in the target consumer's mind". Chinese scholars Sun Ning and Zhang Aimin gave the definition, "The concept of positioning seeks to put a product in a certain position, or place, in the minds of prospective buyers."

The above definitions share one core element in common: <u>A product or brand's position is determined in the minds of consumers</u>, and marketers can use positioning strategies to distinguish their offerings from those of competitors.

Effective positioning can produce positive marketing results. For instance,

> ⊞ 产品或品牌定位
> 是在消费者心目中
> 树立的。

Coca-Cola introduced two virtually identical drinks: Diet Coke and Coke Zero, the former targeting females on a diet and the latter males enthusiastically working out. Though the ingredients of these two drinks are indistinguishable, the market appeals are very different. The different positions are reflected in the packages and TV commercials with distinct male and female elements.

Honda, Toyota and Nissan are deemed by consumers as fuel-efficient, economical brands; BBA (BMW, Mercedes-Benz and Audi) is representative of luxury vehicles, though these brands have recently launched entry-level models priced between RMB 200,000 to RMB 350,000 for the growing lower middle class in the Chinese market; Volvo successfully positioned itself as the safest car (but ironically, a car crash experiment showed that the Volvo car actually did not have the highest level of crashworthiness, but still the brand image of safety has long been firmly established in the minds of consumers). The example of Volvo demonstrates the effects of successful positioning.

A good positioning statement should be clearly stated, delivering messages about the brand, the concept, target group, functions/features, competitive advantage and other information you want to send to customers. Blackberry offered a good positioning statement, "<u>To busy, mobile professionals who need to always be in the loop, Blackberry is a wireless connecting solution that allows you to stay connected to data, people, resources while on the go, easily and reliably—more so than competing technologies.</u>"

田 对于需要始终保持联系的忙碌的、到处走动的专业人士来说，黑莓提供一种无线连接解决方案，比其他技术更能让您在旅途中轻松可靠地与数据、人员和资源保持连接。

Once a company has built a desired position, it must maintain the position through consistent performance and communication. It must closely monitor and adapt the position over time to match changes in consumer needs and the competitive situation.

3.2 Keys to successful positioning

Keys to successful positioning include: clarity, consistency, credibility and competitiveness (see Figure 5.8).

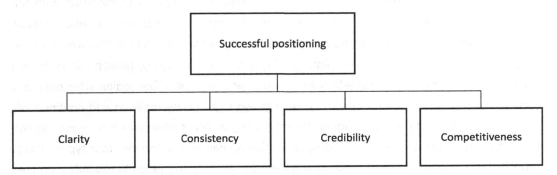

Figure 5.8 Keys to successful positioning

⊞ 营销人员必须非常清楚其目标市场和差异化优势。

Clarity

<u>The idea must be perfectly clear, both in terms of target market and differential advantage.</u> Slogans, such as Panasonic "Ideas for life", LG's "Life is good", Gree's "Master core technology" and Midea's "Life could have been better (with Midea)" send clear messages about the companies' business ideas.

⊞ 营销所传递的信息必须一致，以便受众注意到并记住该信息。

Consistency

As people are bombarded with abundant information every day, <u>a consistent message is required so that the message can be noticed and retained by audiences.</u> For instance, almost in every TV commercial of Gree, the slogan "Master core technology" is always highlighted. If a brand's position is changed frequently, consumers will be confused, which is bad for creating a clear, consistent brand image.

⊞ 所选的差异化优势在目标顾客心目中必须是可信的。

Credibility

<u>The selected differential advantage must be credible in the minds of target customers.</u> A typical example is Toyota created a luxury brand "Lexus" given that it lacked the credibility as an upmarket brand, the same with Nissan's "Infiniti" and Honda's "Accura". The platform selling budget items is rebranded as "TaoTe"—literally meaning Taobao Special.

⊞ 所选的差异化优势必须具有竞争力。

Competitiveness

<u>The chosen differential advantage must possess a competitive edge.</u> In other words, a firm should offer some value to its target customers that its competitors fail to supply. Nongfu Spring has always advertised the competitive advantage of its drinking water as "a little sweet" and "original water from Mother Nature".

3.3 Repositioning alternatives

Though we talked about the necessity of maintaining a consistent position of a brand or product, sometimes changing customer preferences or poor sales performance may necessitate repositioning. Carslan, a Guangzhou-based cosmetic maker which used to position itself as "makeup on a budget", has stepped up its R&D in cooperation with top designer teams at home and abroad, trying to develop more mid-end and high-end products in the hope of becoming one of the top global makeup brands. Carslan is fully aware of the consumers' high requirements on high quality, exquisite packaging, reasonable price and diversification of products. Targeting the consumer group of office ladies who pursue a quality lifestyle, it has been focusing on developing high-quality makeup and continuously upgrading its products and packaging. Repositioning involves changing the target market, the differential advantage or both. Thus, repositioning can be divided into four types: image repositioning, product repositioning, intangible repositioning and tangible repositioning (see Figure 5.9).

Product

		Same	Different
Target market	Same	Image repositioning	Product repositioning
	Different	Intangible repositioning	Tangible repositioning

Figure 5.9 Alternative repositioning strategies

Image repositioning

Image repositioning is to keep the product and target market the same but to change the image of the product. While maintaining the product, a company can reshape its image through marketing campaigns to better appeal to the same target group.

> 田 形象重新定位指保持产品和目标市场相同，但是改变产品的形象。

Product repositioning

Another repositioning strategy involves introducing different products to meet the needs of the same target group. The product repositioning strategy may be necessitated by changing needs, wants, tastes or preferences of the target segment or the changing competitive landscape in the market. For example, Mondeo, a sub-brand of Ford, had a reputation for being dull in appearance, so Ford invested heavily in making its car designs more stylish and appealing to younger car buyers.

> 田 产品重新定位就是推出不同的产品以满足同一目标群体的需求。

Intangible repositioning

Intangible repositioning involves retaining the product but changing the market segment. Intangible repositioning may be required when the position of an offering is wrongly defined. Repositioning to adjust to a more suitable target segment can improve the effectiveness and efficiency of marketing communications.

> 田 无形的重新定位是指保持产品不变，但是改变细分目标市场。

Tangible repositioning

When both product and target market are changed, a company is practicing "tangible repositioning". For instance, a company may decide to move up-market or down-market by introducing a brand new range of products to meet the needs of the newly defined target group.

> 田 当产品和目标市场都改变时，就是"有形的重新定位"。

4. Differentiation

To build profitable long-term relationships with target customers, marketers must understand customer needs better than competitors do and deliver superior value to target customers. Differentiation can give companies competitive advantages over competitors. Especially in highly competitive markets where

> 田 差异化可以为公司带来超过竞争对手的竞争优势。

田 差异化可体现在多个层面和
各个方面,如产品、服务、渠道、
价格、人群、地点和形象等。

supplies exceed demands, whether or not you can differentiate yourself from competitors to some extent determines your success or failure. Differentiation can happen on many levels and in various aspects, e.g. in terms of product, service, channel, price, people, place and image.

Product differentiation

Products can be differentiated on core benefits, features, performance, style, value-added service, delivery or warranty. iPhone differentiates itself on the minimalist design style and the unique operation system IOS.

Service differentiation

Businesses can differentiate themselves by offering speedy, convenient or meticulous services, for instance, Haidilao, a hotpot chain restaurant acclaimed for its superior service.

Channel differentiation

Firms can gain competitive advantage by means of the way they deliver products or services. Amazon and Dell set themselves apart with their smooth direct selling channels. Linshimuye, a Foshan-based furniture manufacturer founded in 2007, is a pioneer of O2O operation (Online To Offline) in the industry. Its offline brick-and-mortar stores are a place to exhibit products and for customers to try out the products. Customers who cannot make decision on the spot can place an order with their online stores later.

Price differentiation

Differentiation can be built on competitive price. Miniso, a Guangzhou-headquartered brand of chain stores selling articles of everyday use, quickly caught on among young people because of low prices for products with acceptable quality. Most of the products sold in a Miniso store are priced at RMB 10.

People differentiation

Some businesses gain differential advantage through its staff. A typical case is Disney—its amiable, joyous and upbeat performers are a big attraction to most visitors.

Summary

This chapter deals with four important marketing strategies: segmentation, targeting, positioning and differentiation. The benefits of segmentation are self-evident. The important thing is how marketers can use feasible segmentation variables to divide the consumer markets into effective, measurable, accessible, actionable and profitable segments.

Among these segments, marketers need to choose one or more segments to serve, in consideration of segment size and growth, segment structural attractiveness as well as the company's objectives and resources available. There are four targeting strategies for marketers to choose from: undifferentiated marketing, differentiated marketing, focused marketing and customized marketing (a derivative variation: mass customization).

The third issue is positioning and repositioning. The position of a brand or product is defined in the minds of consumers. Positioning is important but difficult. It is important because positioning is about linking your products or services to the solutions that consumers seek and ensuring that when they think about their needs or problems, your brand can pop up in their minds. It is difficult because successful positioning strategies must guarantee clarity, consistency, credibility and competitiveness. Marketers need to effectively communicate and deliver the chosen position to the market. Repositioning sometimes is necessary. You may change the product or the target segment or both, so there are four repositioning strategies available: image repositioning, product repositioning, intangible repositioning and tangible repositioning.

Differentiation is about delivering customers something unique and different from your competitors' offerings. It gives companies competitive advantages over competitors. Differentiation can happen on many levels and in various aspects, e.g. in terms of product, service, channel, price, people, place and image.

Key terms

segmentation	customized marketing/individual marketing
market segment	mass customization
niche market	positioning
mass market	keys to successful positioning
segmentation variables	repositioning
criteria for successful segmentation	image repositioning
targeting	product repositioning
undifferentiated marketing/mass marketing	intangible repositioning
differentiated marketing/segmented marketing	tangible repositioning
focus marketing/niche marketing	differentiation

Exercises

Review and discussion

Reference

Socio-economic categories

Marketers use socio-economic categories to describe segments.

Social grade	Social status	Occupation of head of household or chief income earner
A	Upper middle class	Higher managerial, administrative or professional
B	Middle class	Intermediate managerial, administrative or professional
C1	Lower middle class	Junior managerial, administrative or professional; clerical
C2	Skilled working class	Skilled manual workers
D	Working class	Semi-skilled and unskilled manual workers
E	Those at lowest level of subsistence	State pensioners or widows (no other earner); casual or lowest grade workers

Professional, lifestyle and age group

Market segments may also be divided according to professions, lifestyles, or age groups. Some of these are shown below.

Professional market segments	Decision makers	People who have the power to decide what to buy in a company or family
	C-level executives	People who are high in the management structure of a company (CFO, CEO, CMO)
Lifestyle market segments	Metrosexuals	Men concerned with self-image and self-indulgence, living in large modern cities
	The gay and lesbian market The pink market	Homosexuals
Age group market segments	The silver market	Seniors over 70 years old
	Baby boomers	Born between 1946 and 1964
	Generation X	Born after baby boomers
	Generation Y	Born after Generation X
	Twentysomethings	Twenty to twenty-nine years old
	Teens	Thirteen to nineteen years old
	Tweens	Eight to twelve years old

1. Complete the text describing market segmentation for children's art supplies. Consult the "Reference" to help you.

Kids' Arts and Crafts Market Growing

Kids' arts and crafts is brighter than ever, say many retailers. "This _____ segment is growing without question. We're seeing a larger population of young kids entering school than in previous years and creating a great opportunity," said Walgreens' spokesperson Yvette Anne Venable.

An increasing number of products are _____ at parents and grandparents who want their kids to be smart and creative, not just television junkies. Grandparents are a customer segment with strong economic _____. It is relatively easy to _____ to them using positive images of their grandchildren.

Steven Jacober, SHOPA's president, agrees, "Art supplies and crafts continue to grow. This ties into the baby _____ generation, the way they are raising their children and their tendency to make everything a learning experience. There are a lot of different factors, and the demographics support continuing growth of the marketplace."

Arts and crafts are targeted at households with _____, kids aged 12 years and under.

2. Complete the descriptions (1-5) using words from the box. Then match the products with the market segments (a-e). Consult the "Reference" to help you.

affluent	appeal	income	life cycle	lifestyle

_____ 1) Health insurance that covers the needs of people late in the _____.

_____ 2) A hair care range for men with a modern _____ and a self-indulgent attitude.

_____ 3) A new TV channel broadcasting programs that _____ to homosexuals.

_____ 4) A luxury range of executive stationery for an _____ market segment.

_____ 5) Cheap to produce but fashionable sports shoes for a low _____ segment.

---

a. Gay and lesbian market   c. Teenagers   e. C-level executives

b. The silver market   d. Metrosexuals

---

3. Translate the following sentences into English.

1) 市场细分就是在市场调查研究的基础上，根据消费者的需求、购买习惯和购买行为的差异性，把整个市场划分为若干子市场的过程。

_____

_____

2) 人必须生活在一定的地域范围。按地理因素细分，就是按照消费者所在的地理位置、地理环境等变数来细分市场。

_____

_____

3) 企业根据自身的资源和目标，选择对本企业最有吸引力的一个或多个细分市场作为目标市场，有针对性地开展营销活动。

_____

_____

4) 无差异营销策略是指企业以整个市场为目标市场，提供单一产品，采用单一的营销组合方案。

_____

_____

5) 企业产品的市场定位有利于企业深入地了解市场需求，制定合适的市场营销组合策略，更好地为目标市场服务。

_____

_____

6) 重新定位是对销路少、市场反应差的产品进行二次定位。这种重新定位旨在摆脱困境，重新获得增长与活力。

_____

_____

4. Answer the following questions briefly.

1) You have been asked by a client company to segment the ice cream market. Use at least three different bases for segmentation and describe the segments that emerge.

2) Explain which segmentation variables would be most important to marketers of the following products: vitamins, credit cards and coffee.

3) The chapter discusses five requirements for effective segmentation. Suppose you are a product manager in regional fast-food restaurant company. You are listening to a presentation on a new rice burger idea (teriyaki chicken) and it is your turn to ask questions. Write five questions that you would ask the person presenting this product idea. Each question should be directed at one of the five segmentation requirements.

4) Why must firms divide a total market into several homogeneous groups?

5) Under what circumstances might a firm need to reposition its product?

6) How do marketers choose the best types of positioning strategies?

◾ ──────── Projects and teamwork ──────── ◾

1. With a partner, choose a product that you believe might benefit from repositioning—whether it's a favorite food, a form of entertainment, a type of automobile, or electronic equipment. Identify ways in which marketers might reposition the product.

2. Choose your favorite sport. Identify the different market segments for your support. Then write a brief plan for selecting a segmentation strategy for the sport. Once you have selected a segmentation strategy for your sport, try out your idea on your target market.

3. Form a small group and create an idea for a new reality television show in China. What competitive advantage does this show have over existing shows? How many and which differences would you promote? Develop a positioning statement for this television show.

──────── **Case study** ────────

How Red Bull Became an Market Leader of Energy Drink through Precise Positioning

"Drink Red Bull when you are drowsy or tired." ("困了，累了喝红牛") This is a slogan that rings a bell in the minds of most people. Red Bull, since its entry into the Chinese market in 1995, has been keeping a leading position in the functional beverage market. Why is it so popular? What is the key to its success?

Red Bull is one of the world's earliest well-known energy drinks. In the 1970s, the founder of the drink created a tonic drink that contains water, sugar, caffeine, muco-inositol and Vitamin B, and named it "Red Bull". The drink then targeted blue collars such as shift workers and truck chauffeurs, enabling them to keep a clear head when they were working at night. After its launch, Red Bull was enthusiastically accepted by the market, as evidenced by brisk demands for the drink. With the superior quality and function, the drink was widely sold to over 140 countries and regions throughout the world. It has created extraordinary sales performance and topped in terms of sales volume in the global functional beverage market.

In December 1995, Red Bull, a Thai-based brand, decided to enter the Chinese market. With confidence in the Chinese market prospect and a global strategic vision, it quickly expanded the Chinese market through vigorous marketing efforts. The advertisement slogans "Drink Red Bull when you are drowsy or tired" and "Red Bull can refresh your minds and energize your body" ("提神醒脑，补充体力") caught on among the masses almost overnight. The brand was well-known and liked by Chinese consumers. Red Bull has built a sales network that covers the whole country. Upholding advanced business philosophies and management modes, Red Bull placed an emphasis on guiding and nurturing consumer beliefs. With the first-mover advantage in the functional beverage market, it has been gradually established as a leading brand in the Chinese soft drink market.

First, Red Bull explicitly identified its positioning as an energy drink, effectively differentiating itself from competing brands. Second, after its entry into the Chinese market, it employed the localized marketing strategy, which can be reflected by its logo design: a big red sun between two red bulls with their horns pressing against each other. The red bulls represent energy, strength and fighting spirits; the sun radiates heat and energy; the design is painted in red and yellow, the traditional auspicious colors to Chinese people. Third, after entering the Chinese market, Red Bull widely claimed that though it is a Thai brand, the formula of the drink was developed by a Thai Chinese—Chaleo Yoovidhya (许书标). Highlighting the tie between the brand and China strengthened Chinese consumers' emotional identification with the brand. Moreover, as an energy drink, Red Bull linked itself with many sports events including the Olympics by becoming a sponsor. Its presence on sports events enhances the brand positioning in consumers' minds.

Questions:

1. What variables are used by Red Bull to segment the soft drink market?

2. What targeting strategy is adopted by Red Bull? Discuss the advantages of the targeting strategy.

3. Is Red Bull's positioning strategy successful? What are the keys to successful positioning?

Chapter Six

Products, Services and Brands

Objectives:

After studying this chapter, you should be able to:

- Define "product" in marketing terms;
- Distinguish the three levels of a product and know how to differentiate a product at each level;
- Describe the BCG matrix and discuss its limitations;
- Identify which category (star, cash cow, question mark, dog) a product/product line falls into and what marketing strategies are needed for each category;
- Understand the characteristics, marketing objectives and marketing strategies needed for each stage of the product life cycle;
- Describe the typical new product development process;
- Understand the importance of branding;
- Know how to build strong brands and manage brands over time;
- Explain the four distinct characteristics of service;
- Have ideas about how a service firm manages its brands and service quality;
- Truly understand relationship marketing and experiential marketing.

Framework

Chapter Six Products, Services and Brands

Definition of product

Levels of product

- Core product
- Actual product
- Augmented product

Product differentiation

- Core differentiation
- Actual differentiation
- Augmented differentiation

New product development

Branding

- Benefits to firms
- Benefits to consumers
- Brand positioning
- Brand name selection
- Managing brands

Nature and characteristics of service

- Intangibility
- Inseparability
- Variability
- Perishability

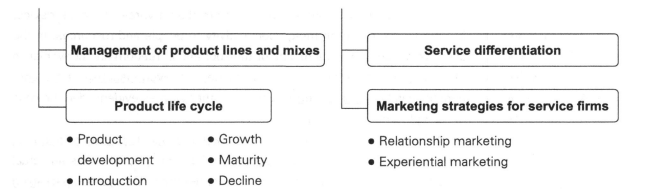

- Product development
- Introduction
- Growth
- Maturity
- Decline

- Relationship marketing
- Experiential marketing

1. Definition of product

When talking about products, people tend to think of tangible objects such as TV set, smartphone, table and toothpaste. However, consumers buying a cellphone are actually buying more than a small case but the convenience of getting connected with people and data anytime, anywhere. <u>Marketers should understand that consumers want that satisfaction of their needs instead of a particular object</u>. Hence, everything related to the satisfaction of consumer needs from features, styling, operability to after-sales service and warranty must be taken into consideration under marketing decisions related to "product". For example, when buying a Xiaomi TV set, people are buying a mix of tangible and intangible entities—the physical form of a TV set, TV programs and an access to video resources online.

<u>In marketing terms, "product" does not refer tangible objects only, but anything that has value and can satisfy customer needs</u>. Philip Kotler defined "product" as "anything that can be offered to a market for attention, acquisition, use, or consumption and that might satisfy a want or need". <u>Broadly defined, products include physical items, services, events, persons, places, ideas or mixes of these entities</u>. Throughout the whole textbook, we use the term "product" broadly to include any or all of these entities. In a word, a product can be anything that is able to satisfy customer needs by providing some form of value.

田 营销人员应该意识到消费者想要的是他们的需要得到满足，而非特定的物体。

田 在营销专业中，"产品"这个术语不仅仅指有形的物体，指的是任何具有价值且能够满足顾客需要的东西。

田 广义上来说，产品包括实物、服务、事件、人物、地点、想法或这些东西的组合。

2. Levels of product

Kotler identified three levels of a product (see Figure 6.1). These three levels are:

Core product: This is the most basic level, standing at the center of a product. It addresses the question: What is the buyer really buying? <u>It consists of the core benefits that people seek to satisfy their needs or solve their problems when they buy a particular product or service</u>. For instance,

田 核心产品包括人们通过购买特定产品或服务寻求满足需要或解决问题的核心好处。

people who buy an iPhone are buying more than a wireless mobile device, but the freedom and on-the-go connectivity to people and resources. In the same vein, cars provide a means of transportation, freedom and convenience of moving around. <u>Products will quickly decline, even disappear if the core benefits can be met most effectively in another way</u>, as evidenced in the case of MP3 players and Kodak films.

Actual product: <u>At the second level, actual product consists of features, design, quality, brand name and packaging.</u> For example, iPhone is an actual product—its name, parts, minimalist design, features, IOS system, packaging and other attributes that have been put together to deliver the core benefits of an iPhone.

Augmented product: <u>Additional benefits offered to consumers around the core and actual products constitute the augmented level.</u> Apart from the core and actual benefits, Apple Inc. and Apple dealers give iPhone buyers a warranty on parts and workmanship, user instructions, after-sales supports and some free-of-charge resources on the app store and iTunes.

⊞ 如果一个产品所提供的核心好处能以另一种方式得到有效满足，这种产品将迅速地衰退，甚至消失。

⊞ 第二个层次的实际产品由产品功能、设计、质量、品牌名称和包装构成。

⊞ 围绕核心产品和实际产品为消费者提供的额外利益，构成了外延产品。

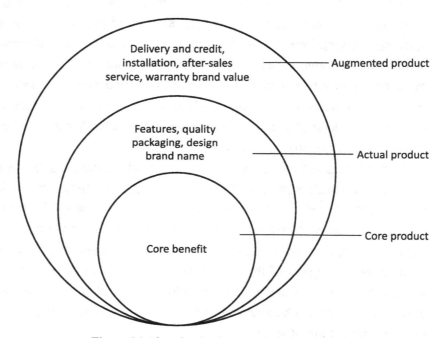

Figure 6.1 Three levels of product

3. Product differentiation

Products can be differentiated at any of the three levels: core, actual or augmented level. <u>Technological advancement or renovation usually leads to product differentiation on core benefits, while marketers of mature products may consider differentiating their products at the augmented level, providing additional benefits to attract and retain customers.</u>

⊞ 技术进步或革新通常会导致产品在核心层次上的差异化，而成熟产品的营销人员可考虑在外延层次上将产品差异化，提供额外的好处来吸引和留住顾客。

Core differentiation

The most radical product differentiation takes place at the core level. As is discussed above, marketers have to see into a product to define its core benefit: CD and VCD are carriers of audio and video resources for entertainment, and lipsticks are more than the color on the lip, but beauty and enhanced self-confidence. As there are other convenient and affordable means of providing the same enjoyment such as digital downloads from the Internet where abundant entertainment resources are available, CD and VDC have quickly become outdated. Another example is the wide use of smartphones which has led to the phase-out of e-dictionary, voice-recorder and MP3 player. The shrinking market of instant noodles can be partly attributed to the rise of the food delivery platforms. In the past, many households purchase instant noodles in case they go hungry late at night when they don't want to go out for a midnight meal. This need has now satisfied by the door-to-door delivery of food offered by the food delivery platforms such as Meituan.

Actual differentiation

Marketers may consider differentiating their products from the following five aspects: features, design, quality, brand name and packaging. You can outcompete your competitors with superior quality (e.g. Gree air conditioner), a well-established brand name (e.g. Starbucks), unique design (e.g. Apple's minimalist design), better or unique features (e.g. the powerful camera of Vivo phones) and unique packaging (e.g. Apple's stylistic and minimalist packaging). A decade ago, the Sanlu poisonous milk powder scandal disastrously destroyed Chinese people's confidence in made-in-China milk powder products for babies. Many parents sought to purchase foreign-branded, foreign-made powdered milk from overseas markets. However, in recent years, Chinese milk powder makers have bounced back with better-quality products and formulas claimed to be specially designed for the physical health of Chinese babies.

OnePlus is a Chinese smartphone brand renowned for its photo-taking features. Amidst fierce competition, OnePlus has been concentrating efforts on developing cellphones with built-in cameras that outshines the competing products in color, filming rate, and professional experience to create the ultimate mobile imaging experience. It has also developed a dedicated Hasselblad Pro Mode in its camera app that will help consumers fine-tune their photos for a natural look and feel.

Augmented differentiation

Most product differentiation efforts take place at the augmented level, especially in a highly competitive market. Firms put greater efforts into intangible entities which cannot be so easily imitated, e.g. quicker delivery, quicker response to customer inquiries and complaints, longer warranty period, more attentive after-sales supports and so on.

4. Management of product lines and mixes

Big companies have a large number of products or brands, which can be categorized in terms of product line and mix. A product line is a group of products that are closely related in terms of their functions and the benefits they provide. All the products, which may be put into different product lines, make up a company's product mix or portfolio. The length of the product line refers to the number of variants offered within the product line, and the width of the product mix can be measured by the number of product lines a company carries (see Table 6.1).

Table 6.1 The product mix of Kweichow Moutai

The length of the product line	The width of the product mix			
	Rice wine	Beer	Red wine	Soft drink
	Kweichow Moutai Moutai Prince Moutai Flying Fairy Moutai Yingbin	Moutai Beer	Moutai Red Wine	No data available

One big challenge for companies is to keep the proper length of the product line. A product line is too short if the manager can increase profits by adding items into the line; the line is too long if the manager can increase profits by dropping a few items. Managers need to conduct regular product line analysis to assess each item's sales and profits and to understand how each item contributes to the line's performance.

Product line length is influenced by the company's marketing strategies. For example, Kweichow Moutai Group offers several rice wine variants for consumers with varying buying powers, Flying Fairy for the high-end market, Prince for the mid-end market and Yingbin for the masses.

The process of managing groups of products to keep the proper length of each product line and the proper width of the whole product mix is called "portfolio planning". This is a very complex and important task. As we know, not every product makes the same contribution to the performance of the product line, and not every product line has the same performance within a product portfolio. So companies need to examine the length of each product line and the width of the product mix, evaluate the performance of each item within a line and each line within a mix and decide how to adjust the distribution of limited resources to support good performers, reduce supports for less satisfactory performers and even drop bad performers.

The best product/business portfolio is the one that best fits the company's

⊞ 产品线由功能和提供的好处相近的产品组成。一家公司的所有产品（可能被放入不同产品线），构成了公司的产品组合。产品线长度是指一条产品线内的产品数量；产品组合宽度是指公司拥有的产品线数量。

⊞ 管理人员需要定期分析产品线，以评估每件商品的销售额和利润，了解其对生产线总体绩效表现的贡献。

⊞ 管理好产品以保持每个产品线长度适中和产品组合宽度适中，这个过程被称为"投资组合规划"。

⊞ 最好的产品/业务组合是指最适合公司优势和劣势以抓住环境机遇的组合。

strengths and weaknesses to opportunities in the environment. Here introduced is a tool that helps companies decide which products to build, to hold, to harvest or to divest—the Boston Consulting Group (BCG) growth-share matrix.

The BCG matrix (see Figure 6.2) is a portfolio-planning method that helps companies make product mix and/or product line decisions in terms of market growth rate and relative market share. Market growth rate forms the vertical axis as an indicator of market attractiveness, while relative market share is represented by the horizontal axis as a measure of company strength in the market. These two dimensions divide a company's business portfolio into four categories: star, cash cow, question mark (also known as "problem child") and dog.

⊞ 波士顿（BCG）矩阵（见图 6.2）是一种投资组合规划方法，旨在帮助公司根据市场增长率和相对市场份额做出关于产品组合和 / 或产品线的决策。

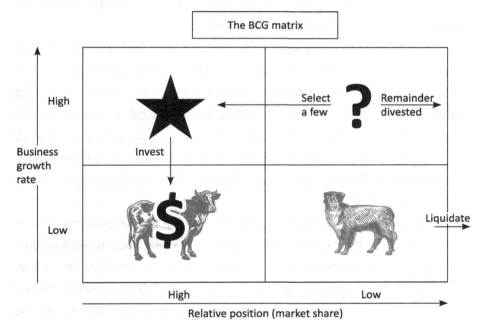

Figure 6.2 The Boston Consulting Group growth-share matrix

Star

Stars are high-growth, high-market-share businesses or products. They are already successful and the prospects for further growth are good. They often require heavy investments to maintain or increase the leading position, but eventually their growth will slow down and they will turn into cash cow.

⊞ 明星产品是指高增长、高市场份额的业务或产品。

Cash cow

Cash cow represents high-market-share businesses or products in a low-growth market. They bring in high profits (cash flows) and require low investment as the market prospects for further growth are not so good. Companies can use the excess cash they generate to fund other categories of products or new product R&D.

⊞ 现金牛产品代表低增长市场，但公司占有高市场份额的业务或产品。

⊞ 问题产品（也称为
"问题儿童"）是指
高增长市场中，公司
占有市场份额低的
业务或产品。

⊞ 瘦狗产品是在市场
增长低且占有市场份
额低的弱势产品。

⊞ 对于一种产品 / 业
务，公司可以投入更
多以扩大其份额；
或者适当投资以保持
现有份额；或者进行
收割，从短期现金流
中获利，不管长期发
展； 或者通过出售
或逐步淘汰来放弃该
产品 / 业务，从而将
资源用在别处。

Question mark/Problem child

Question marks (also "problem child") are low-market-share businesses or products in high-growth markets. The company is not doing well in a fast growing market. Question marks require heavy investments to keep up with the market growth, because the company's weak market position often indicates low profitability. Question marks can be either built into stars or phased out.

Dog

Dogs are low-market-share, weak products that compete in low-growth markets. They may generate enough cash to maintain themselves but do not promise to provide large cashes for other products. One possible way out for dogs is to reposition a dog into a defendable niche.

The BCG matrix clearly shows that each product/business should have its role in the product/business portfolio. Once a company has classified its products/businesses, it must determine the role each will play. The company can invest more in a product/business to build its share; or it can invest just enough to hold the current share; or it can harvest a product/business, profiting from its short-term cash flow regardless of its long-term development; or it may divest it by selling it or phrasing it out and using the resources elsewhere.

It is worth noting that as time passes by, the role of each product/business will change in the matrix. As we will discuss in the next section, each product has a life cycle. Some products start out as a question mark, grow into a star, later become a cash cow and eventually fall into the dog category before they actually die out. Companies need to keep monitoring changes in the positions of products in the matrix.

Problems with the BCG matrix approach

The biggest advantage of the BCG matrix is its simplicity, but it also has very obvious limitations. First, it is difficult to measure market share and growth. Second, the matrix uses market growth rate as an indicator of market attractiveness and relative market share to represent a company's competitive strength, which might oversimplify the market situations. Third, the position of a product in the matrix depends on its market share. This may lead to an unhealthy preoccupation with enlarging market share and an oversight of many other important things such as profitability. Fourth, the matrix overlooks the interconnections between products. For instance, accessories may not be profitable or attractive, but definitely an integral part of a clothes store.

5. Product life cycle

Product life cycle (PLC) is the course of a product's sales and profits over its lifetime (see Figure 6.3). It involves five distinct stages: product development, introduction, growth, maturity and decline. The PLC is built on the idea that nothing lasts forever, and companies have to accept the fact that products will die out and new products should be developed to replace them. Throughout the life cycle of a product, companies need to review their marketing objectives and strategies.

⊞ 产品生命周期（PLC）是指一个产品在其生命周期内，销售额和利润将经历的各个阶段。

⊞ 在产品的整个生命周期中，公司需要不断检视其营销目标和策略。

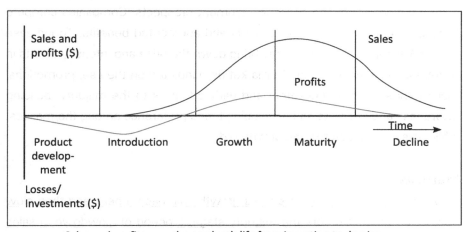

Sales and profits over the product's life from inception to demise

Figure 6.3 The product life cycle (PLC)

Product development

During product development, sales are zero and the company has to make big investments. The next section will introduce the typical process of new product development in detail.

Introduction

Introduction is a period of slow sales growth as the product is introduced into the market. Profits do not exist in this stage because of the heavy spending on product R&D and introduction. Introduction takes time. Some useful, great inventions such as dish washer lingered in the introduction stage for many years before they actually entered the growth stage in the Chinese market. Though widely used western households for many years, dish washers have only started to be accepted by Chinese families in recent years. The marketing objectives for this stage center on creating product awareness among innovators and early adopters. At this stage, there is often one basic version of product. Promotion highlights the core feature or benefit of the product.

⊞ 引入期是指随着产品投入市场，销售缓慢增长的时期。

⊞ 增长期是指市场迅速接受、销售额和利润增长的时期。

⊞ 在某个时点，产品的销售额增长将达到峰值，然后放缓。产品进入成熟期，这时销售额增长放缓，因为该产品已被市场上的大多数消费者广泛接受。

⊞ 成熟期是竞争最激烈的阶段，对营销管理提出了很大的挑战，因此这也是品牌优势作用表现最明显的阶段。

⊞ 当新技术出现，或消费者的品位或偏好发生变化时，产品就会进入衰退期，销量额下降、利润下降。

⊞ 一些公司可能会转向利基市场，专注于提供适合特定小众群体需求的某些改进产品。

Growth

Growth is a period of rapid market acceptance and increasing sales and profits. As a product becomes increasingly accepted by more and more buyers on the market, sales volume rises rapidly during the growth stage. When productions expand and productivity increases, production costs per unit may fall, and promotion costs spread over a larger sales volume. Thus, the average cost per unit stands where it is and even falls. The marketing objectives during this stage are to build sales and enlarge market share. More and more competitors may be attracted into the market during the latter part of the stage by high profits and good development prospects. Companies compete through offering more product variants and augmented benefits. To increase the market share, companies may bring down the price and intensify efforts in distribution channel building. As market demands are on the rise, promotional focus may shift from innovators and early adopters to the majority, building awareness and interests and developing brand preference among the masses, while sales promotion may be downsized.

Maturity

At some point, a product's sales growth will reach a peak and then slow down. The product enters the maturity stage, a period of slowdown in sales growth because the product has been widely accepted by most buyers on the market. Profits level off or decline because of increased expenses to compete with more and more competitors. The maturity stage witnesses the fiercest competition, thus posing big challenges to marketing management, so this is also a stage where the benefits of a strong brand are apparently felt. Strong companies may launch new models or diversify their brands; some resort to price war, cutting down prices to match or beat competitors; some might modify the product—changing quality, style or packing to encourage brand switch; promotion in the stage focuses on brand differences and benefits. All these efforts are to maximize profits while defending the market share. Normally most products stay the longest in the maturity stage. For instance, smartphones are staying in this phase at present.

Decline

When new technology emerges and consumer tastes or preferences change, a product will enter the decline stage, a period when sales fall off and profits drop. As sales and profits fall, some firms may withdraw from the market. Those remaining may drop smaller, less profitable segments, phase out weak items, cut marginal distribution channels, downsize promotional expenses or reduce prices. Some firms may shift to a niche market by focusing on offering certain product variants tailored to the needs of a special group. For instance, though film cameras are no longer needed or wanted by most people, some camera makers have launched instant cameras in bright colors and with cute appearances for teenage girls and a small group of adults with a girlish heart, who can use to the camera to take and produce pictures instantly on special occasions.

Not all products present the same pattern through the five typical stages of the life cycle. Some are introduced and then die out quickly; some stay in the maturity stage for a long time; some enter the decline stage and then cycle back to the growth stage due to strong promotion efforts or product repositioning.

Table 6.2 Summary of characteristics, objectives and strategies of different stages of the product life cycle

		Introduction	Growth	Maturity	Decline
Characteristics	**Sales**	Low sales	Rapidly rising sales	Peak sales	Declining sales
	Costs	High cost	Average cost	Low cost	Low cost
	Profits	Negative	Rising profits	High profits	Declining profits
	Competitors	Few	Growing	Stable number beginning to decline in later part of the maturity stage	Declining number
Marketing objectives		Create product awareness	Maximize market share	Maximize profit while defending market share	Reduce expenditure and milk the brand
Strategies	**Product**	Offer a basic version	Offer product extensions, service and warranty	Diversify brand and models	Phase out weak items
	Price	Use the cost-plus pricing method	Price to penetrate market	Price to match or beat competitors	Cut price
	Place	Build selective distribution	Build intensive distribution	Build more intensive distribution	Go selective: phase out unprofitable channels
	Promotion	Use advertising to build product awareness among early adopters and dealers; use heavy sales promotion to encourage trial	Advertise to build awareness and interest in the mass market; reduce sales promotion to take advantage of heavy consumer demand	Advertise to stress brand differences and benefits; increase sales promotion to encourage brand switching	Reduce advertising to the level needed to retain hardcore loyal customers; reduce sales promotion to the minimal level

⊞ 产品生命周期往往因其倾向于诱使公司或行业快速推动产品通过各个阶段而受到批评。快时尚行业是一个典型的例子。

⊞ 营销人员不应推动产品通过生命周期的各个阶段，而应利用产品生命周期曲线来了解市场形势并制定适当的应对策略。

The PLC is often criticized for its tendency to entice companies or industries to quickly push products through the stages. A typical example is the fast fashion industry. Every season, H&M, Zara and Mango launch a large amount of various new designs while the out-of-season stocks are gone. This arouses some ethical marketing concerns: Is it ethnical to seduce consumers into buying things they don't need at the expense of the environment and resources, just for the sake of sales and profits?

Another problem with the PLC is that in practice it is very difficult for marketers to plan a product throughout the typical stages of the life cycle, because it is hard to forecast the sales level, the length of each stage and the shape of the curve. Instead of pushing a product through the stages of the life cycle, marketers should make use of the PLC to help understand the market situation and develop proper coping strategies.

6. New product development

⊞ 新产品可能与现有产品完全不同，但仅仅改变某些元素的产品也可算是新产品，如带有新香味的香水。

As discussed above, products will die out, and companies need to develop new products. A new product can be fundamentally different from existing products, but a perfume with new fragrance can also count as a new product in marketing. New product development is expensive, risky and time-consuming. Some companies even went bankrupt because of the launch of costly developed new products that are not accepted by the market, for instance, Nokia's Symbian operation system, which is referred to by many people as the culprit of Nokia's quick failure.

After 40 years of reform and opening-up, China has shifted its focus from sheer economic growth to high-quality, all-round development. To get aligned with the state strategy, many businesses have attached great importance to innovation as an approach to quality, sustained development. "Innovation has no end. Only if a company continues to expand its research and development, it can take control of its own destiny," said Dong Mingzhu, chairwoman of Chinese home appliance manufacturer Gree Electric Appliances.

⊞ 典型的新产品研发过程包括七个阶段：创意产生、创意筛选、概念测试、商业分析、产品研发、市场测试和产品商品化。

The typical new product development process consists of seven stages: idea generation, idea screening, concept testing, business analysis, product development, market testing and commercialization (see Figure 6.4). These seven stages will be discussed one by one here, but in practice some of the stages may be skipped and some may be repeated, depending on the specific situation.

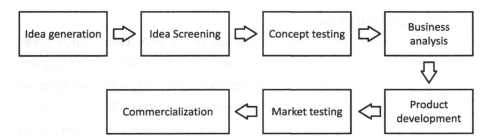

Figure 6.4 The seven-stage process of new product development

Idea generation

Product ideas come from both internal and external sources: scientists, engineers, marketers, sales persons and designers as internal sources, customers, competitors, distributors, social communities on the Internet, key opinion leaders, trade magazines, exhibitions and seminars as external sources. For instance, during the lockdown caused by the COVID-19 outbreak in 2020, demands for long-distant, instant, two-way communication have catalyzed many online videoconferencing, educational and communication platforms and apps, such as Dingding, Tencent Conference and Rain Classroom.

Idea screening

Many ideas may come up during the idea generation stage, and the company will only go ahead with those that are possible to turn into profitable products. Impractical or commercially unviable ideas will be sifted out such as laser-guided scissors.

Concept testing

Once the company deems it worthy to carry on with a certain product idea, it will enter the stage of concept testing. The concept is tested with target potential customers, and views of customers will be taken into consideration during product development. <u>The idea of electric candles may not be useful for practical use during a power outage, but customers may suggest electric candles with exquisite designs and the feature of giving off fragrance can be wanted on romantic occasions.</u>

田 电子蜡烛也许无法在停电期间产生实际效用，但顾客可能会建议商家设计生产外形精美、可散发香味的电子蜡烛，以供浪漫的场合使用。

Business analysis

The business analysis stage is about estimating sales, costs and profits. Besides, the target market, its size and projected product acceptance will be identified during the stage. The management also has to decide on the marketing strategy for the new product. Based on these data, the company is able to analyze and predict the product's financial attractiveness.

Product development

Product development is mostly the job of the R&D team, but requires cooperation from other terms and departments. R&D may produce a prototype or a basic version first, and then test and modify it through repeated communications with prospective buyers and internal people. This is commonly seen in the programing industry. The product development stage needs heavy monetary and resource inputs, which confirms the importance of the previous three stages: idea screening, concept testing and business analysis.

Market testing

During the stage, the new product is launched in a limited way so that consumer response in the marketplace can be monitored and assessed. There are broadly two methods: simulated market test and test marketing.

The basic idea behind simulated marketing tests is to create a simulated shopping environment where the new product is offered side by side with competing products to a sample of customers. The researchers will note down how many consumers choose the new products over the competing products. Later, the shoppers will be interviewed about the reason for choosing or not choosing the new product, their attitude, satisfaction with the product, repurchase intention and so on. Simulated marketing tests may be conducted by companies themselves or more frequently entrusted to market research agencies.

Test marketing takes place in a real-world marketplace—one or a few geographical areas chosen to be representative of the intended market. The idea of test marketing is very simple: Some representative geographic areas or distribution channels are chosen to launch the new product so that its market performance can be measured against its competing products or brands. In this way, the market attractiveness of the product can be predicted and the marketing plan can be tested for its effects and improved for later larger-scale launch.

Commercialization

After going through the previous six stages, the company has finally come to the final stage of commercialization, where it truly introduces its new product into the market. This stage requires large inputs into marketing campaigns. A lot of things need to be decided during the stage. Companies need to carefully consider when, where and how to launch the product. As for target customers, new-to-the-world products initially aim to target innovators and early adopters; while the introduction of modified or improved versions of existing products may start with loyal, heavy users.

田 模拟市场测试背后的基本理念是创建一个模拟的购物环境，在该环境中，新产品与竞争产品并排呈现给抽样顾客以供其选择。

田 市场试销在现实市场中开展，选择一个或几个代表目标市场的地理区域进行产品试销。

田 选择具有代表性的地理区域或分销渠道来推出新产品，可将新产品的市场表现与其竞争产品或品牌进行比较。

7. Branding

"If every asset we own, every building, every piece of equipment were destroyed in a terrible natural disaster, we would be able to borrow all the money to replace it very quickly because of the value of our brand... The brand is more valuable than the totality of all these assets," says a former CEO of McDonald's. The statement highlights the value of a strong brand.

Brands are more than names and symbols. They represent consumers' perceptions and feelings about a product and its performance—everything that the product or service means to consumers. Strong brands are beneficial to both organizations and consumers.

> ⊞ 品牌不仅仅是名称和符号，它代表了消费者对产品及其性能的看法和感受——即产品或服务对消费者意味着的一切东西。

Benefits to firms

Brand is a form of equity for a company. A strong brand can enhance companies' financial value. In marketing, the concept of "brand equity" is used to measure the strength of the brand in the marketplace and high brand equity generates tangible value for an organization in terms of increased sales profits. Franchise fee is the most direct form of brand value. Besides, most consumers are willing to pay premium prices for brands of their choice (e.g. iPhone). In this sense, a good brand represents higher profits.

> ⊞ 高品牌资产能够为机构带来高销售利润，产生有形的价值。

Strong brands can enhance consumers' perceptions and preferences, which in turn promotes brand loyalty because satisfied consumers will continue to purchase a favored brand. It can be observed that in recent years, more and more Chinese consumers have given up Apple products for Huawei smart devices, partially because of the strong brand of Huawei.

> ⊞ 强势品牌可以增强消费者的认知和偏好，进而提升品牌忠诚度，因为满意的消费者会继续购买喜爱的品牌。

When consumers hold strong, positive perceptions about superior brands, it is difficult for new entrants to compete with the brands. In other words, a strong brand can be a barrier to competition. For instance, up till now no brand of caffeinated soda drinks can rival with Coca-Cola and Pepsi. The established brands and their exclusive market acceptance have made it impossible for other brands to compete.

> ⊞ 强势品牌可以阻挡掉部分竞争。

A strong brand lays down a solid foundation for brand extensions. Firms can make use of positive perceptions and reputation from the core brand for brand extensions. Galanz is a well-established brand initially known for its superior-quality microwave ovens. Later as it grew bigger, the strong brand constituted a foundation for its extension into electric ovens, stream ovens and other household electric cookers. Beneunder ("Jiaoxia"), a brand initially known for superior-quality sun-proof umbrellas, is now making and selling other sun protection articles such as sun-proof clothes and accessories.

> ⊞ 强势品牌为品牌延伸奠定了坚实的基础。

⊞ 品牌需要传递关于产品的信息。

⊞ 消费者可以通过选择知名品牌来降低做出错误购买决策的风险。

⊞ 品牌为消费者提供了自我表达的机会。

⊞ 品牌化是公司将其产品与竞争对手区分开来的过程。

Benefits to consumers

Brands also bring consumers benefits. First and foremost, <u>brands send information about a product</u>. For instance, Volvo is representative of safety; Honda and Toyota, fuel efficiency.

Besides, as a good brand is a guarantee for superior quality and features, <u>consumers can reduce the risk of making wrong purchase decisions by choosing an established brand</u>. At the same time, it simplifies the purchase decision making process.

For certain categories of products, <u>brands provide consumers with an opportunity for self-expression</u>. Nike encourages young people to act and pursue their dreams with the slogan "Just do it!" Converse sneakers are a symbol of "winners".

<u>Branding is the process by which companies distinguish their product offerings from the competition</u>. Branding poses big challenges to marketers. The first thing is brand positioning.

Brand positioning

A brand can be dissected from the following six aspects: brand domain, brand value, brand reflection, brand personality, brand assets and brand heritage (see Figure 6.5).

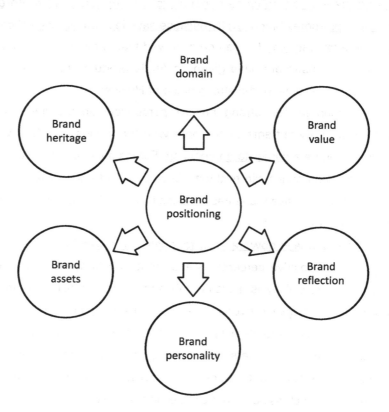

Figure 6.5 The anatomy of brand positioning

Brand domain: the brand's target market, e.g. Clinique targets women in their 30s seeking all-in-one solutions to facial skin care.

Brand value: the core values and characteristics of the brand, e.g. "Ideas for life" of Panasonic and "Life is good" of LG.

Brand reflection: how the brand relates to self-identity, how the customer perceives him/herself as a result of buying or using the brand, e.g. Rolex symbolizes career success.

Brand personality: the characterization of the brand described in terms of people, animals or objects, e.g. Celebrities as spokespersons of brands give brand personality.

Brand assets: what differentiates the brand from other competing brands (symbols, slogans, features, images, relationships, etc.), e.g. the 8-petal sunflower as Huawei's icon.

Brand heritage: the background and culture of a brand, e.g. the over-100-year history of Bank of China.

Brand name selection

Desirable qualities for a good brand name include the following (see Table 6.3):

- A good brand name should evoke positive associations with the product. For instance, "鲜橙多" is a good name for bottled orange juice because it indicates the orange used to make the beverage is fresh and juicy.

- A good brand name should be easy to pronounce, recognize and remember. That's why many brand names adopt the pattern of reiterative syllables.

- A good brand name should suggest product features and benefits. "拼多多" suggests this is a group buying app that offers abundance of products at lower prices.

- A good brand name should be distinctive. However, some businesses go too far in trying to be distinctive to the extent of vulgarity. A campus soft drink store names itself "耍榴芒", which is pronounced the same as "behaving like a hoodlum".

- High-tech products often use numerals to indicate the upgrading of product versions, e.g. Huawei's P-series of cellphones (P20, P30, P40, P50).

- A brand name should not infringe an existing registered name of another brand, which also highlights the importance of registering one's own brand names and trademarks to protect them.

- A brand name should translate well into foreign languages. Sometimes, when literal translation does not produce a satisfactory foreign name, liberal translation or giving a new name may be considered.

⊞ 品牌领域：即品牌的目标市场。

⊞ 品牌价值：品牌的核心价值和特征。

⊞ 品牌认同：品牌与消费者自我认同的关系，即顾客如何通过购买或使用该品牌来看待自己。

⊞ 品牌个性：用人、动物或物体来描述品牌的特性。

⊞ 品牌资产：品牌与其他竞争品牌的区别（符号、口号、特征、图像、关系等）。

⊞ 品牌继承：品牌的背景和文化。

Table 6.3 Brand name considerations

A good brand name should:	Examples
Evoke positive associations	Xianchengduo ("鲜橙多"), Jinliufu ("金六福")
Be easy to pronounce, recognize and remember	Dingding ("钉钉"), Bubugao ("步步高"), Wahaha ("娃哈哈")
Suggest product features and benefits	Renrendai ("人人贷"), Nongfu Spring ("农夫山泉"), Forever 21, Alipay ("支付宝"), Pinduoduo ("拼多多")
Be distinctive	Zhangfei Beef ("张飞牛肉"), Lao Gan Ma ("老干妈"), Jiang Xiao Bai ("江小白"), OnePlus (一加)
Use numerals when emphasizing technology	iPhone, Audi, Huawei Honor
Not infringe an existing registered brand name	Hanwang, a market leader of e-book reader in China, registered the trademark "i-phone" in 2004
Translate well into foreign languages	Rejoice ("飘柔"), Thermos ("膳魔师"), Diet Coke ("健怡可乐"), 微信("WeChat")

Managing brands

⊞ 值得注意的是，维持品牌靠的不是广告，而是品牌体验——消费者购买和消费该品牌的体验。良好的品牌体验有助于建立品牌偏好甚至品牌忠诚度。

As time passes, companies must manage their brands carefully. First, the positioning of a brand must be continuously communicated to consumers so that consumers are clear of the brand's positioning, especially when the brand is repositioned. Firms often spend huge amounts of money on advertising to create brand awareness. However, it is worth noting that brands are not maintained by advertising but by brand experience—consumers' experience in buying and consuming the brand. Good brand experience can help build brand preference and even loyalty.

Second, brand image and goodwill require efforts of everyone in the company. For instance, consumer preference with JD.com is grounded on their buying experience on the platform, which relies on efforts of everyone from programmers, art designers, quality controllers to after-sales service personnel and hotline people.

⊞ 品牌延伸是指在同一市场领域内，将已有的品牌名用于新产品或新产品类别。

Third, firms need to periodically examine their brands' strengths and weaknesses, and, where needed, make adjustment to their brand strategies. A brand may be extended, stretched, globalized, localized or glocalized.

Brand extension means the use of an established brand name on a new product or new product category within the same broad market. For instance, Galanz extended the brand from originally microwave ovens to other household electric cookers. Beneunder ("Jiaoxia") extended the brand from sun-proof umbrellas to other sun protection articles.

In 2019, Chinese on-demand service platform Meituan launched a new delivery brand as part of its broader efforts to boost overall delivery efficiency. The latest brand, namely Meituan Delivery (美团配送), will open its delivery platform, including the technology platform, delivery network and value chain, to partners within its ecosystem. The extension and opening of Meituan's delivery network will help establish a more flexible delivery platform. With the platform, Meituan aims to offer a more customized platform for different industries and meanwhile bolster its own delivery infrastructure and dispatch.

Brand stretching means the use of an established brand in unrelated markets. For example, Huawei, originally a communication infrastructure builder, has been stretched into a brand renowned for cellphones, personal computers, tablet PCs and other smart devices.

⊞ 品牌扩张是指在不相关的市场中使用已有的品牌。

Another example is provided here to help readers tell brand extension apart from brand stretching. New Oriental, originally known for English training, has diversified its courses into other foreign languages—this is brand extension. But the practice where a translation service company starts to provide language training services is called "brand stretching".

Global branding, also standardized branding, means the adoption of globally uniform marketing strategies for the brand. A case in point is H&M. In spite of physique differences between Europeans/Americans and Asians, H&M insists on selling virtually the same products in all outlets throughout the world. Global branding can help reduce campaign costs and create global uniformity, but the drawbacks are also very apparent, as proved by those unusually large clothes offered in an H&M outlet that are unfit for most Asian consumers.

⊞ 品牌国际化，也称为品牌标准化，指在全球范围内某个品牌采用统一的营销策略。

Localized branding is the opposite of global branding. Marketing and management decisions for the brand are tailored to the local market's characteristics and specific conditions.

Glocalized branding is perhaps a more practical strategy for multinational corporations. Glocalization is a blended word of "globalization" and "localization". For example, McDonald's and KFC adopt the glocalized strategy. While offering the basic items that are almost the same in all restaurants, they also launch localized foods tailored to the taste of consumers on the target market, e.g. porridge and rice meals for the Chinese market and foods more spicy for the Thai and Malaysian markets. Probably the old saying "Think globally. Act locally" is a good manifestation of globalization.

⊞ 品牌本土化，是指品牌的营销和管理决策根据当地市场的特点和具体情况而定。

⊞ 品牌全球本土化，对于跨国公司来说，可能是一种更实用的策略。

8. Nature and characteristics of service

The distinction between goods and services is not always clear-cut. Many services contain goods elements (e.g. A hair solon also sells shampoos while offering haircut services), and manufacturers and dealers of most goods also provide auxiliary services (e.g. Customers who purchase an air conditioner also get installation service). In spite of this, services can be defined as deeds, efforts and performances, not an objective, device or thing, with the following four characteristics that may differentiate them from goods (see Figure 6.6).

⊞ 服务可以被定义为行为、付出和表现，而非物体、装置或事物，以下四个特征可以将服务与有形商品区分开来。

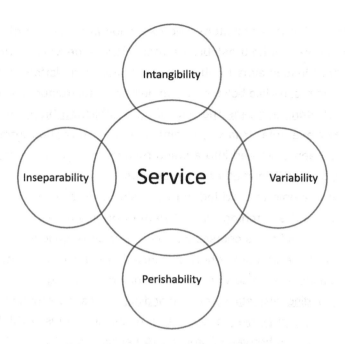

Figure 6.6 Four distinct characteristics of service

Intangibility

⊞ 与椅子、桌子等有形产品不同，服务在被购买和体验之前是无法被看到、感受到、听到或闻到的。

Unlike tangible products such as a chair or a table, services cannot be seen, felt, heard or smelled before they are bought and experienced. The intangibility means that a customer may find it hard to evaluate a service before purchase and the service provider may find it difficult to make prospective customers believe that its service is of good quality. For example, it is almost impossible to know how good the handcraft of a hair stylist is before you actually have your hair cut by him; and there is also no way to truly know how enjoyable a spa is before you actually have one. Of course, service providers can send the right cues about quality such as presenting testimonials from customers who have consumed their service. That also explains the importance of managing post-purchase feedbacks and complaints from consumers. Despite all this, feelings about one same service may vary from person to person—that means a customer has no ideas whether a service can truly satisfy his needs or wants before truly experiencing it.

Intangibility poses threats to service firms in winning over first-time consumers, but it also brings chances of retaining satisfied consumers. As it is hard for consumers to evaluate the service quality before purchase, service consumers are often highly concerned about the service quality of those service providers they have no prior experience with. Nevertheless, once they try a service item and have a good impression about it, they are more likely to come back for repeat purchases. That explains why many service-oriented businesses such as hair solons, holiday resorts and spa centers offer big discounts for first-time consumers as an important promotional technique for new launch.

Inseparability

It is common sense that goods are first produced, then sold, and finally consumed, whereas services are sold first and then produced and consumed simultaneously. In other words, <u>production and consumption take place at the same time</u>. For instance, a haircut, financial consultation, legal advice, a pop concert are produced and consumed at the same time. <u>"Inseparability" also means services cannot be separated from their providers</u>, whether the providers can be people or machines. It highlights the importance of the service provider, which is an integral part of customer satisfaction. The service must be provided at the right time, in the right place and in the right way.

<u>Apart from the service provider, other customers present at the consumption premises may affect a customer's experience of services</u>. This is apparent with restaurant meals, air, rail or boat travel, hotel, amusement parks and so on. For instance, some cafeterias may lose customers if they fail to properly control the number of people dining at the same time. Therefore service providers need to identify possible sources of nuisances (e.g. crowdedness, noise, smoke, queue jumping) that may arouse dissatisfaction and try to reduce such nuisances.

田 服务的产生和消费是同时发生的。

田 "不可分离性"还意味着服务不能与其提供者分开。

田 除服务提供者外，同在一个消费场所的其他顾客会影响顾客的服务体验。

Variability

<u>Service variability means that the quality of services depends on who provides them as well as when, where and how they are provided</u>. For example, Haidilao is a Chinese hotpot brand renowned for its superior-quality service. But from time to time we may hear news that customers dining at a particular Haidilao restaurant are accidently hit by noodles in the Haidilao-featured noodle juggling performance conducted by less careful or less skilled performers. Customers hit by noodles may hold bad impressions about the restaurant. The quality of each and every single Haidilao employee's service varies according to his energy and frame of mind at the time of each customer encounter.

<u>The variability of service quality highlights the need for rigorous selection, training and rewards/punishments of front-line staff members in direct contact with consumers</u>. Staff training should emphasize the standards of service and the evaluation of service quality. Moreover, service standardization is an approach to tackling the variability problem. For example, massage services offered by different masseurs can by no means be identical, but the massage shop can develop a set of standardized procedures of delivering services and have some guidelines about the length, the strength and skills of delivering massage.

田 服务变化性意味着服务质量取决于提供服务的人以及提供服务的时间、地点和方式。

田 服务质量的变化性凸显了对与消费者直接接触的一线员工进行严格选拔、培训和奖惩的必要性。

田 易消失性意味着服务不能保存以供日后销售或使用；未使用的服务能力无法保留，服务本身无法存储。

Perishability

<u>Perishability means services cannot be saved for later sale or use; unused</u>

capability in services cannot be reserved, and services themselves cannot be stored. A hotel room or an airline seat that is not occupied today represents lost income that cannot be gained tomorrow; unconsumed working hours of a masseur in a massage shop cannot be made up for later. This poses a problem to service providers when there are times of peak and sluggish demands. For manufacturers of tangible goods, the problem can be easily solved by putting unsold goods into warehouses. But as services cannot be inventoried, service firms often find themselves faced with short supplies during peak times and short demands during slack seasons.

The problem can be solved by devising a flexible pricing system. It is quite common to see that hotels, restaurants and airlines have different prices for different periods of time. In this way, demands can be smoothed through differential pricing to encourage customers to consume during off-peak hours. Another alternative is to use part-time workforce during peak periods. But service firms have to ensure that part-time employees are well-trained to deliver up-to-standard services. Besides, the wide application of smartphones has enabled service providers to use an effective ordering and queuing system, which sends notification to waiting consumers when it is time for them to receive service so that they can shop around before that without having to line up at the premises.

9. Service differentiation

As many companies find it increasingly difficult to differentiate themselves on physical goods, many companies have shifted the focus to provision of added value in terms of service components. For instance, hotpot restaurants may not rely on the hotpot soup and foods to differentiate themselves, as the foods are not cooked by the restaurant's cooks, but provide additional services such as free-of-charge manicure, snacks and drinks for customers waiting. Companies can also differentiate themselves in terms of service delivery by having more competent and reliable customer-contact people.

10. Marketing strategies for service firms

Like providers of tangible products, service firms also need to manage service quality, properly attend to marketing strategies such as segmentation, targeting, positioning and differentiation, deliver values to win customer satisfaction, and try to build long-term profitable relationships with customers. Everything discussed in the previous chapters applies to service firms. There are two forms of marketing especially relevant to service firms: relationship marketing and experiential marketing.

Relationship marketing

The intangible nature of services indicates customers can have value through having a close relationship with a service provider. For example, if you are satisfied with the handicrafts of a hair stylist, there is a big chance that you will revisit the hair salon for the same stylist. It is the relationship with the stylist that keeps you revisiting the hair salon. It is not surprising that many customer-contact persons often want to befriend first-time customers on WeChat, especially in those service sectors where ongoing or periodic services are needed such as dental service, haircut, electric appliance repair and so on.

The efforts in building good relationships with customers so that they continue to buy a company's products or services over a long period of time are collectively referred to as "relationship marketing". Relationship marketing is good for service firms in apparent ways: increased repeat purchases, lower operational costs as attracting new customers is always more expensive than retaining existing ones, higher lifetime consumer value brought by customers staying in a long-term relationship with the business, sustainable competitive advantage as it is not easy to copy good relationships, possible word-of-mouth promotion, and higher job satisfaction of employees as a result of good relationships with customers.

⊞ 鉴于上述原因，许多与顾客直接联系的企业人员通常希望与新顾客添加微信好友，尤其是那些需要提供持续或定期服务的领域，如牙科服务、理发、电器维修等。

⊞ 与顾客建立良好关系，使他们长期持续购买公司产品或服务，这个过程称为"关系营销"。

Experiential marketing

Creating good experience for customers is another way of delivering value and creating customer satisfaction. Experiential marketing is particularly relevant to service firms organizing concerts, art exhibitions and music festivals. Apart from guaranteeing delivery of considerate services during the process, service providers conducting experiential marketing should also focus on pre-publicity and post-services.

⊞ 开展体验式营销的服务商除了要保证提供贴心的服务外，还应注重售前宣传广告和售后服务。

Experiential marketing is also very popular in the retail trade as stores seek to find new ways of appealing to potential customers and of pleasing regular buyers. That explains why high-end cosmetic brands and luxury goods are still insisting on opening brick-and-mortar outlets in department stores despite the high rents, when online shopping is prevalent nowadays, for it is not only the tangible product but also the service and shopping experience that retain those less-budget-conscious buyers.

Summary

Broadly defined, "product" refers to any form of value offered to customers, including tangible products and intangible services in the marketing sense. Product contains three levels: core benefits, actual product and augmented product. The core level is the most basic benefit or feature of a product that addresses consumers' needs; the actual level consists of product features, quality, packaging, design and brand name; the augmented level covers delivery, installation, after-sales service, warranty and brand value—forms of added value. Companies can differentiate their products at any of the three levels.

A company's product mix contains all of its products, which can be divided into several product lines. Product line is a group of products that are closely related in terms of functions and benefits. The length of the product line is the number of variants offered within the line, and the width of the product mix can be measured by the number of product lines a company carries. How to manage the product lines and the product mix is a big challenge for marketers.

The BCG matrix is introduced to help with managing the product mix. By the dimensions of relative market strength and market growth rate, a company can divide products into four categories: star, cash cow, question mark and dog. Different marketing considerations and strategies are required for each of these categories.

Like people, products also have their life cycle. Typically, the product life cycle (PLC) consists of five stages: product development, introduction, growth, maturity and decline. As each stage shows different patterns of sales and profits, companies have different marketing objectives and strategies for each stage.

Since products die out, new products must be created and introduced. The typical product development process has seven steps: idea generation, idea screening, concept testing, business analysis, product development, marketing testing and commercialization.

An issue closely related to product and service is branding. The benefits of a strong brand are very obvious for both organizations and consumers, and the importance of brands can never be overstated. Branding concerns two aspects: how to build strong brands and how to manage brands over time.

For building strong brands, there are mainly two issues: positioning a brand and naming a brand. When defining the positioning of a brand, companies must define brand domain, brand value, brand reflection, brand personality, brand assets and brand heritage. When naming a brand, companies need to consider whether a brand can evoke positive association, is easy to pronounce, can be easily recognized and remembered, suggests product features and benefits, is distinctive, uses numerals when emphasizing technology, does not fringe an existing registered brand name and translates well into foreign languages.

As for managing brands over time, an established brand can be developed in terms of brand extension, brand strengthening, globalized branding, localized branding and glocalized branding. Companies must audit their brands periodically and make due adjustments to brand strategies.

Service is distinguishable from tangible products ("product" in the narrow sense) in terms of four characteristics: intangibility, inseparability, variability and perishability. Firms can always differentiate themselves from competitors with unique or superior services.

As we have clarified, product in the broad sense includes service. Hence, everything we have discussed by far in the previous chapters also applies to firm services. Two new forms of marketing—relationship marketing and experiential marketing are briefly talked about, for they are highly relevant to service firms.

Key terms

product	actual differentiation
core product	augmented differentiation
actual product	product line
augmented product	length of product line
core differentiation	product mix

width of product mix	brand
BCG matrix	branding
star	brand positioning
question mark/problem child	brand domain
cash cow	brand heritage
dog	brand asset
product life cycle (PLC)	brand personality
product R&D	brand reflection
introduction	brand value
growth	brand extension
maturity	brand stretching
decline	global branding
new product development	localized branding
idea generation	glocalized branding
idea screening	characteristics of service
concept testing	intangiblity
business analysis	inseparability
product development	variability
market testing	perishability
commercialization	

Exercises

Review and discussion

1. Make sentences using one part from each column. Then match the sentences (1−5) with the stages of the development process (a−c).

_____ 1) We should carry	date and now need to prepare the distribution	plan.
_____ 2) We have completed the alpha	rollout across	research.
_____ 3) The results will allow us to fine-	test and are now ready for beta	network.
_____ 4) We have planned the market	tune our marketing	testing.
_____ 5) We have set a launch	out some sensory	Europe.

a. Test marketing
b. Commercialization
c. Product development and optimization

2. Complete the description of product development using words from the box.

date	prototype	flaws	representations
forecast	resources	launch	success
manage	time	product	

After we get the OK for the product concept we need to allocate _____ to the next stage: product development. We start by _____ modelling. We have to create a _____ which we use to identify and eliminate product _____ in order to increase the likelihood of _____. We use CAD to create 3D _____. Although there is always pressure to reduce our _____ to market, I think it is important to _____ risk well so that the product launch is success. At the end of the product development and optimization stage, the project moves into test marketing, used to _____ sales. In the last project we worked on, we carried out a test of the market before the full _____. At the end, a commercialization _____ is set and the product is launched, successfully we hope.

3. Put the words in italics in the correct order to complete the sentences.

1) *Boston Consulting matrix The Group* is used as a planning tool.

2) It concerns the *cycle life product*.

3) A product with *a market relative high share* and *market growth rate low* is a cash cow.

4) Cash cows can be used to fund *development research* and for new products.

5) Stars may *cash high flows generate* but are not always profitable.

6) Dogs may *cash negative flow generate*.

7) It may be necessary to *line the drop*.

8) Question marks will consume resources before *a return investment on giving*.

4. Decide where the following services can be place on the BCG matrix: as question mark/ problem child, star, cash cow or dog.

1) Network Protection Protect your network from hackers and viruses. Contact us today for the latest in network protection. Now over 5,000 happy clients. Join the fastest growing safe online community.	**3) Summer Sale Book Now** Visit our online store to find reductions on weekend breaks in North Wales. Hurry: Some of our hotels are being converted into private apartments. Offer ends October 31st.
2) Join the Diet Club Lose weight quickly and safely. Millions of slimmer clients. Read their testimonials. The Diet Club: trusted nutritionists delivering sound advice for generations.	**4) New Service** You can now raise money for your favorite charities by using CharitySearchClick.com. All you need to do is use CSC every time you search on the web, and we will donate half your profit to your selected charity. Try it today and tell your friends.

5. Match the examples (1-4) with the summaries (a-d).

_____ 1) Apple invented the iPod. They started to market it.

_____ 2) After a successful launch, Google got more and more market share.

_____ 3) Coca-Cola created new products (Diet Coke, Blak, Etcs) using the same brand.

_____ 4) Beaner's coffee changed the company name to Biggby Coffee at the beginning of 2008. The new name appears on signs and marketing material.

a. They rebranded.	c. They launched the brand.
b. The brand became established.	d. The stretched the brand.

6. Choose the correct word from the brackets to complete each brand value statement.

1) Our (trustworthiness / outlook / flexibility) means you can easily adapt the service to your needs.

2) We value (fresh / simplicity / inspirational) and we design our products with this in mind.

3) Our product is (easy to be / easy to use/ easy to cost).

4) We are (knowledgeable / luxury / heritage) about food.

5) We are a low cost, value for (lifestyle / fun / money) brand.

7. Answer the following questions briefly.

1) What are the three levels of a product?

2) List and explain the three product levels of a cellphone, a notebook, or a shampoo.

3) Explain why many people are willing to pay extra money for specialty goods? What does this tell you about human motivations described by the needs hierarchy?

4) What product category do you think has the longest life cycle? What products now on the market do you think are fads or fashion that will soon disappear?

5) Define the terms: services, and goods.

6) Why do many goods producers nowadays turn to the service to generate additional revenue for their firms?

7) What strategies should an insurance company utilize in its attempt to minimize the effects of intangibility? Of the companies that have actively attempted to minimize the effects, have some companies done a better job than others? Please explain.

8) What is a brand? Describe the value of branding for both the buyer and seller.

9) Think of five brand names. To what extent do they meet the criteria of good brand naming? Do any of the names legitimately break these guidelines?

10) Examine a product like bottled water through the lens of the core, actual and augmented product. What types of differentiation strategies are being used by brands in this sector? Can you suggest any new sources of differentiation?

11) Discuss the role of service staff in the creation of a quality service. Can you give examples from your own experiences of good and bad service encounters?

▬▬▬▬▬ Projects and teamwork ▬▬▬▬▬

1. Form a small group. Generate ideas for a new consumer product that fills an existing need but does not currently exist. Select the one idea that you think is best. What process did your group use for idea generation and screening?

2. Work in teams. Briefly describe how the unique service characteristics of intangibility, inseparability, heterogeneity, and perishability apply to your educational experience in your marketing classes.

3. Perishability is very important in the airline industry: unsold seats are gone forever, and too many unsold seats mean large losses. With computerized ticketing, airlines can easily use pricing to deal with perishability and variations in demand.

   Call a travel agent or use an online service to check airline fares in Chinese airline industry. Get prices on the same route for 60 days in advance, two weeks, one week, and today. Is there a clear pattern to the fares?

   What are airlines doing to their prices as the seats get close to "perishing"? Why? What would you recommend as a pricing strategy to increase the total revenue?

4. With a classmate, visit the website of a domestic company that interests you—say, Huawei. Measure the company's product mix according to width, length, and depth. If the firm is small, you can list all of its products or product lines. If it is large, try to identify the product lines and give a few samples of individual products.

▬▬▬▬▬ Case study ▬▬▬▬▬

Green-packeded Wanglaoji vs Red-canned Wanglaoji

"Worried about getting inflamed? Drink Wanglaoji!" ("怕上火，就喝王老吉") As the slogan widespread across the country, Wanglaoji has become a popular choice on Chinese people's dinner table. The glory shined over the red-canned Wanglaoji, while its twin brother—the green-packed Wanglaoji remained in obscurity.

The herbal tea Wanglaoji was invented during the Qing dynasty with a history of over 170 years. It is widely recognized as the origin of Chinese herbal teas. However, at the beginning of the 1950s, due to some political reasons, the Wanglaoji business was split into two establishments: one was reformed into public ownership and evolved later into what we know now as Guangzhou Wanglaoji Pharmaceutical Company Limited ("Wanglaoji Pharmaceutical"), and the other was taken to Hong Kong by the offspring of the Wanglaoji founder. Today, the brand Wanglaoji is owned by Wanglaoji Pharmaceutical, while in countries and regions outside the Chinese mainland, the brand is owned by the Wanglaoji family.

With the recipe provided by the Wanglaoji family, the production of canned Wanglaoji drinks was franchised by Wanglaoji Pharmaceutical to JDB Company, while the box-packed drink continued to be manufactured and sold by Wanglaoji Pharmaceutical.

However, as we know Wanglaoji Pharmaceutical is mainly engaged in making and marketing medicines, and the green-packed Wanglaoji, as a soft drink, requires vastly different distribution channels, promotional efforts and marketing strategies. For years, the company has neither attached enough importance to nor input enough efforts into marketing the drink. As a result, the market performance was unsurprisingly subpar.

The red-canned Wanglaoji produced by JDB caught on almost overnight due to the rigorous marketing campaign. Wanglaoji rose from a Guangdong-based brand into a national renowned brand. At the same time, its green-packed counterpart underperformed on the market. Wanglaoji Pharmaceutical was pretty anxious about the situation.

Starting from 2004, after obtaining consents from JDB Company, Wanglaoji Pharmaceutical also used the slogan "Worried about getting inflamed? Drink Wanglaoji!" in its advertising campaigns, but the result was not as good as expected.

Meanwhile, the pharmaceutical company started to subconsciously regard the red-canned Wanglaoji as the biggest threat to its green-packed drink and speculated that its segmented market should be part of the target groups of the red-canned drink.

At the end of 2005, Wanglaoji Pharmaceutical authorized a marketing agency to conduct a market research designed to figure out how the packed Wanglaoji can grab part of the market from the canned Wanglaoji and to develop marketing promotion guidelines for it.

In the minds of consumers, there is virtually no difference between the packed Wanglaoji and the canned Wanglaoji in the drink itself, and they are only two versions of the same drink with different packages and prices. Though the two variants are produced by two manufacturers, to consumers they are the same drink of the same brand put into different containers. The price difference is only because of the different packaging.

From the perspective of the product itself, the different packages and prices to some extent determine differences in target consumers and consumption occasion. The canned Wanglaoji, put in a red aluminum can, appears classic and fashionable, meets Chinese people's etiquette protocols, and thus are suitable for social occasions such as gatherings and banquets. Hence, the red-canned Wanglaoji was massively distributed into the catering industry. In contrast, the packed Wanglaoji cannot compete with its canned counterpart in the catering industry due to the low-profile package.

However, putting aside the catering industry, is there any chance for the packed Wanglaoji in the open-and-drink segment and the household consumption (non-social occasion) segment?

Both the segments are characterized by consumer preference for lower-priced, easy-to-carry products, for there is no need of social considerations. In the open-and-drink segment, the red-canned Wanglaoji is priced at RMB 3.5 per can, which, compared with other drinks, is relatively higher. It may not be a good choice for those price-sensitive, low-income groups such as students and labor workers. The price of the packed Wanglaoji is RMB 2. For people who like Wanglaoji but are budget-conscious, the packed drink is no doubt a better choice. In the household segment, without consideration for "face", lower price for the same quality is a big push for household buying. Therefore, the packed Wanglaoji, instead of being a competitor, can be a complement to the canned Wanglaoji in these two niches.

From the perspective of competition, the red-canned Wanglaoji has done most jobs for market exploration and expansion. The herbal tea market is growing rapidly, with space and potential for further exploration. Because of the rigorous marketing efforts of JDB, the red-canned Wanglaoji has become the first choice of herbal tea drinkers and established itself as a leading brand. The packed Wanglaoji, with a sale volume of less than 1/10 of the red can's, apparently is incapable of market expansion.

In sum, consumers do not see virtual differences between the two versions of Wanglaoji, and the market expansion task is mainly assumed by JDB, the producer of the red-canned Wanglaoji. Instead of trying to grab a bit from the red can's market, Wanglaoji Pharmaceutical should position the green pack as a complement to the red can by focusing on the niche markets that are overlooked by the latter—the open-and-drink segment and the household consumption segment.

Since the marketing strategy has been clarified, how can Wanglaoji Pharmaceutical implement the strategy?

First, it is important to point out that the difference between the two products that matters is not that known by the manufacturers, but that perceived by consumers. Consumers see the packed and canned variants as the same product only in different packages and at different prices. Marketing promotions of the two should be congruent to avoid confusing consumers.

Second, the target groups of the packed Wanglaoji should be determined. As discussed above, the open-and-drink segment and the household consumption segment are the niches for it, so its target groups could be price-sensitive, budget-conscious consumers for individual and household uses, such as students and working-class families. Housewives, most of whom are the main buyer of household grocery shopping, should be the target of promotional campaigns.

Third is about the promotion strategy. Promotion of the packed Wanglaoji should achieve two primary purposes: reassuring consumers that the packed version contains the same drink as the canned version; telling consumers that the packed version is different from the red can only in terms of specifications. Based on this, the advertising slogan for the green-packed Wanglaoji was adjusted into: "Wanglaoji has a pack version" ("王老吉，还有盒装"). The new round of marketing campaigns turned out to be quite effective, and resulted in a big increase in the sales of the green pack.

In modern marketing, price war, fights for distribution channels, flooding advertisements and big sales are no longer guarantees for market success. Instead, formulating and implementing successful brand strategies is the key to winning the battle.

Questions:

1. On what product level is the green-packed Wanglaoji differentiated from its red-canned counterpart?

2. Analyze the segmentation, targeting and positioning strategies of the green-packed Wanglaoji in terms of product.

3. Use the brand positioning anatomy to dissect the packed Wanglaoji.

Chapter Seven
Pricing

Objectives:

After studying this chapter, you should be able to:

- Identify factors affecting a company's pricing strategy and understand how they affect the price;
- Distinguish between cost-based pricing and value-based pricing and understand their pros and cons;
- Understand that in practice neither cost-based pricing result nor value-based pricing result is used alone, but as price floor and price ceiling;
- Discuss how the price is interconnected with the company's positioning strategy;
- Explain what is price elasticity of demand (PED) and its marketing implications;
- Distinguish between market skimming pricing and market penetration pricing;
- Discuss price adjustment strategies and decide when to initiate or respond to price changes.

Framework

Chapter Seven Pricing

Factors affecting the company's pricing decision

- Production cost
- Positioning strategy
- Customers' perception on product value
- Market demand
- Competitors' marketing strategy

Price adjustment strategies

- Discount and promotional pricing
- Segmented pricing
- Psychological pricing
- Geographical and international pricing
- When to initiate or respond to price changes

New product pricing strategies

- Two major pricing strategies for new products
  - Market skimming pricing
  - Market penetration pricing

- Product mix pricing strategies
  - Product line pricing
  - Optional product pricing
  - Captive product pricing
  - By-product pricing
  - Product bundle pricing

Pricing is an important aspect in marketing, and also the most important element in determining a company's market share and profitability. Among the 4Ps (product, price, promotion and place), price is the only element that represents income while the other three represent costs. In a narrow sense, price is the amount of money or value given up by customers to exchange for the benefit of obtaining or using a product or service. This chapter discusses the factors affecting the company's pricing decision and the various types of pricing strategies.

Pricing compliance is critical to a business's marketing operations. In 2021, China's top market regulator fined e-commerce giant JD.com, Alibaba Group's business-to-customer platform JD.com and Tmall 500,000 yuan ($77,200) each for irregular pricing, as JD.com, Tmall and Vipshop were complained by consumers about their irregular conducts during the November 11 shopping bonanza, such as raising prices before offering discounts, sales tricks, seduced deal closing and so on. China's online economy has flourished, but competition has become increasingly fierce in some sectors, and the problem of unfair competition has also emerged. Unfair competition not only damages the legitimate interests of businesses and consumers, but also distorts and destroys normal market competition mechanisms, ultimately affecting high-quality economic development.

1. Factors affecting the company's pricing decision

There are internal and external factors that influence the firm's pricing decision. Internal factors include the firm's production cost and its overall strategies (marketing strategy, objectives and market mix). And external factors include the value customers place on the product, the market demand, and competitor's marketing strategies and costs. This section discusses five major factors influencing a company's pricing decision: production cost, positioning strategy, customers' perception on product value, market demand and competitors' marketing strategy.

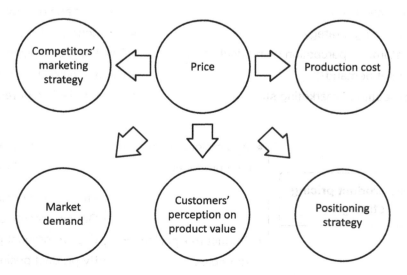

Figure 7.1 Factors affecting the company's pricing strategy

1.1 Production cost

Cost is an important basis for setting price. In order to break even or earn a profit, the firm needs to look at the production costs. Total costs include fixed costs and variable costs. Fixed costs are those that do not vary with production or sales volume, such as property maintenance expense, management salaries, depreciation, and rental expenses, etc. Variable costs are costs that vary directly with production or sales level, such as assembly line workers' salaries, cost of materials and packaging, etc. Given that cost is an important consideration, cost-based pricing is a typical pricing approach. It refers to setting prices based on all the costs for producing, distributing and selling the product plus a reasonable profit margin. The company designs product features that it considers attractive to customers, calculates the costs (including fixed and variable costs), adds a target profit it hopes to earn, and then formulates the price. After designing the product features and setting the price, the company will have to convince consumers that it's a good price that justifies their purchases.

Cost-based pricing has its problems. One major problem of cost-based pricing is that price will increase when sales level drops. A simple case will explicitly illustrate this point. In the first year when sales are expected to reach 100,000 units, fixed costs of $300,000 are spread among the 100,000 units and average fixed costs are $300,000/100,000=$3. By adding up average fixed costs, average variable costs and a 10% markup, marketers set the price at $5.5.

By comparison, in the second year, sales are predicted to drop to 50,000, the same fixed costs of $300,000 are spread among fewer units and average fixed costs are $300,000/50,000=$6, which is twice of that in the first year. Thus, by adding up all the costs and markup, the price should be $8.8, higher than that in the first year.

田 固定成本是指不随生产或销售量变化的成本，如物业维护费、管理人员工资、折旧、租金等。可变成本是指随生产或销售水平变化而变化的成本，如流水线工人的工资、材料和包装成本等。

田 基于成本定价法是一种典型的定价方法，根据生产、分销和销售产品所产生的所有成本加上合理的利润空间来确定价格。

Table 7.1 Price setting under the cost-based approach

Year 1	
Fixed costs	=$300,000
Expected sales	=100,000
Cost per unit	
Average variable costs	=$2
Average fixed costs ($300,000/100,000)	=$3
Average total costs	=$5
Markup (10%)	=$0.5
Price (cost plus markup)	=$5.5

Continued

Year 2	
Fixed costs	=$300,000
Expected sales	=50,000
Cost per unit	
Average variable costs	=$2
Average fixed costs ($300,000/50,000)	=$6
Average total costs	=$8
Markup (10%)	=$0.8
Price (cost plus markup)	=$8.8

The calculation indicates that poor sales lead to higher price, which is abnormal in practice and may hurt sales further. Moreover, a sales projection is made before the price is set, which is illogical. Furthermore, this pricing approach is production-driven instead of market-driven or customer-driven. It's based on the production cost instead of the value perceived by consumers. But in fact, it is consumers' perception of the product value that ultimately determines the maximum price companies can charge. In reality, cost-based pricing is seldom applied alone. It's normally used to supplement other pricing strategies in that it can help specify the minimum price for the company to break even. Theoretically, when the price is set above the value perceived by customers, there would be no demand; below the production cost-based price, there would be no profit.

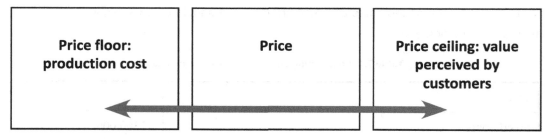

Figure 7.2 Price ceiling and price floor

1.2 Positioning strategy

The second factor relevant to pricing is the firm's marketing strategy, including its positioning strategy. Paired with the firm's positioning strategy, price can be a key marketing tool to appeal to different segments. Specifically, a firm adopts low price if it targets its product at the middle- or low-income, price-sensitive segments, and positions its product as low-grade. In contrast, it can set a high price if the product targetes at high-income, price-insensitive groups, and positions itself as high-value. For instance, Vipshop, a B2C platform positioning itself as a good-value discount shop, offers big discounts for quality branded products to the budget-conscious middle class who values life quality.

Price is a powerful positioning tool in that it indicates quality in customers' mind. For example, Walt-mart puts forward a strategy of "everyday low price" since the targeted customers are price-sensitive, so it positions itself as a budget supermarket. In comparison, Louis Vuitton sets very high prices for its bags because it's positioned as a high-end luxury brand. A price cut on such luxury brand, instead of attracting customers, may indicate reduced product quality or corporate financial distress, resulting in loss of some existing customers. Furthermore, some customers buy such brand as a way of demonstrating their social status, they may stop buying it as the positioning is blurred because of the price cut. Therefore, high-end brands must be very careful with price cut as it may undercut the brand value and competitiveness.

田 价格是强大的定
位工具，价格体现产
品在顾客心目中的
质量。

田 高端品牌在降价
时必须非常小心，因
为降价可能会削弱
品牌价值和竞争力。

1.3 Customers' perception on product value

Good pricing is based on a clear understanding of customers' perception of product value, which determines the maximum they will pay for the product, called customers' willingness to pay. Value-based pricing refers to the pricing strategy that is based on the value perceived by customers rather than on the production costs. As opposed to cost-based pricing, value-based pricing guides companies to set the target price based on product value. They then design product features and determine the appropriate costs to incur based on the target price. This method starts from analyzing customer needs—a typical feature of a market-oriented organization.

田 基于价值定价法是
指基于顾客感知到的
价值而非生产成本进
行定价的策略。

One challenge in value-based pricing is measuring the customers' perception of product value to be quantified, which is very difficult, if not impossible at all. In practice, some companies ask customers about the price they will pay for the basic product and each additional feature. Other companies may conduct experiments to find out how many customers are willing to pay for different product offerings. The second challenge in value-based pricing is that value perceived by customers varies from person to person on different occasions.

One particular method of value-based pricing is good-value pricing, which refers to offering just the right combination of quality and good service at a fair price. The key is to make the product affordable to a large number of customers. An important type of good-value pricing is "everyday low pricing" (EDLP). It involves charging constant low prices every day with few or no temporary price discounts. In comparison, high-low pricing involves charging higher price regularly and offering discounts or other forms of promotion temporarily on all or selected items. To offer everyday low price, the company needs to maintain low costs. The reason for Wal-Mart's ability to do so lies

田 超值定价法，是指
以公平的价格提供
质量和服务的合适
组合。

田附加价值定价法：一些公司通过提供具有附加价值的功能和服务来保持相对较高的价格，以将其产品与竞争对手区分开来，这些附加价值能支撑高价格。

in its great bargaining power with suppliers. However, the retail giant is often criticized for its "oppression" of the weak, small manufacturers.

The other form of value-based pricing is <u>value-added pricing</u>. When facing fierce competition and price war, <u>some companies keep the relatively high price by attaching value-added features and services to differentiate their offers and justify the higher price</u>. The freedom of not cutting prices comes from pricing power, the power to escape from fierce competition, maintain high price and profit margin without losing market share. Such power comes from the unique product value created by the company. In the competitive market of smartphones, Apple is still able to charge higher prices for iPhones because it boasts a unique operation system—IOS, the minimalist design and other added values. Gree guarantees a 10-year warranty for its air conditioners, which to some extent justifies the higher price it charges.

1.4 Market demand

田 需求的价格弹性 (PED) 是指需求量变化相对价格变化的程度，通常用百分比表示。

The nature of the product and the corresponding elasticity of demand also influence the pricing strategy. <u>Price elasticity of demand (PED) refers to the percentage of change in the quantity demanded in relation to a percentage of change in price</u>. PED measures the responsiveness of demand to a change in price. It is determined by availability of close substitutes, nature of the product, and time horizon, etc. Products that have no or few substitutes have smaller elasticity of demand. For example, if the supplier of a product monopolizes the market and there are no similar products in the market, the supplier has a great power to set a high price to rip off big consumer value.[1] In contrast, elasticity of demand is much greater in a perfectly competitive market, in which numerous buyers and sellers are trading identical products. When customers have substitutes to choose from, they are more sensitive to the price change, and any slight increase in price will lead to a significant reduction in quantity sold. The price elasticity of demand is calculated as:

田 需求的价格弹性 (PED) = 需求量变化的百分比 / 价格变化的百分比

<u>PED = % change in quantity demanded/ % change in price</u>

The example below illustrates the calculation of PED:

Table 7.2 Calculation of price elasticity of demand

Product X	Original price	New price
Quantity demands	1,000 units	800 units
Price	$4	$5

---

[1] There are four types of market, i.e., perfect competition, monopolistic competition, oligopoly and monopoly. In perfectly competitive market, there are numerous buyers and sellers trading identical products. Perfect competition is idealistic and no market in the real world is truly perfectly competitive. In monopolistically competitive market, there are numerous buyers and sellers trading products that are similar but not identical. In oligopoly, there are several suppliers in the market so that each needs to act strategically. Monopolistic competition and oligopoly are called imperfect competition. In monopoly, there is only supplier in the market and the market has a barrier to entry.

Change in demand: –200 units

% change in demand: –200/1000 = –20%

Change in price: $1

% change in price: $1/$4 = 25%

PED = –20%/ 25% = –0.8

The above example shows how PED is calculated. In cases where the absolute value of PED is greater than 1, suppliers need to reduce the price to increase revenue, because the rise of quantity sold is proportionately greater than the drop in price. And vice versa when the PED is smaller than 1.

Table 7.3 Interpretation of PED value

	PED	Interpretation
Price elastic	> 1	Change in demand is greater than the change in price.
Price inelastic	< 1	Change in demand is smaller than the change in price.
Unitary price elasticity	=1	Change in demand is equal to the change in price.

1.5 Competitors' marketing strategy

In oligopoly, there are only a few sellers in the market, so that each seller is an important player in the game. The profit of any seller depends not only on its own strategy, but also on the strategies of others. In such cases, companies need to look at the competitors' marketing strategy when setting its own price. The same applies to the other type of imperfectly competitive market, monopolistically competitive market.

In the case of undifferentiated commodities, businesses tend to adopt the going-rate price—the average price in the industry. This is a typical method of the competition-oriented pricing. This pricing method has some advantages: higher acceptance by customers as the average price is often deemed as reasonable, peaceful coexistence with competitors, moderate profit margins and wide applicability. However, the shortcomings are obvious too. First, firms with differential advantages may lose the opportunity to charge higher prices that are grounded on the differential advantages. Second, following the going-rate price, some firms with a cost position weaker than its competitors' may not be able to break even.

> ⊞ 对于无差别商品，企业倾向于采用通行价格——行业平均价格。

2. New product pricing strategies

Pricing strategies are different at different phases through the product life cycle, and the introductory phase is the most challenging. Since the product is new to the market, it's difficult for the company to predict the market response to its pricing. When setting prices for new products, generally companies can follow two approaches, i.e., market-skimming pricing and market-penetration pricing. Moreover, this section discusses the methods of setting pricing for product line, optional product, captive product, by-product and product bundle.

2.1 Two major pricing strategies for new products

Two major strategies are introduced for pricing new products: market skimming pricing and market penetration pricing. The two strategies are briefly demonstrated in the table below.

Table 7.4 Two major new product pricing strategies

	Skimming pricing	Penetration pricing
Price level	High	Low
Applicability	For products that have high quality, are truly unique, or are patented	For other products that are not truly unique, or are positioned as being cost-effective
Profit margins	Big	Small
Target customers	Price-insensitive	Price-sensitive

Market skimming pricing

⊞ 市场撇脂定价法是指将新产品价格定得很高，从愿意支付高价的顾客身上攫取最大利润的策略。

In cases where the company positions its product as a high-end one, with better quality, unique design or features that appeal to the market, it can adopt market skimming pricing and set a high price. Market skimming pricing refers to the strategy of setting a high price for a new product to skim maximum profits layer by layer from customers willing to pay a high price. The purpose is to get a considerable return on the company's initial investment quickly, before there is fierce competition. After profits from the keenest customer group are reaped, it will lower down the price to target at the new layer of customers who are willing to pay a lower price for the product. This is also the time when competitors start to join in.

For example, when mobile phone was first introduced to China in the form of "Dageda" in the 1980s, it was priced at over RMB 20,000. It was clumsy, with limited functions, yet it was chased by successful businessmen who were price-insensitive and in real need to keep in touch anytime, anywhere. High prices were charged for "Dageda" because it was unique, brand new, and with no substitute. The price dropped later on when competitors joined in and there were greater varieties of mobile phones in the market. Now a smartphone, the improved version of mobile phone with far greater functions, costs only RMB 3,000—7,000.

Market skimming pricing is appropriate for products that have high quality, are truly unique, or are patented. <u>In other words, the new product must have some qualities that shield it from competition and thus justify the high introduction price</u>. Apple adopted the skimming strategy for introducing each edition of iPhone. However, when rivals do join in the market, the company should be able to adjust its price quickly to better cope with competition. One thing that companies need to keep eyes on is that the number of price-insensitive customer needs to be large enough for the company to stay profitable.

> 田 换言之，采用撇脂定价法的新产品必须具备一些能够屏蔽掉竞争的特性，这些特征能够支撑高额的上市价格。

Market penetration pricing

For other products that are not truly unique, or are positioned as being cost-effective, companies follow the other type of pricing strategy, <u>market-penetration pricing, which means setting a low price for a new product to penetrate the market, attracting a large number of buyers and taking up a large market share</u>. The purpose is to seize the market quickly and maintain the competitive advantage by keeping a low price. Miniso, a Japanese-inspired lifestyle product retailer that offers high-quality household goods, cosmetics and snacks at affordable prices, adopted the market penetration pricing strategy when entering the Chinese mainland market. As a result, it quickly caught on, opened numerous chained outlets and seized a large market share.

> 田 市场渗透定价法，指为了新产品能够渗透市场，将其价格定得比较低，从而吸引大量购买者，占据较大的市场份额。

Price can be kept low because by producing a large quantity of the product, the company achieves economies of scale and average total costs are lowered. Consequently, the first condition for adopting market-penetration pricing is that the company is able to achieve economies of scale through scaling up production. Secondly, customers are price-sensitive so that a lower price induces a rise in quantity sold that is proportionately greater. Thirdly, a low price does not lead to price wars, which means it's difficult for rivals to charge competitively low price as the company does. Otherwise, the low price brings competitive advantages only temporarily.

2.2 Product mix pricing strategies

In some cases, pricing strategies are important not only for a single product but also for the product mix of which it is a part. Products in the same mix are related in terms of demand and costs. Thus, when selecting or changing the pricing strategy of a certain product, marketers will target at maximizing the profit of the whole product mix. There are generally five types of product mix pricing, i.e., product line pricing, optional product pricing, captive product pricing, by-product pricing, and product bundle pricing.

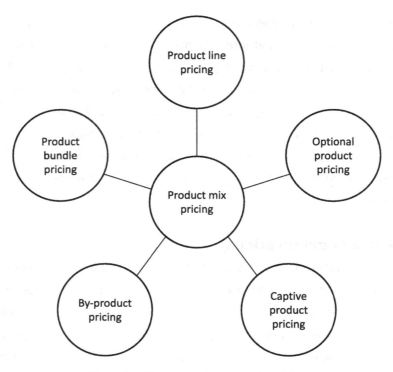

Figure 7.3 Five types of product mix pricing

Product line pricing

Product line pricing refers to setting different prices for different products in a product line based on cost differences among the products or the value customers place on each product, so as to maximize the profit of the product line. Marketers may use price points for the products in the same line. Price points refer to the different points on a scale of prices instead of the price itself. For example, clothes stores may set three price levels, or price points, of ¥260, ¥320, and ¥410 for the ladies' dresses. The three layers help create images of high-, mid-, and low-end dresses in customers' minds. Different segments of customers choose the level that suits them. Even if the three prices increase at the same time, they will choose the same level as before. Setting a range of price points instead of a single price helps companies realize different marketing goals. Products at low price points are priced at the break-even level or even lower than average costs to attract a large number of customers, seize the market and beat competitors. Products at high price points help establish good brand image and earn a high return. And products at average price points can help realize economies of scale and gain reasonable profits, supporting the functioning of the company. Companies need to be careful in setting the price points, i.e., the number of layers and the price gap between different layers should both be appropriate.

Optional product pricing

Some companies offer to sell optional products together with the main

⊞ 产品线定价法是指根据产品的成本差异或顾客对每个产品感知到的价值，为产品线中的不同产品设定不同的价格，以使产品线整体利润最大化。

⊞ 价格点是指价格尺度上的刻度点，而不是具体价格本身。

product. <u>The pricing of such optional or accessory products along with the main product is called optional product pricing</u>. For example, when restaurants sell wines and cigarettes along with meals, wines and cigarettes are optional products. Cellphones are also sold with a number of accessories like AC adaptors that customers can choose from. There are two pricing strategies for optional products. One is to charge a low price for the main product to attract customers and a high price for optional products to generate a lot of revenue. The other is to charge a low price for optional products to attract customers and a high price for the main product. Companies need to be careful in deciding which items to be included in the main product and which items to offer as optional. Including too many in the main product drives up prices and may intimidate customers, while including too few may lead to a basic product that functions not satisfactorily or is not attractive enough.

田 可选或配套产品与主产品一起定价称为任选产品定价法。

Captive product pricing

<u>Captive products are those products that need to be used along with a main product. The pricing of such products is called captive product pricing</u>. For example, captive products of computer printers include printer ink cartridges. Companies normally set low prices for main products and high prices for captive products to earn high markups. Some companies even design main products that can only be matched with captive products made by them. For example, the new generations of iPhone headphone jack can only be matched with its own headphone plug. Customers buying iPhones have to buy iPhone headphones as well, which bring high markups to the company.

田 附属产品是指那些需要与主要产品一起使用的产品，此类产品的定价称为附属产品定价法。

By-product pricing

Some industries produce by-products, such as petroleum, chemicals, agricultural product, processed meats, etc. Companies need to spend money getting rid of them and that may influence the profitability of the companies and their decision in pricing the main products. They can instead choose to sell the by-products to save the cost of disposal. <u>By-product pricing means setting the price for by-products to cover the cost of storing and delivering them, so as to make the main product's price more competitive</u>.

田 副产品定价法是指设定副产品的价格以覆盖副产品存储和交付的成本，使主产品的价格更具竞争力。

Product bundle pricing

<u>Sometimes several products are grouped together as a bundle and sold at a price lower than the sum of all individual prices. That is product bundle pricing</u>. For example, fast-food restaurants like MacDonald's and KFC offer "value meal" by combining a burger, fries and a soft drink into a set and sell it at a reduced price. Family cinema is offered as a bundle that includes a television, a DVD player, and stereos. The bundle is priced at a reduced level.

田 有时几种产品被组合捆绑在一起，以低于所有产品单独价格总和的价格出售，这就是产品捆绑定价法。

Offering the second ice cream for 50% of its original price is also regarded as product bundle pricing, as the two ice creams are bundled together at a reduced price. Product bundle pricing can encourage customers to buy a greater number or variety of products, but the price should be low enough to create incentives for customers in buying the bundle.

3. Price adjustment strategies

Since the market is dynamic, marketers need to adjust the prices from time to time, as a result of a need to initiate the price change or is prompted by the competitors' strategic move. This session discusses the different price adjustment strategies and when to initiate or respond to price changes.

3.1 Discount and promotional pricing

⊞ 折扣是购买特定商品所享受的直接降价。

⊞ 进货折扣是企业提供给及时付款的客户，通常是分销商的折扣。

⊞ 数量折扣是提供给购买大量商品的客户的折扣。

Most companies reward customers for large quantity purchase, early payments, and off-season purchase, etc. by reducing the quoted price in the form of discount or allowance. Discount is a straight reduction in price for particular purchases. There are different types of discounts. Purchase discount is discount offered to customers, usually distributors, who make payments promptly. Discount offered in the form of "3/10, net 30" indicates that the credit period, the period within which the payment is due, is 30 days, and customers enjoy a 3% discount from the total payment if they pay within 10 days. A quantity discount is offered to customers who buy a large quantity. Purchase discounts are provided to encourage early payments, and offering quantity discounts can motivate customers to buy a greater quantity.

⊞ 推广定价法指产品的价格偶尔会低于正常价格甚至低于其成本，以营造一种购买的兴奋感和紧迫感。

Promotional efforts to boost sales include promotional pricing. The product is occasionally priced lower than its regular price or even below its cost to create a sense of excitement and urgency of purchase. Supermarkets may offer some items at discounted price from time to time to attract customers, hoping that they will also buy other items selling at normal price. Sellers also make use of special events or dates, such as Valentine's Day, National Holiday, and November 11 (called Double 11), etc. Discounts are offered on such occasions to induce much greater enthusiasm than ever in making a large number of purchases.

3.2 Segmented pricing

⊞ 在差别定价法中，公司以不同的价格销售同个产品或服务，是基于多种因素而非成本的考虑，这些因素包括顾客、产品和地点等。

Companies sometimes divide the market into several segments and offer different prices in different segments. In segmented pricing, the company sells a product or service at different prices based on differences in a variety of factors rather than costs, such factors including customers, products and locations, etc.

In customer-segment pricing, different customers are charged different prices for the same product or service. For example, museums, parks, and cinemas charge lower entrance fees for children, students and the elderly, even if the services all the customers enjoy are the same. However, marketers must be very careful with using the customer-segment pricing method. Didi, a car pooling platform with market dominance in the Chinese mainland was reproached by the public and investigated by the regulator for secretly charging more frequent and regular users higher prices for the same trip. In product-form pricing, different versions of the product are offered at different prices according to the product form but not the costs. For example, by changing the design and packaging, the bottle of water can be sold at a much higher unit price at department stores. In location pricing, products offered at different locations are charged differently, even if the cost of selling in different locations is the same. For example, movie tickets are sold at a higher price in cinemas in busy downtown and a lower price in remote areas, even if the cost of providing one seat is the same. The same bottle of beverage is priced much higher at fancy restaurants than at convenient stores. Time pricing means offering the products or services at different prices in different seasons, months, days or even hours. Airlines are skillful users of time pricing. A seat booked weeks before departure will be much cheaper than the one booked at the last minute. Supermarkets offer big discounts for foods that are about to expire.

The effectiveness of segmented pricing depends on several conditions. Firstly, different segments must show enough differences in demand so that charging different prices is possible. Secondly, the costs of segmenting the market and following through the segmentation should not outweigh the benefit. Also, the price in each segment should accurately reflect the customers' perceived value in that segment, so that customers will not resent or resist the price differences.

3.3 Psychological pricing

When marketers are pricing their products, they take into account the psychological effect such price has on customers' minds. Psychological pricing refers to the pricing strategy that considers the psychological effect of prices. A higher price may indicate better quality or some added value, especially when customers don't have other relevant information or the experience or competence to judge the quality of the product. For example, clothes sold at high prices in department stores are regarded as having better quality. Also, people are willing to pay almost RMB 2,000 for a pair of basketball shoes simply because such shoes used to be worn by a NBA player in the basketball game, even if the economic value of such shoes is only RMB 400.

One typical strategy of psychological pricing is the manipulation of reference prices. Reference price is the price in customers' mind that they

⊞ 在顾客差别定价法中，相同的产品或服务针对不同的顾客收取不同的价格。

⊞ 在产品形式差别定价法中，根据产品形式而非价格对不同版本的产品收取不同的价格。

⊞ 在地点定价法中，在不同地点提供的产品定价不同，即使在不同地点销售该产品的成本相同。

⊞ 时间定价法是指在不同的季节、月份、日子甚至时间段，以不同的价格提供产品或服务。

⊞ 心理定价法是指考虑到价格产生的心理效应的定价策略。

⊞ 参考价格是客户在考虑特定产品的价格时心目中所参考的价格。

refer to when they look at the price of a particular product. It can be the price of a comparable product, or the one formed by customers' experiences. Companies can skillfully manipulate reference prices in setting price. For example, they can display a target product along with other more expensive products to send a psychological signal that such product belongs to the same price range but is now offered at a bargain price. Or, the seller can list a higher manufacturer's suggested price together with the current quoted price, to show that the quoted price is much lower. In other cases, retailers offer products that customers are familiar with at low prices, indicating that all of the products are at bargain prices, and then price the less familiar product higher. Since the product is new, it's difficult for customers to judge whether it's expensive. What they can do is to look at other prices in the same store as reference prices. Another common practice is to make use of the psychological effect of digits. For example, a pack of biscuit is price at RMB 19.99 instead of RMB 20.00, in that most people tend to regard RMB 19.99 belongs to the 10.00 spectrum while RMB 20.00 belongs to the 20.00 spectrum. The psychological difference between the two prices is much greater than one cent. Couples celebrating the wedding ceremony in restaurants may choose packages of meals that are priced at RMB 8,888 or RMB 18,888 even if they know that those are not bargain prices, for 8 is an auspicious number in the Chinese culture. Similarly, companies avoid pricing their products at the number of 4 since the number sounds like death in Mandarin.

3.4 Geographical and international pricing

⊞ 地理区域定价法是指针对不同地理区域的顾客定价不同。

Geographical pricing refers to setting prices for customers located in different geographical areas. Companies can choose to set a single price for different locations or vary the prices according to different locations. Such practice also applies to international pricing. Companies can choose to set a uniform price worldwide or change the prices in specific countries. Factors that lead to price differences include economic conditions, market competition, consumers' preference and perception, laws and regulations, etc. Besides, companies may adopt different marketing strategies in different countries, such market penetration or market skimming strategy, depending on factors like the economic conditions and price sensitivity of consumers. The cost of delivery, transportation and tax will also influence the price in a certain country as well. For example, cars, luxury bags and clothes, and perfumes are sold at lower prices in the place of origin and at higher prices abroad, because of the additional transportation cost and tariffs. In other cases, exporters of certain goods get refunds of tax like value-added tax from the government, making it possible for the goods to be sold at lower prices abroad. In such cases, companies need to guard against parallel importing.

⊞ 平行进口，是指将拟销往国外的货物重新进口回到国内市场，并以低于公司目标价格的价格销售。

which refers to re-importing the goods that are destined to be sold abroad back to the domestic market and selling them at lower prices than the company's target one.

3.5 When to initiate or respond to price changes

Another issue to consider is whether or not to initiate or follow the price change. Companies sometimes find it desirable to initiate a price cut or a price increase. A price cut is necessary when the company faces excess production capacity and there is an urgent need to boost sales. Also, when falling demand affects the profitability of the company, it will cut the price to increase quantity sold, especially when price elasticity of demand is greater than 1. In addition, companies are willing to cut the price when they can achieve economies of scale through a large sales volume. On the contrary, when the company is faced with cost inflation, it will have to raise the price to cover the higher costs. Besides, excess demand brings the company bigger bargaining power and the incentive to raise the price. When initiating the price change, the company needs to keep an eye on buyers and competitor reactions to the change.

If the price change like a price cut is initiated by competitors, the company needs to decide how to respond to the change. There are several ways that the company can respond to a price cut initiated by rivals. Firstly, the company can follow the price cut, especially when customers are price-sensitive, and when such move does not lead to severe price war. Secondly, the company can raise the perceived value of the product instead, through effective promotion efforts or other forms of communication with customers. The company can even raise the price and improve the quality, positioning its brand at the higher end. Apart from that, the company can also launch low-price "fighter brand" to fight against competitors. For instance, Armani Jeans is a lower-price brand launched by Armani to fight against the mid-end rivals.

Summary

Price is an important element in the marketing portfolio as it is the only one that represents revenues while the other three all represent costs for companies. This chapter focuses on issues related to price, including factors affecting companies' pricing decisions, pricing approaches, new product pricing strategies and price adjustment strategies.

Factors affecting pricing decisions that are explored in this chapter include: product cost, positioning strategy, customers' perceived value, market demand and competitors' marketing strategy. Product cost forms the basic ground for setting prices. The cost-based pricing approach, though simple and convenient, has some limitations. The biggest one is that price goes up when sales are predicted to go down, which goes against what is happening in reality. As opposed to cost-based pricing, value-based pricing depends on the value perceived by customers. It justifies higher prices charged by companies with differential advantages. Besides, price is a key positioning tool. Firms that intend to change its position (upward or downward) will necessarily increase or reduce prices. Price is also subject to market demand. In a market where supplies exceed demands, price goes down; in a market where supplies fall short of demands, price goes up. However, different products vary in terms of demand responsiveness to price change. PED, price elasticity of demand, is used to measure the responsiveness of demand to change in price. Adopting the competitor-oriented pricing approach may be simple and easy, but is risky especially when your cost position is weaker than your rivals'. However, following the going-rate price could be doable for undifferentiated commodities.

Market skimming and market penetration are two general new product pricing strategies. Market skimming pricing refers to the strategy of setting a high price for a new product to skim maximum profits layer by layer from customers willing to pay a high price. In contrast, market-penetration pricing means setting a low price for a new product to penetrate the market, attracting a large number of buyers and taking up a large market share. This chapter also introduces five types of product mix pricing: product line pricing, optional product pricing, captive product pricing, by-product pricing and product bundle pricing.

Apart from setting price, price adjustment is also an important pricing issue. The chapter discusses some price adjustment strategies: discount and promotional pricing, segmented pricing, psychological pricing, geographical and international pricing. Firms also have to decide when and how to initiate price change or respond to price change initiated by competitors.

Key terms

production cost	market penetration pricing
fixed cost	product line pricing
variable cost	optional product pricing
cost-based pricing	captive product pricing
value-based pricing	by-product pricing
good-value pricing	product bundle pricing
value-added pricing	segmented pricing
price elasticity of demand (PED)	psychological pricing
going-rate price	reference price
market skimming pricing	

Exercises

Review and discussion

1. Complete the text using words from the box.

bargain	points	significance	fair	solutions
premium	costs	sensitive	unique	

When deciding on the price of a product or service you have to consider the product or service itself. For example, does it have _____ benefits? Does the consumer have any alternative _____? What is the monetary _____ of the product or service? You also have to think about the possibility of complementary _____, and how price _____ the consumers are to these and the product or the service cost.

Then you need to think about the pricing strategy and how this relates to the brand. For a luxury brand it is essential to follow a _____ pricing strategy in order to maintain the brand image. A no-frills low price would not be suitable for a brand such as Cartier.

Finally, you need to carry out a price test to check the price _____ you are considering. The _____ price is the amount that the consumer is prepared to pay for the product or service. A _____ price is a low price that may be used during special offers or for promotional pricing.

2. Reading the descriptions and name the pricing strategies that are being used. Consult the "Reference" to help you.

Reference

Premium pricing: Use a high price where there is a substantial competitive advantage—for example, rooms in Savory hotels.

Penetration pricing: The price charged for products and services is set artificially low in order to gain market share. Once this is achieved, the price is increased.

Economy pricing: Marketing and manufacturing costs are kept to a minimum. Supermarkets often have economy brands for soups, spaghetti, etc.

Price skimming: Charge a high price because you have a new product type. However, the high price attracts new competitors into the market, and the price falls due to increased supply. DVD players were launched with this strategy.

Psychological pricing: The consumer responds on an emotional, rather than rational, basis. For example, charging 99 cents instead of 1 dollar.

Captive product pricing: Companies will charge a premium price where the consumer cannot choose a competitive product.

Product bundle pricing: Sellers combine several products in the same package. This also serves to move old stock.

_____ 1) Charging a high amount for bottles of water inside a football stadium during the World Cup

_____ 2) Charging $ 2.95 instead of $ 3

_____ 3) Charging a low price to win sales in a new market

_____ 4) Packaging shampoo, conditioner and hair gel from the same hair care product line together, and charging one price for the lot

3. Match the questions about pricing strategy (1-7) to the pricing considerations (a-g). Consult the "Reference" to help you.

_____ 1) What is the value of the product or service for the consumer?

_____ 2) What is special or different about the product or service?

_____ 3) Is it difficult to compare the price and quality of similar products or services?

_____ 4) How many people want to buy the product or service?

_____ 5) How many similar products or services are there on the market?

_____ 6) What else does the consumer need to pay for in order to used the product or service?

_____ 7) How much does a change in price affect consumer demand for the product or service?

---

a. Alternative solutions   e. Demand

b. Ease of comparison   f. Price sensitivity

c. Unique benefits   g. Complementary costs

d. Monetary significance

Reference

The marketing team for Stick Tea are preparing for a meeting about the price of a new range of tea that comes in a stick instead of a bag. They make notes on pricing considerations.

a. Alternative solutions: Our stick packaging is unique.

b. Ease of comparison: Easy to compare price but difficult to compare taste.

c. Unique benefits: Quality of teas; stick format.

d. Monetary significance: Tea is cheap, but the innovative packaging has a high value.

e. Demand: Tea consumption is stable, but sales in speciality shops are on the rise.

f. Price sensitivity: Consumers are very price sensitive—sales decrease when prices increase.

g. Complementary costs: None—the customer doesn't even need a spoon!

---

4. Translate the following sentences into English.

1) 价格与需求直接相关，通常价格越高，需求越小；价格越低，需求越大。

_____

_____

2) 需求在很大程度上为企业确定了一个最高价格限度，而成本则决定价格的下限。

_____

_____

3) 在纯粹寡头垄断的条件下，市场价格往往不是由市场供应关系直接决定，而是由少数寡头通过默契所确定的。

_____

_____

4) 所谓"撇脂定价法"，是指将产品的价格定得较高，尽可能在产品生命初期，在竞争者研制出相似产品以前，尽快地收回投资，并且取得相当的利润。

_____

_____

5) 消费者购买产品过程中大都受到其心理因素的影响，因此企业可以根据消费者购买心理的特点对产品价格进行一定的调整。

_____

_____

5. Answer the following questions briefly.

1) The chapter points out that many companies do not handle pricing well. Beyond focusing too much on cost, what are some of the other difficulties that marketers have in setting prices?

2) What are the differences between cost-based and value-based pricing?

3) Four recent MBA graduate are starting their own financial services firm. They plan to promote a "good value" pricing strategy to their customers. Would you recommend this pricing strategy?

4) Explain why elasticity of demand is such an important concept to marketers who sell a "commodity" product.

5) Discuss the difficulties an international company would encounter if it set a uniform worldwide price for a commodity-type product? What are the advantages and disadvantages of worldwide standard price?

6) Distinguish between a skimming pricing strategy and penetration pricing strategy.

7) How would you justify the price differences for a cup of coffee that you might encounter if you purchase it in a local coffee shop versus a top-class hotel?

Projects and teamwork

1. What does the following positioning statement suggest about the firm's marketing objectives, marketing-mix strategy, and costs? "No one beats our price. We crush competition."

2. You are an owner of a small independent chain of coffee houses competing head-to-head with Starbucks. The retail price your customers pay for coffee is exactly the same as at Starbucks. The wholesale price you pay for roasted coffee beans has increased by 25 percent. You understand that you cannot absorb this increase and that it must be passed on to your customers. However, you are concerned about the consequences of an open price increase. Discuss three alternative price increase strategies that address your concerns.

────────────────── **Case study** ──────────────────

Nongfu Spring's Pricing Strategy

In 2000, Nongfu Spring initiated a wide debate over "natural water vs purified water". As a result, the brand skyrocketed to fame and turned into a representative of high-quality, healthy water. One of its main rivals—Wahaha was beaten down in the campaign.

However, it never occurred to Nongfu at that time the sales pitch "nature" would one day become an obstacle to its nationwide expansion. Sticking to producing natural water, Nongfu was restricted by many factors when choosing water sources and the location of bottling plants. The bottling plants must be close to the water sources, which should live up to the standard of "zero pollution and natural origin" as advertised.

Nongfu had only four water bottling plants in the country, which are close to its four water sources: Jilin, Heyuan, Danjiangkou and Qiandao Lake. The limited number of the plants not only restricted the production capacity, but also increased transportation costs in distribution. Most of Nongfu's products were shipped over a long distance. Though the four plants were located in railway terminals, rail transport was relatively costly as compared to road transport, and many of its points of sale were located in places uncovered by railways.

According to an insider from Nongfu, as Nongfu's rail-dependent transport was three or even more than three times the cost of Wahaha's road-dependent transport, Nongfu dealers had to pay for part of the transportation cost, adding to their operational costs. Compared with Nongfu which had only four plants, Wahaha had a nationwide network of 15 manufacturing plants, which delivered products by truck directly to terminal shelves and warehouses of wholesalers. High transport efficiency saved Wahaha dealers a lot of money.

Another advantage of road transport is higher responsiveness to the market, resulting in shorter time needed for executing orders and payments. At the consumer end, terminal dealers and consumers had more convenient, quicker access to products. Doubtless it enhanced sales volume, as most Chinese consumers did not have the habit of preordering things with grocery shops, but they chose among those available instead.

Nongfu's high-price strategy was, on the one hand, a natural choice accompanying its product differentiation, and on the other hand, a way to cover the high transportation cost and make up for profits of its own and its channel distributors.

Now the problem is Nongfu's high price did not stand firm in fierce market competition. The high price was built upon high quality as the selling point, which seemed not strong enough to keep consumers willingly paying premium prices. As a result, it had to reduce the retail price of Nongfu Spring bottled water.

Nongfu Spring, which was positioned as a substitute better than purified water, had higher production costs than competing products. As introduced by an employee from Nongfu's procurement department, Nongfu's wide-mouthed bottle costs five times of Wahaha bottles. Besides, Nongfu did not use artificial sweeteners as most of drink manufacturers did, but the more expensive refined cane sugar in its soft drinks under the brand Nongfu.

In a highly competitive sector, Nongfu had small profit margins. "We rely on sales volume to keep business," an employee said.

Nongfu Spring is now trapped in a dilemma. In the beginning, it adopted the high-price strategy because it believed that the high price is supported by higher value delivered to customers and consumers are willing to pay higher prices for good-quality products. However, the less satisfactory sales volume, plus high transportation costs and cash flow pressure, forced the mineral water producer to bring down prices to increase sales. But regular consumers were not necessarily happy to see a price cut for they might think the product quality was compromised as well.

Price reduction is not the only way to promote sales. It is only short-term sales incentives, but not a long-term pricing approach for business. Many real-life marketing cases tell us appropriate prices, instead of low prices, are a guarantee of sales.

Questions:

1. What are the three main pricing strategies? Discuss the possible perils of the cost-based pricing strategy.

2. Analyze the reasons Nongfu Spring lowered the price.

3. Could you provide some suggestions for Nongfu Spring's pricing?

Chapter Eight
Place

Objectives:

After studying this chapter, you should be able to:

- Understand the importance of managing marketing channels;
- Identify the different types of marketing channels;
- Master the concepts of vertical marketing system, multichannel distribution system and disintermediation;
- Understand intensive distribution, selective distribution and exclusive distribution and give examples of each;
- Talk about how channel conflicts arise and how they can be solved;
- Name some major types of retailing, e.g. supermarket, department store, specialty shop, discount house, convenient store, automatic vending and online retailing;
- Talk about marketing decisions that are important to retailers.

Framework

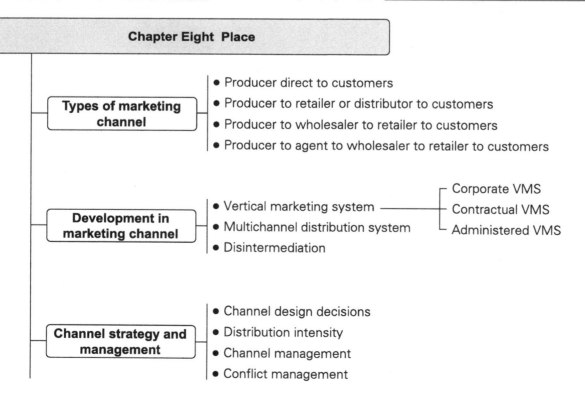

Chapter Eight Place

Types of marketing channel
- Producer direct to customers
- Producer to retailer or distributor to customers
- Producer to wholesaler to retailer to customers
- Producer to agent to wholesaler to retailer to customers

Development in marketing channel
- Vertical marketing system — Corporate VMS / Contractual VMS / Administered VMS
- Multichannel distribution system
- Disintermediation

Channel strategy and management
- Channel design decisions
- Distribution intensity
- Channel management
- Conflict management

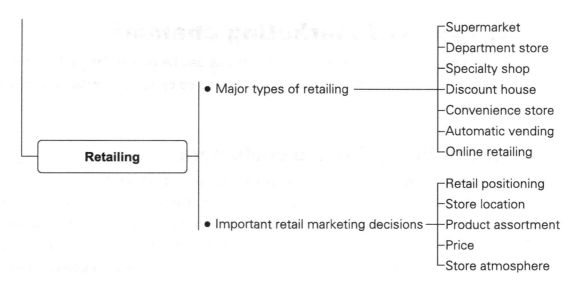

Marketing channel is the access through which consumers buy the product. Marketing channel is part of the company's supply chain, which consists of the upstream and downstream partners. Upstream business deals with suppliers, while downstream side refers to the marketing channel which connects the company with customers. <u>Marketing channel (or distribution channel) consists of a group of independent organizations that help to make the product available or accessible to consumers or business users.</u> Marketing channel decisions must be integrated with other marketing mix decisions, including pricing and promotion, to deliver maximum marketing effects. For example, depending on the cost of different channels, pricing strategy can be varied. Besides, promotion efforts such as sales force and means of communication are also subject to channel choices.

⊞ 营销渠道（或分销渠道）由多个独立的、帮助消费者或企业用户获得或使用产品的机构组成。

Careful design of marketing channel is important for the success of a brand. There's nothing worse than building enough consumer awareness of the brand through massive promotion, only to discover that consumers cannot find it from supermarkets or stores where they usually do the shopping. Producers normally rely on intermediaries in distributing their products to locations they are not familiar with or remote areas they lack the access to, or because it's too costly to build direct sales teams there. Besides, each producer provides limited types of goods in large quantity, while consumers need a variety of goods in small quantity. The gap is then filled by intermediaries in the channel. To be specific, each producer sells limited assortments of products in large volume, which are purchased by intermediaries in different markets. The intermediary in each market breaks them down and sells broad assortments of products in small volume to customers. <u>Channel members add value to the supply chain by improving efficiency and reducing costs in delivery through their contacts, experience, specialization and scale of operation.</u>

⊞ 渠道成员通过他们的关系、经验、专业和运营规模提高供应效率并降低交付成本，从而为供应链增加价值。

1. Types of marketing channel

Depending on its length, marketing channels can be divided into different types, ranging from direct sales to end users to being mediated by agents, wholesalers, retailers, or distributors.

1.1 Producer direct to customers

Producers may rely on their own sales force to connect with customers. The producer cuts all the intermediaries out of the channel so that it avoids sharing profits with distributors, saves costs and may offer a lower product price. Direct selling is necessary when the goods require immediate delivery like fruits. They are also required by business customers who need close connections with the supplier in solving technical problems or maintenance. Such method is also popular in the service industry, where distribution channel is always short. Direct sales are facilitated by the popularity of the Internet. Now an increasing number of products are sold online, such as books, clothes, food, appliances and services. This at the same time posts threats to traditional distributors since online distribution reduces costs substantially and thus lower prices can be offered to end users, draining customers away from traditional distribution channels.

1.2 Producer to retailer or distributor to customers

A producer may choose to sell to consumers indirectly through retailers or to business customers indirectly through distributors. As is mentioned earlier, intermediaries like retailers break the bulk purchase from producers into smaller quantities and provide wide assortments for customers to choose from. Such advantage is more prominent when a number of retailers gathered in large shopping centers, which are perfect places for consumers to shop as well as to relax and have fun with friends or colleagues. Supermarkets are an important type of retailers which provide almost every kind of daily necessities. Busy businessmen may spend the weekend shopping in a supermarket to buy all the foods and drinks for the upcoming weekdays, which has gradually become a lifestyle. Apart from selling furniture in its stores, IKEA also gathers food and snack stalls there, as it realizes that this is an effective way to attract and keep customers on the premises longer, which increases the chance of purchase.

When dealing with business customers, producers may use distributors to help provide less expensive and frequently bought business-to-business products. Such effort enables business customers to buy small quantities locally. In other cases, the producer may rely on agents to connect with business customers. The agent (in a certain market) has the experience and contacts in that market, which is helpful for producers whose costs of establishing a sales network in that market is too high. The disadvantage is the lack of control over the agent and less autonomy in doing business in that area.

1.3 Producer to wholesaler to retailer to customers

When selling to consumers, producers may use wholesalers and retailers in the marketing channel at the same time. This makes sense when retailers are small and with limited buying capacity. Wholesalers buy in bulk from producers and further distribute to different retailers in smaller quantities. Japan has complicated distribution networks composed of various layers of intermediaries and numerous retailers in various locations. The advantage is that consumers can buy products conveniently from stores near their locality. The risk of multiple distribution layers lies in the conflict between channel members. There're possibilities for large retailers to cut the wholesaler from the chain and purchase from the producer directly. The lower input costs enable them to sell the product at a lower price than that offered by competitors, who buy from wholesalers.

1.4 Producer to agent to wholesaler to retailer to customers

This is by far the longest marketing channel and is applied when the producer deals with consumers, especially when the consumers are located in foreign markets. In such case, the producer is unfamiliar with the foreign market or the foreign culture, and an agent is thus very helpful in reducing obstacles. The agent contacts local wholesalers or (retailers) and receives commission fees. Agents sometime are even required by the country's regulation. For example, companies planning to make investment or do business in some Arab countries will have to find a contact person in that country.

2. Development in marketing channel

There's a shift of marketing channels from loosely connected independent intermediaries to greater integration into other members. Channel integration refers to the pattern of integration among channel members, ranging from conventional marketing channels consisting of independent producers and intermediaries, to ownership of the channel by one channel member. There are tendencies towards vertical marketing system, multichannel distribution system and disintermediation.

⊞ 渠道整合是指渠道成员之间进行整合的模式，既包括由独立生产商和中间商组成的传统营销渠道，也包括由一个渠道成员拥有的整个分销渠道的所有权。

2.1 Vertical marketing system

Historically, producers follow conventional marketing channels—channels consisting of loosely connected independent producers, wholesalers and retailers, each operating to maximize their own profits. Such system leads to conflict among members since one member's profit may come at the expense of profits of another member or even the whole system. Channel conflicts are not unusual although channel members depend on each other.

As opposed to conventional marketing channels, a vertical marketing system (VMS) has one member that dominates the whole distribution channel

⊞ 传统的营销渠道由松散连接的独立生产商、批发商和零售商组成，每个角色都以最大化自己的利润为目标。

⊞ 垂直营销系统 (VMS)
由一个渠道成员控制整个
分销渠道，生产商、批发
商和零售商统一行动。控
制权有三个来源，即某个
成员对渠道的所有权、成
员之间的契约或源自大规
模或庞大运营规模的经济
权力。

⊞ 企业的垂直营销系统由
某个渠道成员拥有整个营
销渠道，该成员会整合协
调生产和分销。

⊞ 合同式垂直营销系统是
由个体生产商和中间商通
过合同联合在一起，目的
是实现规模经济。

⊞ 管理式垂直营销系统是
指一个渠道成员源于其规
模或运营规模获得控制。

⊞ 当生产商使用不同的分
销渠道将产品销往不同的
市场时，就形成多渠道分
销系统。

and the producers, wholesalers and retailers act in an integrated unity. The power of domination comes from three sources, i.e., ownership by one member, contracts among members, or economic power from size or scale of operation. The dominating member can be the producer, wholesaler, or retailer that provides leadership in coordinating the efforts of channel members. A corporate VMS consists of one member that owns the complete marketing channel, then integrates and coordinates production and distribution. Channel conflict management and control over other channel members are easier under such single ownership. However, there's risk of such organization becoming too cumbersome because of overexpansion. Keeping it lean and efficient is thus the key to success.

The second type of VMS is contractual VMS, which is formed by individual producers and intermediaries joining together through contracts so as to achieve economies of scale. Franchising is one type of contracts between producer, called the franchisor, and the intermediary, called the franchisee. The franchisor provides expertise, and specifies the uniform procedure and standards of production, services and store decoration, etc., so as to maintain a consistent brand image in different markets. Besides, by utilizing local franchisee, the producer saves costs and improves efficiency. This is a popular form of channel organization adopted by McDonald's, Coca-Cola, and Toyota, etc.

The third type of VMS, administered VMS, results from the dominating power of one channel member from its size or scale of operation. Famous producers can get the support from retailers or distributors easily and maintain bargaining power. Also, large retailers like supermarket chains may dominate the marketing channel because of their purchasing capacity. Examples include Procter & Gamble, Wal-Mart, and others.

2.2 Multichannel distribution system

Producers used to have one single channel to connect to a certain market. Nowadays, there're increasing efforts in adopting multichannel distribution network. Multichannel distribution system is formed when a producer uses different distribution channels to reach different markets. A producer may choose to make direct sales to consumer segment 1, since it's geographically close to such market or it has experiences dealing with such market directly. It then uses retailers to connect to consumer segment 2 because it's too costly to build a sales team in that market. Besides, it has business customers located in another country, so that it relies on agents and distributors in making its products available to them. Alternatively, a producer may grant franchise to local franchisees in one part of the country while use retail outlets in another part. Differentiating the distribution efforts in different segments results from the fact that each segment has its own typical customer needs, preferences and market situation. Multichannel distribution model is ideal when producers want to expand into more customer segments. For example, when a cosmetic brand was previously sold to higher-income group, it used specialty store as the retailer. Afterwards when it wants to expand its business to lower-income customers, it cooperates with supermarkets or small retail stores, since those are places where the new targeted group commonly shops.

2.3 Disintermediation

Thanks to the advancement of technology and popularity of online marketing, there's a tendency of disintermediation in the marketing channel. Disintermediation occurs when the producer cuts traditional intermediaries such as retailers, wholesalers and distributors out of the channel and reaches end users directly or through new type of intermediaries like the Internet. Disintermediation has its advantages in saving costs for producers and helping maintain lower prices. But caution needs to be taken in solving channel conflicts, since the new form of intermediaries such as the Internet posts threat to traditional retailers.

3. Channel strategy and management

Depending on company strategy, producers choose different channel strategies to maximize value. In this section, we first examine the process of channel design decision making, in which the producer chooses different strategies based on the internal and external factors. One important aspect of channel strategy concerns channel intensity. After the strategies have been decided, producers need to manage the channels properly to realize their value.

3.1 Channel design decisions

In designing marketing channels, several factors need to be considered, including customer needs, company resources, and channel objectives, etc. The producer starts by analyzing customer needs in determining the structure of the channel. It then looks at the company resources available for supporting the structure, since it's sometimes not feasible to build complicated channels due to the lack of resources. In other words, the producer must strike a balance among customer needs and preferences, available resources and costs, and the pricing appropriate for customers. The third step is determining the channel objectives. This is related to the level of services the producer wishes to deliver to the target market and the costs of providing such services. Higher level of services requires more resources and higher costs. The producer then lists the available options of channel structures, including producer direct to customers, producer to retailer/distributor to customers, and producer to agent to wholesaler to retailer to customers, etc., among others. The final step is to evaluate each option based on criteria including economic benefits such as potential revenues, costs and profits, the extent of control by the producer, and the flexibility of the channel in response to market dynamics.

⊞ 密集型分销旨在通过向各个市场的大量经销店供应商品来扩大市场覆盖率。

....

⊞ 选择性分销是指生产商在某个市场中选择有限数量的特定经销店来销售其产品。

....

⊞ 独家经销是指生产商在某一特定市场只选择一个批发商、零售商或分销商来销售其产品。

3.2 Distribution intensity

One important decision in designing marketing channel is the choice of distribution intensity. There are broadly three types, intensive distribution, selective distribution, and exclusive distribution. Intensive distribution aims to bring extensive coverage of the market, by supplying goods to a large number of outlets in various markets. This strategy can be applied when convenience in purchase is the priority of customers. Examples include the sales of daily necessities. Selective distribution is the strategy whereby a producer selects a limited number of outlets in a certain market to sell its products. It enables the producer to focus on the best outlets and maintain closer relations with a limited number of outlets, which also helps to reduce costs. In exclusive distribution, only one wholesaler, retailer or distributor is selected to sell the producer's products in a certain market. Those intermediaries receive exclusive rights in selling the product. Such practice is common in the distribution of luxuries or high-value goods including Haute Couture, high-end cosmetics, and cars, etc. For example, a car manufacturer may offer one dealer the exclusive right to sell its cars in each territory such as a town or city, and consumers can only buy from this dealer. The practice enhances the brand image and helps achieve higher profit margin. It also enables the manufacturer to maintain close cooperation with the dealer in servicing, pricing and promotion. In industries where counterfeiting is prevalent, the exclusivity in distribution channel guarantees consumers an assured way to purchase genuine products.

3.3 Channel management

Channels need to be managed properly once the channel strategy has been decided. Channel management includes the selection of channel members, the motivation, training and evaluation of them. The producer sets the criteria in selecting channel members, including the years of experience in the trade, size, growth, profitability and reputation, etc. Effective motivation on channel members is built on the understanding of their needs. Possible sources of motivation include financial rewards, exclusive rights in retailing, involvement in joint decision making and resources support from producers, etc. Training is welcomed by small retailers, while large wholesalers or retailers may regard the offer of training by producers as a signal of mistrust. Finally, evaluation on channel members is necessary. Evaluation helps the producer to decide the channel members to retain and those to be replaced. Criteria for evaluation include the sales records, average inventory levels, delivery time, customer satisfaction, and cooperativeness, etc.

3.4 Conflict management

Given that channel members are independent, conflicts may arise from time to time. Proper management of channel conflict facilitates the health development of marketing channel. Firstly, conflicts may result from the different goals of members, in that each is driven by self-interests. Take the split of profits between producers and retailers as an example, a greater proportion of profits assigned to retailers means smaller proportion for producers. When each wants to maximize its own profits, conflict arises. Besides, resellers may want to add additional product lines to help expand their business, which will undercut the sales of the original product line. For example, a retailer previously specializing in selling professional sports outfits may want to step into children's clothing, stationery and school bags, etc. The move may help the retailer capture new customers, but it also tarnishes the original brand image and leads to dissatisfaction of original customers, which does harm to suppliers of sports outfits. Similarly on the producer's side, it may want to use multichannel distribution to access more customer segments. Conflicts may arise among members in different channels. For example, when the producer adopts cost-efficient online marketing or sells directly from its own outlets at discounted prices, retailers purchasing from wholesalers will be irritated since they cannot afford to sell at that low price.

> 田 独立的渠道成员
> 之间可能会不时出
> 现冲突。妥善管理
> 渠道冲突，有利于营
> 销渠道的健康发展。

4. Retailing

Retailing is an important form of marketing distribution. This section discusses some major types of retailing and important marketing decisions that should be made by retailers such as location, product assortment, price, to name a few.

4.1 Major types of retailing

Most retailing is handled by brick-and-mortar stores like supermarkets, department stores and specialty shops, while non-store retailing like online marketing and automatic vending is also an important type of retailing.

Supermarket

Supermarkets are familiar to most consumers as they sell a great variety of daily necessities such as food, drinks, kitchen supplies and toiletries, etc. Large supermarkets also sell clothing, home appliances, cosmetics and pharmaceuticals. Supermarkets are popular because of the wide range of products they provide, as well as the locations that are always close to living communities and prices that are competitive. Large supermarket chains may dominate the channel and exert great bargaining power against producers.

Department store

Department stores sell different categories of products in separate departments, such as cosmetics, women's or men's clothing, jewelry and appliances, etc. Some department stores provide superior services to distinguish themselves.

Specialty shop

Specialty shops specialize in selling a narrow range of products. Some specialty stores sell only one product line. By selecting and focusing on a limited number of products, specialty stores are able to provide quality and personalized service.

Discount house

Discount houses provide substantial discounts to encourage quantity purchases. An important form of discount houses is manufacturer's outlets. Owned directly by manufacturers, they sell out-of-season products for the manufacturers or unsold products from department stores. Big discounts are offered to sell out the goods quickly. To guarantee profits, convenient location and higher inventory turnover are key to discount houses.

Convenience store

Convenience stores are usually located near customers' homes or central business districts and open for long hours so that customers can buy from them conveniently. They are small in size and large in numbers. Because of the limited scale of operation, prices offered are comparatively higher than that of supermarkets. They succeed when the benefits (less time, energy, trouble required to buy goods) obtained by customers, especially busy businessmen, outweigh the problem of higher prices. Seven-Eleven is a convenience store brand that operates successfully in large cities where people live a high-pace life.

Automatic vending

Automatic vending machines sell drinks, snacks or newspapers, and can be found in stations, airports, cinemas or even school teaching buildings. Customers put money into the machine and the product comes out automatically. No salesperson is required. Problems arise when the machine breaks down or goods are out of stock.

Online retailing

Online retailing is popular today due to the wide coverage of the Internet. An increasing number of products are sold online, such as clothing, food, appliances, computers, or even services. A product can be ordered and delivered online, or it can be ordered online and delivered through physical stores. In other cases, owners of physical retailers also operate online stores under the same brand names. This applies to many leading brands like Tesco and Marks & Spencer. Online retailing is powerful thanks to its cost saving and large capacity in carrying stocks.

Embedded in e-commerce platforms such as Taobao and JD.com, a livestreaming channel is an effective and powerful distribution tool as it allows "real-time connection". During livestreaming, audiences can have Facetime-like interactions with the broadcasters, when answers can be instantly answered, products be presented in an all-round way and promotional activities made more convincing and pressing. This business form in combination of livestreaming and e-commerce is referred to as "Live Commerce". The combination of key opinion leaders or KOLs in Live Commerce seems to be very effective, as product reviews and brand recommendations embedded in live video hosted by KOLs (key opinion customers) or KOCs increase product exposure and brand recognition.

Many businesses have realized the huge market potential of this burgeoning business form. Ymatou, a Shanghai-based cross-border e-commerce platform, is beefing up efforts to provide supply chain service for livestreaming platforms and KOLs. Ymatou said it is banking on China's rapidly growing segment of e-commerce via livestreaming to present it new growth opportunities.

4.2 Important retail marketing decisions

A retailer operating under the name of a brand needs to weigh and make marketing decisions that are discussed under Chapter 6. However, there are some other issues related to retailing that are worth separate discussions.

Retail positioning

Retailers differ in their positioning strategies, which depend on their overall strategies and target marketing. Successful positioning depends on a clear understanding of the needs of targeted market segment. Once the target segment is decided, the retailer also has to consider and develop its differential advantages.

Store location

Location is a vital decision to make for some type of retailers like convenience stores and supermarkets. Busy customers will be discouraged to shop in stores that are too far away. Or, if the store is out-of-town, it should be in or near the shopping center where customers spend their weekends or leisure hours. Besides, producers need to choose between large cities and smaller towns—the decision also depends on the producers' target marketing and positioning strategy.

Product assortment

Retailers have to decide the breadth and depth of their product assortment. Some retailers such as supermarket offer a wide range of product lines like food, drink, toiletries, clothing and other daily necessities; others such as specialty shop provide a limited number of deep product lines. The decisions depend on various factors, such as the marketing objectives and strategies, resources available, target segments and others.

Price

Pricing strategy depends on the retailer's target marketing and positioning. For price-sensitive customer segments, it's profitable for retailers to offer lower prices. There's an increasing tendency for retailers to charge low prices, at least at the beginning of new product launch as a means to attract new buyers, rather than high prices supported by heavy promotion.

Store atmosphere

Customers nowadays put more emphasis on purchasing experience than ever before. Under such context, retailers pay more attention to store decorations such as lighting, layout, color, smell and music to bring atmospheres of relaxation and increase the comfort of staying in the store. For example, cosmetic and clothing stores use fragrance to attract customers, and the smell from the bakery in supermarket attract hungry shoppers.

Summary

Place, as an element of the marketing mix, concerns how to deliver goods from the producer to end users. To this end, some intermediaries may be involved during the distribution process. This chapter deals with important issues related to distribution channels. First, depending on the length of the distribution chain, marketing channels can be divided into several types: producer direct to customers, producer to retailer or distributor to customers, producer to wholesaler to retailer to customers, producer to agent to wholesaler to retailer to customers.

There's a shift of marketing channels from loosely connected independent intermediaries to greater integration into other members— this is called channel integration. The chapter also introduces vertical marketing system, multichannel distribution system and disintermediation.

It is never easy to decide on channel strategies and manage channels. For instance, various factors, internal and external, need to be taken into consideration in designing marketing channels. Distribution intensity also has to be decided by choosing among intensive distribution, selective distribution and exclusive distribution. Channel management includes the selection of channel members, the motivation, training and evaluation of them. Besides, conflicts between channel members should be properly managed.

As an important form of distribution, retailing is worth discussions in a separate section. First, some major types of retailing are briefed including supermarket, department store, specialty shop, discount house, convenient store, automatic vending and online retailing. Then important marketing issues related to retailing are discussed: retail positioning, store location, product assortment, price and store atmosphere.

Key terms

marketing channel	contractual VMS
channel member	administered VMS
producer direct to customers	channel conflict
producer to retailer or distributor to customers	multichannel distribution system
producer to wholesaler to retailer to customers	disintermediation
producer to agent to wholesaler to retailer to customers	intensive distribution
	selective distribution
vertical marketing system (VMS)	exclusive distribution
corporate VMS	

Exercises

Review and discussion

1. Put the steps in the distribution chain in the correct order.

_____ 1) The goods arrive and can be sold to the consumer.

_____ 2) The franchise sends the order to the warehouse in South America.

_____ 3) Road haulage is used to ship the goods from Southampton to Brighton.

_____ 4) The goods land in Southampton.

_____ 5) The container ship is loaded with the parts.

_____ 6) A franchise in Brighton places an order for car accessories.

2. Complete the passage using phrases from the box.

direct distribution	distribution chain	indirect distribution	distribution costs	distribution intermediary

_____ were very high last year so this year we have advised all project managers to use air freight as little as possible. Another possible source of high costs has been the length of the _____ for our product. Although we have been trying to develop _____ by attracting more customers to our website and encouraging them to order from us, most of our products get to market through an _____ channel. We have been seeking ways to cut down the number of wholesalers and other types of _____. We are beginning to deal directly with retailers and in the long run this will reduce our costs.

3. Make word combinations using words from the box. Then use the word combinations to complete the text below. Consult the "Reference" to help you.

commercial	deals	licensing	partners	products	team

David Beckham started his career as a footballer. He has signed _____ all over the world and has made a fortune for himself and his _____. When he started playing for Real Madrid, sales of _____ such as football shirts rose rapidly.

Reference

Sports clubs can develop additional revenues by selling team products, such as shirts and memorabilia, at a premium price. They can also sign merchandising deals or licensing deals with sponsors or other commercial partners. The club authorizes, or licenses, the partner to use the club's logo on their products. For example, Lego bought the right to use the NBA league logo on their figurines.

---

4. The owner of a small business is thinking about putting her catalogue online, and is presenting the business case to her bank manager. Correct the mistakes in her PowerPoint slides. Consult the "Reference" to help you.

Pros
1) Customers can put an order 24 hours a day.
2) No need for already paid envelopes.
3) We can still have a hot telephone line.

Cons
1) The ordering form must be simplified for older users.
2) Older customers may prefer using mailing order to ordering online.

Reference

Mail order is a system of buying and selling goods through the post. Customers normally select their goods from a catalogue. The instructions below tell customers how to order a product from a company's catalogue:

Please complete the order form and return it to us in the prepaid envelope provided—you don't need a stamp. Alternatively, you can call your telephone hotline and place your order. Calls are free on your Freephone number.

5. Translate the following sentences into English.

1) 密集分销是指制造商尽可能地发展批发商和零售商，并由他们销售其产品。

_____

_____

2) 选择分销是指制造商根据自己所设定的交易基准和条件精心挑选最合适的中间商销售其产品。

_____

_____

3) 独家分销渠道是一种最为极端的分销渠道。这种渠道有利于维持市场的稳定性，有利于提高产品身价，有利于提高销售效率。

_____

_____

4) 垂直分销系统是指制造商、批发商和零售商等形成一个统一体。他们服从于一个领导者，或是制造商，或是批发商，或是零售商，取决于其能量和实力的大小。

_____

_____

5) 采用多渠道分销系统，公司可以获得三个方面的好处：扩大市场覆盖面；降低渠道成本；增加销售特征，使其更适合顾客的要求。

_____

_____

6. Answer the following questions briefly.

1) Define distribution channel. What is its alternative name?

2) What are the major differences between wholesaler and retailer?

3) What marketing channels are often used by tangible goods producers?

4) What are some of the product factors affecting distribution intensity selection?

5) What does technology advance contribute to the efficiency and effectiveness of logistics management?

6) Discuss the impact of the growth of online retailing on other retail formats.

7) What factors does a cosmetics company need to consider when designing its marketing channel for a new low-priced line of cosmetics?

8) Identify the primary challenges an organization faces in managing its channel members. What are some of the methods companies use to motivate channel partners?

────────────────── **Projects and teamwork** ──────────────────

1. Work with a classmate and visit the website of one of the Chinese companies you are familiar with to learn about its products and its choice of marketing channels. Then determine which factors—market, product, organizational, and/or competitive—influenced the selection of the distribution channels. Discuss your findings in class.
2. Choose three retailers that you buy from often. Classify these retailers in terms of the characteristics presented in the chapter and categorize each retailer.

────────────────── **Case study** ──────────────────

What Is the Way Out for Community-based Group Buying?

Community-based group buying (CBGB) is an emerging e-commerce mode. Based on offline physical communities, this retail mode relies on individual residents living in the community or owners of shops around ("group leaders") as the "transfer station" of goods.

CBGB works in this way: A group leader, who works for a certain CBGB platform, poses merchandise information to people in the community via WeChat group, WeChat mini-program or special-purpose Apps. Consumers who want to buy the products place an order and make payment via mobile payment platforms such as AliPay, WeChat Pay, etc. The group leader collects and sorts out the orders, and forwards the orders to the CBGB platform. The platform has the ordered goods sent to the transfer point. The goods may either be distributed to the buyers door-to-door by the group leader or collected by the buyers at the transfer point.

Figure 8.1 The operation mode of the community-based group buying

CBGB is mainly specialized on goods that serve consumers' frequent daily needs such as tissues, detergents, foods (especially fresh foods like vegetables, fruits, fish, meat, seafood)—these are fast-moving daily necessities. The current CBGB market is dominated by four competitors: Didi, Meituan, Pinduoduo and Xingsheng Youxuan.

The emergence of this business mode can be attributed to several factors. First, the mature WeChat ecosystem that comprises WeChat payment, WeChat mini-program, WeChat group, the Moment, etc.

makes it possible for the business. The high popularity of WeChat among Chinese people enables it to quickly widespread among consumers.

Second, the perfection of the supply chain is also a perquisite. Without the warehousing and distribution foundation built earlier through the development of takeout service and fresh food e-commerce, this business mode would by no means be possible.

Third, CBGB depends on geographic segmentation of consumers. People living in tier-1 cities (and some tier-2 cities) lead a fast-paced life and thus attach great importance to time-saving and convenience. Though goods can be delivered to the community even to the door, consumers have to keep eyes on and rummage through massive sales messages, which may be too troublesome and time-consuming for them. CBGB platforms mainly target at community residents in tier-3 and tier-4 cities (and some tier-2 cities) where there are more budget-sensitive and time-rich people.

CBGB is also grounded on segmentation based on life cycle stage. For instance, young couples who have neither babies nor parents living with them tend to order takeout foods instead of cooking by themselves and buy groceries from the convenience store nearby instead of waiting for group-purchased goods. Families with children are more likely to buy in bulk and store fast-moving consumer goods to save money.

Fourth, Chinese people are now very comfortable with socialized buying. The development of Xiaohongshu, Pinduoduo and WeChat Business has validated the influence of "groups" on individual consumers. Consumer buying behaviors are vulnerable to group influence.

CBGB platforms compete with offline brick-and-mortar food stores and grocery stories on price and channel. Lower price is the major appeal to most first-time users, so CBGB platforms often have to invest a great deal of money into attracting new customers by offering big discounts, free samples and coupons. However, as an old saying goes, things that made you can also break you. The platforms somewhat become prisoners of their own low-price strategy. The bright side is the big data technology, if properly exploited, can enable the platforms to develop more precise customer profiles and search for more cost-effective goods for them. Many platforms are now facing the challenge of losing customers once they stop subsidizing the products and the price returns to the normal level. As for distribution, now dry goods are sent to the transfer point in a community, and fresh foods that are supposed to be sent to the door are often dropped at the gate of the community because of the pandemic control measures. It would be a problem for time-poor consumers, but if the CBGB platforms want to expand their customer base to cover the less price-sensitive but time-poor segment, this is a real problem they need to address.

What should the platforms do? Probably they have to focus on several key links of the business mode. First is the group leader. Don't forget community-based group buying is heavily dependent on social networking of group leaders. How to segment the group leaders? How to develop group leaders of various types? Second is the management of the supply source and the supply chain. To save costs is to pass on more value to customers. Fresh goods such as seafood incur additional costs as they rot easily. In other words, perfecting the supply chain can reduce such costs. Third is the retention of existing customers. Low price serves as short-term incentives but by no means is a long-term strategy. To retain customers, a business can offer other forms of value than price value, such as brand value, performance value, emotional value and so on. An in-depth understanding of the target group's psychological needs can help with developing strategies for keeping customers. For example, the lonely, isolated modern city dwellers may still secretly yearn at the bottom of their heart for a close relationship with their neighbors. Why not turn the buying-purpose group into a real "group"? This requires a lot of wisdom and efforts from the platform and the group leader.

Questions:

1. Read the article critically and summarize the reasons behind the emergence of community-based group buying. Could you think of other possible reasons?

2. Evaluate how the business mode of community-based group buying delivers value to end consumers.

3. What challenges are CBGB platforms facing? In your opinion, how could CBGB platforms cope with the challenges?

Chapter Nine
Promotion

Objectives:

After studying this chapter, you should be able to:

- Name the major promotion tools including advertising, sales promotion, publicity, sponsorship, direct marketing, digital marketing, personal selling, etc.;

- Define "integrated marketing communication" (IMC), know its process and discuss its advantages;

- Understand the importance of socially responsible marketing communication;

- Discuss issues related to the major advertising decisions: objectives setting, budget decision, message decision, media decision and advertising evaluation;

- Name the major sales promotion techniques and know how they can be applied to promotional practices;

- Understand the importance of public relations to a company and distinguish publicity from advertising;

- Have some ideas about sponsorship, direct marketing, digital marketing, buzz marketing, personal selling and their application in real-life business scenarios;

- Talk about the new promotion trends.

Framework

Chapter Nine Promotion	Tools in the promotion mix	• Mass communication techniques	┌ Advertising ├ Sales promotion ├ Public relations and publicity └ Sponsorship
	Integrated marketing communication		
	Effective marketing communication process	• Direct communication techniques	┌ Personal selling ├ Direct marketing └ Digital marketing
	Socially responsible marketing communication		
	Major marketing communication tools	• Other communication techniques	┌ Product placement ├ Exhibition ├ Ambient advertising └ Guerrilla marketing
	New marketing communication trends		

Up till now we have discussed issues related to "Product", "Price" and "Place", the last "P", "Promotion", in the 4Ps mix concerns communication with the market about value. This chapter will explore tools available for marketing communications, how to make use of these tools for effective communications, the existing application of new technologies including social media, the Internet, etc. to marketing communications and some ethical issues related to the field.

1. Tools in the promotion mix

All the tools a company employs for marketing communications are collectively referred to as "promotion mix", which consists of a specific combination of advertising, sales promotion, publicity, personal selling and direct marketing tools (see Table 9.1). Definitions of the major promotion tools are as follows:

Table 9.1 Major tools in the promotion mix

Category	Promotion tool	Definition
Mass communication techniques	Advertising	Any paid form of non-personal communication about products, services or ideas in mass media, e.g. television, press, poster, radio and cinema.
	Sales promotion	Short-term incentives to boost the purchase or sale of a product or service.
	Public relations	The process of building and managing good relationships with all stakeholders by obtaining favorable publicity, building a good corporate image and handling or defusing unfavorable rumors and events.
	Publicity	Communications about a product or business by placing information about it in the media without paying directly, e.g. media interviews and blogs.
	Sponsorship	The association of a company or its products with an individual, event or organization.
Direct communication techniques	Personal selling	Personal communication with prospective purchasers by a firm's sales force with the intention of closing a deal.
	Direct marketing	Direct communications with carefully selected target consumers to obtain an immediate response and cultivate lasting customer relationships through using direct mail, the telephone, direct-response television, e-mail, the Internet and other tools that allow interactive communication with specific consumers.
	Digital marketing	The distribution of products, information and promotional benefits to consumers and businesses through digital means, such as the use of telephone, e-mail, the Internet and instant messages.

Continued

Others	Exhibition	Commercial settings that bring buyers, sellers and competitors together for face-to-face communication about prospective business.
	Product placement	The deliberate placing of products and/or their logos in movies, TV series, songs and video games, usually in the paid form.
	Ambient advertising	Advertising carried on outdoor media that do not fall into the established outdoor categories such as billboards and bus signs, e.g. advertisements on shopping bags, balloons or banners towed by airplanes and other ambient places.
	Guerilla marketing	The delivery of advertising messages through unexpected means and in ways that almost "ambush" the consumer to gain attention.

Though the elements of the marketing mix (4Ps) have been discussed one by one under separate chapters, it is worth noting that <u>the entire marketing mix—product, price, place and promotion—must be coordinated for greatest communication effects</u>.

田 营销组合的各个要素，产品、价格、地点和推广，必须协调以实现最大的营销传播效果。

2. Integrated marketing communication

In the past decades, marketers relied heavily on mass communication techniques as there were not many choices available. With the advancement in digital technologies, more direct digital tools are now available for marketing communications. Few companies nowadays are using a single marketing communication tool. However, when several different communication tools are used, it is important that they should be consistent and complement each other, because conflicting messages from different sources can result in confusing company images, unclear brand positioning and uncertain customer relationships.

<u>The process of carefully integrating the delivery of clear, consistent and competitive messages through different communication channels is called "integrated marketing communication"</u>. Integrated marketing communication strategies are adopted by an increasing number of companies. <u>The application of this concept leads to improved consistency and clearer positioning of companies, their brands and products in the minds of consumers</u>.

田 仔细整合通过不同的渠道传递的清晰的、一致的、能够体现竞争力的信息，这一过程称为"整合营销传播"。

田 这一概念的应用提高了公司、品牌和产品在消费者心目中的一致性和清晰定位。

3. Effective marketing communication process

An effective marketing communication process typically consists of five steps: identifying target audience, setting communication objectives, designing messages, choosing a promotional mix and collecting feedbacks (see Figure 9.1).

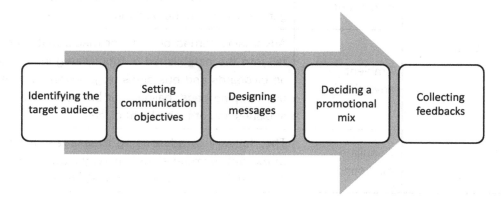

Figure 9.1 Effective marketing communication process

Step 1: Identifying target audience

Decisions to be made in this step concern the target audience to which marketing messages are to be communicated in a campaign, including the geographical area of the target audience, individuals, groups, special publics or the general public, existing buyers or potential buyers, heavy users or light users, and so on. Decisions about target audiences are determined by the purpose and goal of the campaign. The target audience in return will affect the communicator's decisions on what will be said, how it will be said, when it will be said, where it will be said and who will say it.

Step 2: Setting communication objectives

Once the target audience has been defined, marketers must decide what results they seek. Of course the ultimate goal is to close a deal, but marketers may have smaller, periodical objectives during the long process of consumer decision making before purchase is made. For instance, you may want a marketing campaign to bring your product to consumers' awareness, increase their knowledge about it, enhance their liking or multiply the number of consumers who like it, strengthen product/brand preference or conviction, or help to bring about a purchase.

Step 3: Designing messages

The third step is to design messages with effective contents. <u>The content of the message should be appealing, interesting and suggestive, and conducive to the realization of the communication objectives</u>. A promotional message may appeal to the target audience in three ways: rational, emotional and moral.

⊞ 信息内容应具有吸引力、趣味性和启发性，并有利于实现传播目标。

Rational appeals encourage self-interests by claiming certain benefits of a product or stress one unique selling point or distinct feature in terms of quality, performance, economy or value. For instance, Nongfu Spring's slogans—"Nongfu Spring, a little sweet!" and "We do not produce water; we are just porters of nature"—highlight the natural quality of its mineral water.

Emotional appeals seek to stir up negative or positive emotions that will motivate purchase. The promotional message can contain an emotional selling proposition. For example, TV commercials of anti-dandruff shampoos often depict how dandruffs can put a person in an embarrassing social situation. This may stir up some people's negative emotional associations with similar experience.

Moral appeals are directed to the audience sense of what is "right" and "wrong". They are more often used in advertisements for social causes, such as waste sorting, environmental protection, gender equality and so on. We are not unfamiliar with such slogans as "Protecting the environment is saving lives"; "Maintaining ecological balance on the planet is protecting the mankind"; "A grain on the table, a drop of sweat from the face of famers".

> ⊞ 理性诉求鼓励人们的自利行为，声称产品具有某些好处或强调其在质量、性能、经济性或价值方面的独特卖点或突出特征。
>
> ⊞ 感情诉求试图调动人们悲观或乐观情绪作为购买动机。
>
> ⊞ 道德诉求针对人们的正义感。

Step 4: Deciding a promotional mix

The fourth step is to make media decisions, including media class and media vehicle. If it is decided the message is to be delivered via TV, the specific media vehicles such as CCTV 1, Guangdong TV should be decided. Media decisions are based on several considerations: the size of the campaign budget, the competitors' campaigns, readership/viewership figures and charging standards of specific media vehicles, etc.

> ⊞ 媒体决策基于几个考虑因素：活动预算、竞争对手的活动、读者／观众人数和特定媒体形式的收费标准等。

Step 5: Collecting feedbacks

The communication process is ended with collecting feedbacks—the audience's response. During the process, unfavorable factors such as wrong media vehicles, inappropriate message contents and limited target coverage will undercut the effects of marketing communication. Collecting feedbacks allows marketers to evaluate the effectiveness of the communication and make modification where necessary.

4. Socially responsible marketing communication

A large body of legal and ethical issues surrounds marketing communication in practice. Most marketers work hard to communicate openly and honestly with consumers and resellers. However, it is not uncommon to see malpractices in advertising, sales promotion, personal selling and direct marketing activities.

Policy makers and trade associations have developed a substantial body of laws, regulations and standards for advertising. Law forbids false or deceptive advertising.

⊞ 广告商不得做出虚假、误导或夸大的声明，例如暗示某种产品可以治愈其不能治愈的某些疾病，或在传递的信息中隐瞒重要事实。

⊞ 除了要避免欺骗性广告等法律陷阱，公司还可以通过广告和其他推广方法来传播其社会责任行为。

Advertisers must not make false, misleading or exaggerated claims, such as suggesting a product can cure some disease when it cannot, or conceal important facts in the message delivered. For instance, a weight-loss pill cannot be advertised as being capable of removing 15 kilograms within one month unless it is so on most people under regular conditions.

Beyond avoiding legal pitfalls such as deceptive advertising, companies can use advertising and other promotional techniques to spread their socially responsible actions. For example, Huawei launched a CSR micro-film advertising its commitments and actions to the nature, the society and people across the world. In the film, the IT technology giant hailed its social responsibility conviction of "bridging the digital divide" through presenting a series of socially responsible programs and actions including building green power generation infrastructures, bringing digital hospital solutions to underdeveloped countries and regions, providing equal access to the Internet for poor people and making charitable donations to disaster-struck areas.

As for personal selling, laws and regulations outlaw some sales acts, including offering bribes, obtaining technical or trade secrets of competitors through bribery or industrial espionage, or disparaging competitors or competing products by suggesting things that are not true.

5. Major marketing communication tools

5.1 Mass communication techniques

Advertising

⊞ 广告是由特定赞助商付费，进行非个人展示和推广创意、产品或服务的一种推广形式。

Advertising is defined by Philip Kotler as "a paid form of non-personal presentation and promotion of ideas, goods or services by an identified sponsor". When developing an advertising campaign, marketers must make four major decisions: defining advertising objectives, setting the advertising budget, making decisions about the message to be delivered and the media through which the message is to be delivered and evaluating the advertising campaign (see Figure 9.2).

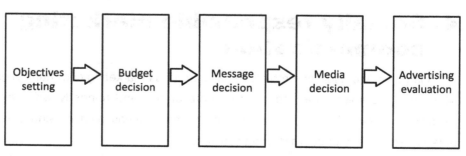

Figure 9.2 Major advertising decisions

A. Objectives setting

Generally speaking, all advertising is to build good customer relationships by communicating customer value. Here we talk about the specific objectives of an advertising campaign. <u>The specific advertising objectives may be creating awareness of a brand or product, stimulating trials, positioning/ repositioning products, correcting misconceptions, reminding customers of sales or special offers and providing supports for the company's sales force.</u> Advertising objectives can be classified by primary purpose into three types: informative advertising, persuasive advertising and reminder advertising (see Table 9.2).

⊞ 具体的广告目标包括建立品牌或产品的知名度、促进消费者试用、定位／重新定位产品、纠正误解、提醒顾客商品减价或特价以及为公司的销售人员提供支持。

Table 9.2 Three types of advertising

Informative advertising	• Communicating customer value. • Telling the market about a new product. • Explaining how a product works. • Suggesting new uses of a product. • Informing the market of a price change. • Describing available service. • Correcting false impressions. • Building brand/corporate image.
Persuasive advertising	• Building brand preference. • Encouraging switch to your brand. • Changing customer perception of product attributes. • Persuading customers to purchase now. • Persuading customers to receive a sales activity. • Calling convinced customers to tell others about the brand.
Reminder advertising	• Maintaining customer relationships. • Reminding customers that the product will soon enter off-seasons. • Reminding customers where to buy the product. • Keeping the brand in customers' minds.

⊞ 告知型广告旨在创造对产品、服务、组织、人员、地点、创意或事业等的初始需求。

⊞ 说服型广告试图增加人们对现有产品、服务、组织、人员、地点、创意或事业的需求。

⊞ 提醒型广告在公众面前反复提及产品、服务、组织、人员、地点、创意或事业，以增强先前推广活动的效果。

<u>Informative advertising seeks to develop initial demand for goods, services, organizations, persons, places, ideas or causes. Persuasive advertising attempts to increase demands for existing goods, services, organizations, persons, places, ideas or causes. Reminder advertising strives to reinforce previous promotional activity by keeping the name of goods, services, organizations, persons, places, ideas or causes before the public.</u>

B. Budget decision

An advertising budget is closely related to the stage in the product life cycle. A newly developed product typically requires large advertising budgets to build awareness and to encourage trials. In contrast, mature products or brands need lower advertising budgets relative to sales. Besides, building the market or taking market share from competitors requires more advertising spending than simply maintaining the current share.

There are several methods of setting advertising budgets: the percentage of sales method, the competitive parity method and the affordability method, each with its own weaknesses. Probably the most effective one is the objective and task method. Instead of setting advertising budgets based on the sales figure, competitors' advertising spending or the company's maximum resources available, the objective and task method links the budget with communication objectives and the costs of the tasks required to achieve them.

⊞ 目标和任务匹配法不是根据销售额、竞争对手的广告支出或公司可用的最大资源来设置广告预算，而是将预算与传播目标和实现这些目标所需的任务成本联系起来。

C. Message decision

Advertising messages translate a company's value propositions into an advertising platform, which refers to the words, symbols and illustrations that are attractive and meaningful to the target audience. For example, the advertising slogan of Vipshop—"Affordable prices for top-end brands" ("全是傲娇的品牌，只卖呆萌的价格") highlights the value proposition of the B2C platform; the slogan of Industrial and Commercial Bank of China (ICBC)—"Integrity Leads to Prosperity" indicates its underlying core value; Midea's advertising slogan "Life could have been better with Midea" stresses that Midea electric appliances can make people's life better. In addition to advertising the benefits or performance of a product or brand, advertisers can also appeal to consumers' emotions. A typical case is that widely-known and well-remembered line for diamond advertising: "A diamond can last forever" ("钻石恒久远，一颗永流传").

⊞ 除了宣传产品或品牌的好处或性能，广告商还可以迎合消费者的情感诉求。

D. Media decision

As for media decisions, marketers must decide on the coverage, frequency and impacts, choose media types and decide on media timing. First, the advertising coverage, frequency and impacts are related to choices of media class (e.g. TV commercial vs press advertising) and media vehicle (e.g. a particular magazine or TV channel).

TV advertising is more effective for establishing brand image and creating awareness, as a typical TV commercial lasts less than 30 seconds and costs a lot. Press advertising is suitable for providing factual information. For instance, magazines or newspapers placed on airplanes or railways, especially those heading for a tourist city, contain articles about hotels, restaurants, scenic

⊞ 电视广告对树立品牌形象和创造知名度更有效。

⊞ 平面广告适合于提供事实信息。

spots and local-featured entertainments. The Internet is now increasingly used for advertising as well. Any Internet surfer will find it quite often to encounter pop-up windows or website banners that advertise something.

Once the media class is determined, the next decision to make is the specific media vehicle (see Table 9.3). The product category to be advertised must be in alignment with the positioning and target audience of a specific media vehicle. For example, *Bazaar*, a famous fashion magazine, is a good choice for advertising fashion clothes, footwear, cosmetics, jewelries, perfumes, luxury bags and so on, as the advertised items can be fully presented in color pictures and elaborate wording.

⊞ 需要宣传的产品类别必须与特定媒介的定位和目标受众保持一致。

Table 9.3 Media classes and vehicles

Media class	Media vehicle
Television	CCTV (1, 2, 9...), Guangdong TV, Guangdong News
Radio	Classic FM (FM 91.4...), CNR
Newspaper	*China Daily*, *The Economist*, *Yangcheng Evening News*
Magazine	Bazaar, Rayli
Outdoor	Billboard, bus shelter, Guangzhou Underground
Internet	iQIYI, Tencent Video, Youku
Cinema	Cinema Palace (Parc Central)
Exhibition	Canton Fair, Frankfurt Book Fair

E. Advertising evaluation

Advertising results include two types: the communication effects and the sales and profit effects. A variety of data can be obtained for the evaluation such as TV viewing rate, newspaper/magazine sales volume, past and current sales and profit figures, results of market research conducted by the internal marketing department or a market research agency and so on. In practice, advertising effectiveness and return on advertising investment can be measured by conducting a pre-test and a post-test and comparing results of the two tests.

⊞ 广告效果体现在传播效果和销售额及利润。

Sales promotion

Sales promotions are short-term incentives to encourage consumers or the trade to purchase or sell a product or service through a great variety of promotional tools such as money off, free gifts and discounts. Compared with advertising, which offers reasons to buy, sales promotion offers reasons to buy now.

Despite the fact that sales promotion provides short-term incentives to

⊞ 促销是一种短期激励措施，旨在通过各种促销手段（例如优惠、免费礼品和折扣）来鼓励消费者购买或贸易商销售产品或服务。

⊞ 尽管促销能够在短期内刺激当下的购买，但其长期影响可能是积极的、中性的或消极的。

buy now, the long-term effects can be positive, neutral or negative. If the promotion has succeeded in attracting new buyers who find that they like the product or brand, repeat purchases from them add to the long-term effect of the promotion. If customers are only seduced by lower prices into buying the product and the product fails to change their purchase preference, the sales promotion has neutral long-term effects. Where a big sales promotion has devalued the brand in the minds of consumers, the long-term effect may be negative. For instance, Cadillac, an American high-market motor brand, was a late entrant into the Chinese market compared with BMW, Benz and Audi. To capture a share of the competitive market where most consumers were not familiar with the brand, Cadillac resorted to the penetration pricing strategy for new models and offered a big discount for some old models in order to attract new buyers. Some Cadillac fans may think the marketing strategy has devalued the brand.

⊞ 哪种促销技术有效取决于预算规模、促销的具体目标、当前市场状况、竞争情况和顾客条件。

Major consumer promotion tools include: money off, bonus packs, free sample, prize, loyalty card, give-away, allowance, competition, discount, coupon and premium (see Figure 9.3). Which sales promotion technique is effective depends on the budget size, specific objectives of the promotion, current market conditions, the competitive scenario and customer conditions.

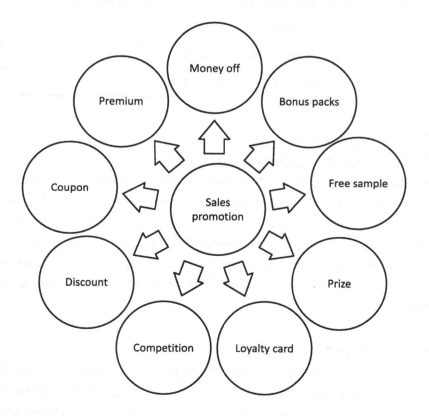

Figure 9.3 Consumer sales promotion techniques

Money-off provides direct value to consumers by means of price reduction. Money-off works particularly on budget-conscious buyers, but marketers should also watch out that price reduction cannot devalue the positioning of the brand in the minds of existing customers. Bonus packs give added value by giving extra quantity at the same price, and often used in drinks, detergents, toothpastes and so on. A bonus pack may be several items banded together with such lines as "Buy 5 and get 2 free". Premiums are goods offered either free or at low costs as incentive to consumers, such as phone cards attached to a cellphone and a one-year membership card guaranteeing free access to digital resources for a newly purchased TV set.

Free samples are given out to encourage trial. It is an effective, also expensive way to introduce a new product. The sample may be delivered door to door, sent by mail, distributed in a store or attached to other products of the same category, as we often see in the case of shampoos, body washes or lotions. Coupons are certificates that give buyers savings when they purchase specified goods. Hard-copy coupons are less and less seen nowadays, and coupons are often distributed in electronic forms. Unlike money-off that incentivizes trials, coupons are more effective to encourage repeat purchases. Discount is the offering of a product at a reduced price. Discounts are often applied to food, drink, personal care or cosmetic products that have an approaching expiration date.

Competitions, sweepstakes and games give consumers chances to win something such as cash refunds, trips or goods, by luck or through extra efforts. The soft drink brand Master Kang once swept the Chinese mainland market through launching the "One More Bottle" campaign. Customers who find "One More Bottle" printed inside the twisted cap of Mater Kang drinks can get one more bottle for free instantly from the point of sale. Prizes are offered to contest winners in the form of sponsored trips, free merchandizes and even money.

As a popular promotional tool for service businesses, loyalty cards are effective to attract customers back to the store and can be used to collect consumer information. Businesses offer loyalty cards to accumulate points from each purchase of a customer that can later be exchanged into some gifts or other forms of benefits. More importantly, businesses can use customer information collected through the loyalty card for better-targeted marketing communications and launch of better-designed

⊞ 减价优惠通过降价直接为消费者提供价值。

⊞ 优惠包装通过提供额外的产品数量但保持价格不变的形式提供附加值，通常用于饮料、洗涤剂、牙膏等。

⊞ 优惠价是为了激励消费者购买而提供免费或低价格的产品。

⊞ 店家也可通过分发免费试用装来鼓励消费者试用新产品。

⊞ 优惠券是购买者在购买指定产品时获得优惠的凭证。

⊞ 与鼓励试用的减价优惠不同，优惠券更能有效地鼓励重复购买。

⊞ 折扣是指以较低的价格提供产品。

⊞ 竞赛、抽奖和游戏让消费者有机会凭运气或额外的努力赢取现金退款、旅行或礼品等。

⊞ 比赛获胜者获得奖品的形式包括赞助旅行、免费商品甚至现金。

⊞ 会员卡是服务行业流行的促销工具，可以有效地吸引顾客再次回到店里消费，并可以用来收集消费者信息。

⊞ 第一，营销人员必须决定激励的规模并设定参与条件。

⊞ 第二，营销人员必须决定如何推广以及如何分发推广活动信息。

⊞ 第三，确定合适的推广活动时长。

⊞ 第四，公司应在促销结束后评估促销效果，这一步很重要。

⊞ 公共关系 (PR) 是通过积极正面的宣传、树立良好的企业形象、处理或消除对企业不利的谣言和事件，与所有利益相关者建立和管理良好关系的过程。

⊞ 与媒体广告相比，宣传保证了所发送信息的高可信度，不产生直接的媒体成本，但其风险在于对所发布的信息控制很小。

⊞ 赞助旨在进行宣传、创造娱乐机会、促进与品牌或公司的积极联系、改善社区关系并创造促销机会。

promotional campaigns.

How to develop a sales promotion program? First, marketers must decide on the size of the incentive and set conditions for participation, e.g. for everyone or just for selected groups. Second, marketers must decide how to promote and how to distribute the promotion program. For instance, is a coupon to be given out at the store, attached to wrappers of the products on sale or distributed via the Internet? Third, a proper length of the program is to be determined. A length that is too short or too long does no good to the effects of the promotion program. Fourth, upon the end of a sales promotion, it is important that companies should evaluate its effects. Common questions that should be asked in the evaluation include: Did the promotion attract new customers or create more purchases from current customers? Can we retain these new customers and purchases? Does the promotion do any good to our long-term relationship with customers?

Public relations and publicity

An organization is associated with a variety of stakeholders, such as employees, customers, shareholders, the local community, the media, government bodies and pressure groups. Public relations (PR) is the process of building and managing good relationships with all of these stakeholders by obtaining favorable publicity, building a good corporate image and handling or defusing unfavorable rumors and events. Major PR tools include: publicity, speeches, special events, written materials, audio visual materials, corporate identity, public service activities and word-of-mouth.

Publicity is a major element of PR. Publicity is the communication of information about a product or organization by means of news in the media without directly paying for news exposure. Compared with media advertising, publicity guarantees high credibility of message sent, generates no direct media costs, but contains the risk of little control over publication.

Sponsorship

Sponsorship has been defined by Sleight in his widely cited article published in 1989 "Sponsorship: What It Is and How to Use It" as "a business relationship between a provider of funds, resources or services and an individual, event or organization which offers in return some rights and association that may be used for commercial advantage". Potential sponsors may choose to fund sports, arts, community activities, teams, tournaments, celebrities or events, competitions, fairs and shows. Sponsorship aims to gain publicity, create entertainment opportunities, foster favorable associations with a brand or company, improve community relations and create promotional opportunities.

The advantage of sponsorship is very apparent: high visibility and extensive media coverage. But it is also not without its risks, especially when the sponsorship is linked with a celebrity. Many times we have witnessed how the image of a brand or company is dampened by its chosen image representative who is being mired in a scandal. Moreover, at many events, <u>category exclusivity is quite common—an event has only one sponsor from each product category</u>. For example, if a sports event chooses Coca-Cola as the sponsor in the soft drink category, it cannot take Pepsi as sponsor at the same time. This often results in sky-high sponsorship costs.

⊞ 品类独家赞助权非常常见，即在一个活动中，每个产品类别只能有一个赞助商。

5.2 Direct communication techniques

Personal selling

<u>Personal selling—personal representation by the firm's sales force for the purpose of making sales and building customer relationships</u>, is one of the oldest marketing practices. <u>Unlike the one-way, non-personal communication means such as advertising and publicity, personal selling involves two-way, interpersonal communication between salespeople and individual customers</u>. Salespersons listen to their customers, assess customer needs and organize the company's efforts to solve customer problems. Today, most salespeople are well-educated and well-trained professionals who work to build and maintain long-term customer relationships. For instance, sales representatives of pharmaceutical companies and publishing houses spend much time and effort in organizing academic conferences or exchange programs.

⊞ 人员推销，由公司的销售人员进行产品推销，以卖出产品和与顾客建立关系。

⊞ 与广告和公共宣传等单向、非一对一的沟通方式不同，人员推销是销售人员与单个顾客之间的双向人际沟通。

In most companies, the sales force plays a major role. In companies that sell business products and services such as Huawei Technologies and Johnson & Johnson Medical Devices Companies, their salespeople work directly with organizational customers. In consumer product companies like P&G and Nike, the sales force deals with wholesalers and retailers. Though the major part of salespeople's job is making sales, salespeople are concerned with more than that—they should work with others in the company to create customer value and satisfaction and obtain company profits in return. Salespersons need support from everyone in the company from the technical team to the after-sales service center.

Direct marketing

<u>Direct marketing involves direct communications with carefully targeted consumers to obtain an immediate response</u>. Except for personal face-to-face selling, direct marketing can be conducted through TV, direct mail, telephone, new forms of telecommunications and computer-based media. Early direct marketers collected customer information and sold goods mainly via direct mail or telephone. Today, with the rapid advancement in information technologies, databases and big data technologies, direct marketing has undergone a big transformation.

⊞ 直接营销涉及与精心确定的目标消费者直接沟通，在沟通过程中可得到立即回应。

⊞ 直邮营销是指通过邮政服务将信函、小册子、样品、CD和 DVD 等材料寄到收件人的指定地址。

Figure 9.4 shows the major forms of direct marketing. <u>Direct mail marketing involves sending materials such as letters, brochures, samples, CDs and DVDs through the postal service to the recipient at a particular address</u>. Direct mail is suited to direct, one-to-one communications. It facilitates targeting at specified individuals, and allows personalized communications and easy measurement of results.

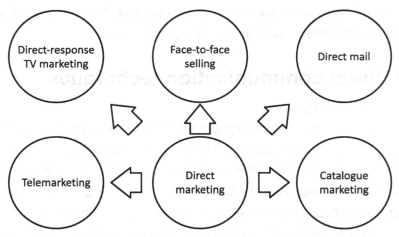

Figure 9.4 Major forms of direct marketing

⊞ 目录营销是指通过邮寄或在商店中将产品目录分发给代理商和顾客的方式来销售产品。

⊞ 电话营销是指使用电话直接向客户销售产品。

⊞ 直接响应电视营销包括直接响应电视广告和家庭购物频道两种形式。

<u>Catalogue marketing refers to the sale of goods through catalogues distributed to agents and customers, usually by mail or at stores</u>. For instance, in an outlet of Gloria, a Chinese female fashion clothes brand, consumers can access colored catalogues of new products of the season. Today, print catalogues are increasingly replaced by web-based catalogues, which are more cost-saving, efficient and convenient.

<u>Telemarketing means using the telephone to sell directly to customers</u>. It has a number of advantages: lower costs per contact than face-to-face selling, less time-consuming, the availability of more sophisticated telecommunication technologies that make telemarketing a lot easier, and two-way, personalized communications. Many banks use telemarketing to promote credit cards or other financial services.

<u>Direct-response TV marketing includes two forms: direct-response TV advertising and home shopping channels</u>. Television viewers find a lengthy advertising program lasting 120 seconds or even 30 minutes for a single product and conspicuously displaying a toll-free telephone number or a website address for ordering. Such TV advertising programs are aired through regular TV channels, and there are also channels dedicated to direct-response TV marketing. In real life, direct-response TV marketing is especially attractive to retired old people, who, unlike young people heavily depending on smartphones for shopping, sit in couch and watch TV a lot throughout the day. You will find that commodities advertised through direct-response TV marketing are often those things that appeal to old people, such as health products, sneakers specially designed for old people, frying pan, etc.

Digital marketing

Digital technology-based marketing is referred to as "digital marketing". By media, digital marketing can be divided into Internet marketing, social media marketing, mobile marketing and email marketing (see Figure 9.5).

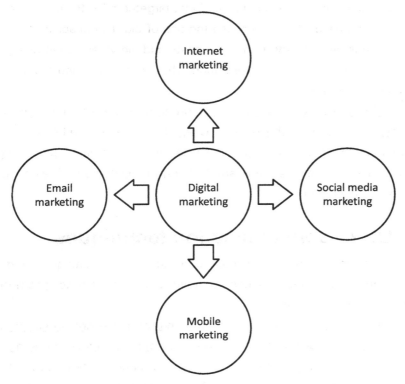

Figure 9.5 Major forms of digital marketing

Internet marketing, also online marketing, is increasingly popular nowadays as the Internet is a powerful marketing tool. On the one hand, consumers can directly order products and services from online stores such as Taobao and JD.com. On the other hand, marketing information can be easily distributed and obtained online. <u>Online marketing can be conducted through four types of online business platforms: B2B, B2C, C2B and C2C</u> (see Figure 9.6).

田 在线营销可以通过四种在线业务平台进行：B2B（企业对企业）、B2C（企业对个人）、C2B（个人对企业）和 C2C（个人对个人）。

	From business	From consumer
To business	B2B (re.1688.com)	C2B (Yaoshao.com)
To consumer	B2C (Taobao, JD.com, Vipshop)	C2C (Xianyu)

Figure 9.6 Online business platforms

Online advertising takes various forms including display advertising (e.g. website banner), rich media adverts (e.g. pop-up webpage) to email advertising, search advertising (paid search adverts on Baidu or Google) and online video advertising (e.g. Youku). All these forms of online advertising are common to regular online surfers.

田 社交媒体营销是
使用社交媒体在线
对顾客进行营销传
播，并让他们参与这
个传播过程。

田 移动营销是指通
过移动设备（包括智
能手机和平板电脑）
进行的营销传播。

田 产品植入广告是一
种新的非面对面销售
形式，产品和／或其
标志被故意植入在电
影、电视、歌曲和视
频游戏中，通常是需
要付费的。

田 展览是一种在商业
环境中将买家、卖家
和竞争对手聚集在一
起的促销工具。

田 环境广告是指在不
寻常的物品上或通常
不会看到广告的不寻
常的地方投放广告，
例如购物袋、邮政包
裹的包装纸、汽油泵
喷嘴、街道人行道和
公路的广告牌上。

田 游击营销是指通过
低成本、创造性的非
常规手段，用几乎"伏
击"消费者以吸引他
们注意力的方式来传
递促销信息。

Social media marketing is the use of social media for marketing communications with and engaging customers online. Social media provide a platform for marketers and businesses to distribute messages on the one hand, and allow them to collect customer information on the other. For instance, Sina microblog users will find that targeted adverts are inserted into their personal page—this is because the use of big data enables businesses to detect customer needs from their posts and views and then design and deliver relevant advertising information. The same marketing practices are also common on WeChat.

Mobile marketing refers to marketing communications through mobile devices, including smartphones and PC tablets. As people are becoming more and more dependent on their mobile devices in their daily life, it provides great opportunities for flexible, well-targeted communications with existing and prospective customers.

5.3 Other communication techniques

Apart from the traditional mass communication techniques and new promotional techniques discussed above, a variety of other promotional techniques are also available.

Product placement is a new form of non-personal selling where products and/or their logos are deliberately placed in movies, television, songs and video games, usually in return for money. In product placement, marketers should carefully choose the movies or TV shows whose viewers are the target segment and design appropriate amounts of exposure so that the product can be noticed by the viewers without annoying them.

Exhibitions are a promotional tool that brings buyers, sellers and competitors together in commercial settings, providing chances for participants to identify prospective buyers and determine their needs, build relationships, demonstrate and display products, make sales, collect competitive intelligence and foster the corporate image.

Ambient advertising refers to placing ads on unusual items or in unusual places where you wouldn't normally see an advertisement such as on shopping bags, wrappers of postal parcels, petrol pump nozzles, street pavements and highroad billboards. Ambient advertising can be found anywhere and everywhere! The key to a successful ambient media campaign is to choose the best media form that can be combined with effective message.

Closely related to ambient advertising is guerrilla marketing—the delivery of promotional messages through low-cost creative unconventional means and in ways that almost "ambush" consumers to gain their attention. Most people who have ever used the washroom of a motorway service station or a scenic spot may see advertisements pasted or printed on the inside surface of the toilet door. <u>Ambient and guerrilla tactics are favored by advertisers with limited budgets or as a complement to a bigger campaign.</u>

Ethical marketing practices in promotional activities are topics worth discussion. Over-exaggerating, fake and deceptive advertising is now overtly banned by law, but there is a gray zone where a business's marketing ethics is tested. Choices related to ethical issues made by companies are receiving more and more attentions from the regulators, trade associations, consumer protection organizations and consumers.

KFC recently launched a new promotional campaign in collaboration with top domestic blind box toymaker Pop Mart to offer 260,000 dolls with its 99 yuan ($15.60) family-sized chicken bucket. The doll set features seven models of Dimoo, a popular character created by Pop Mart, with six regular ones and one hidden model, meaning customers have to pay at least 594 yuan to collect a complete set. Such marketing can lead to impulsive and excessive consumption, and KFC has been criticized for using a limited number of blind box sales to lure customers into over-purchasing its food, thereby causing food waste. KFC's marketing practice is now questionably against "the spirit of the law", as the *Anti-food Waste Law* adopted in April 2021 clearly stipulates that food operators should resist food waste, prompt customers to consume moderately and take measures to prevent waste rather than induce or mislead them to purchase excessively.

6. New marketing communication trends

As the market is further fragmented, more and more marketers are shifting away from broadcasting communications to narrowcasting communications. More and more marketing programs are designed to build closer relationships with customers through more personalized, two-way communications. <u>Unlike the "one size fits all" approach in advertising, marketing via microblog, WeChat and other social media platforms allows more efficient delivery of customized information to more narrowly defined micromarkets.</u> With the advancement in information technologies and the application of the big data technology, marketers are now able to feed targets with messages tailored based on their personal data.

Advertisers can supplement the traditional mass media with more specialized and highly targeted media that cost less, target more effectively and encourage customers more fully. For example, in the Chinese mainland market where almost everyone holds a smartphone and uses WeChat as an instant messaging tool, many brands, apart from their traditional marketing channels and approaches, have input many resources and efforts into WeChat marketing, such as running an official subscription account, pushing regular

⊞ 环境广告和游击营销通常受预算有限的企业的青睐，或是把它们作为一项大型广告活动的补充。

⊞ 与广告"一刀切"的方式不同，通过微博、微信和其他社交媒体平台进行营销可以更有效地将定制信息传递到定义更狭小的细分市场。

> ⊞ 营销人员现在不但可以利用传统大众媒体，还可以利用各种令人兴奋的、更有针对性的和更个性化的传媒手段进行营销沟通。

feeds to subscribers, launching a WeChat-inbuilt program, and having their selling persons "befriend" and keep contact with existing and potential customers.

In sum, under the new marketing communication landscape, <u>marketers can now rely on a mix of traditional mass media and a wide array of exciting, more targeted and more personalized media.</u>

Summary

This chapter centers around one of the 4Ps in the marketing mix—promotion. Simply put, promotion is communications of customer value. The promotional mix can be broadly divided into three categories: mass communication techniques (advertising, sales promotion, public relations, publicity and sponsorship), direct communication techniques (personal selling, direct marketing and digital marketing) and others (product placement, exhibition, ambient advertising and guerilla advertising).

An important concept—integrated marketing communication (IMC) is introduced. IMC is the process of carefully integrating the delivery of clear, consistent and competitive messages through different communication channels. The effective marketing communication process consists of five steps: identifying target audience, setting communication objectives, designing messages, deciding a promotional mix and collecting feedbacks. Socially responsible marketing communication is also an important issue. Marketers must abide by the laws, regulations, trade codes and standards governing marketing communications.

A large proportion of this chapter is distributed to discussions on the major promotional tools. For advertising, marketers must make major decisions about advertising objectives, budget, messages to be delivered, media and post-evaluation. As short-term incentives to encourage consumers to buy, sales promotion takes a variety of forms: money off, bonus packs, free sample, prize, loyalty card, give-away, allowance, competition, discount, coupon and premium. Public relations (PR) is about managing good relationships with a variety of stakeholders, such as employees, customers, shareholders, the local community, the media, government bodies and pressure groups. Sponsorship is an expensive promotional tool, but effective to promote corporate/brand image and build awareness.

Direct marketing involves direct communications with carefully targeted consumers. It takes various forms: personal face-to-face selling, direct mail marketing, catalogue marketing, telemarketing and direct-response TV marketing. Digital technologies are increasingly used for marketing purposes—this is called "digital marketing". The four major forms of digital marketing in heavy use today are Internet/online marketing, social media marketing, mobile marketing and email marketing. The application of database, information and big data technologies allows marketers to carry out better targeted, more personalized and flexible communications with micromarkets. Under the current marketing communication landscape, marketers are shifting away from broadcasting to narrowcasting.

Key terms

promotion mix	sponsorship
integrated marketing communication	personal selling
rational appeal	direct marketing
emotional appeal	digital marketing
moral appeal	social media marketing
advertising	product placement
sales promotion	exhibition
publicity	ambient advertising
public relations	guerrilla marketing

Exercises

Review and discussion

1. Complete the texts about TV and radio advertising using words from the box.

channels	listeners	programs	reaching	station

TV plays a huge role in our lives and even in these days of 200-plus _____, ITVI continues to be the most watched. In 2005, a massive 885 of the 1,000 highest-rating _____ were shown on ITVI.

Classic FM is the largest commercial radio _____ in the UK, _____ almost 6 million people every week. Most of the station's _____ are not connoisseurs of classical music and come to us because of the way Classic FM makes them feel, regardless of age, sex or income.

2. Complete the news report using words from the box.

catching	coverage	graphics	hung	shelters	wrapped

Commuters in Bristol were surprised by an invasion of out-of-home advertising last Tuesday. The opening of a new concert hall was announced by huge banners _____ on prominent sites around the city. Buses were _____ in the concert hall's logo and colors. Bus _____ were treated to new eye-_____ interactive ads that lit up and made noises as pedestrians waled past. A spokesperson for the new concert hall said that the public reaction had been good. "We got greater _____ than we had imagined," he added. One commuter said that she had been pleasantly surprised to find herself walking on floor _____ instead of the ordinary floor.

3. Anna Bounty works for a major record company. Complete the extract from an interview using words from the box.

cflyers	grassroots	posters	swag	word	word of mouth

Meet the woman who organizes _____ promotional efforts for your favorite artists.

What do you do?

I run the street team. They get the _____ out about events such as album releases and tour dates. I have street teamers in every city putting up _____, handing out stickers and _____ and giving out free CDs. Street teamers also pass on information by _____. The fans are rewarded with free records, tickets to show and other _____.

4. Match the two parts of the sentences and write a–h on the lines before the numbers 1–8.

_____ 1) Procter & Gamble has released viral

_____ 2) In addition to launching the Noscruf.org website, the campaign includes paid search ads, and two viral videos on the peer

_____ 3) The Sony Bravia advert with pain exploding over a block of flats spread

_____ 4) The general

_____ 5) The film has been uploaded onto peer to peer sites and widely discussed in chat

_____ 6) The JetBlue airline recruited a network of buzz

_____ 7) Influential students pass

_____ 8) A portal allows ambassadors to share ideas and communicate with other students in their social

---

a. agents called CrewBlue Campus Ambassadors

b. rooms

c. along the airline's brand message on university campuses

d. public was allowed to attend the shooting of the new campaign and the film was released on the Bravia website

e. commercials that aim to persuade men to shave

f. on the Internet

g. to peer site YouTube.com

h. networks

5. Make word combinations using a word or phrase from each box. One word can be used twice. Then use the word combinations to complete the sentences below. Consult the "Reference" to help you.

an element	coupons
money-off	offer
no	of skill
online	promotions
seasonal	purchase necessary
special	two
three for	

1) Some _____ can be found on the Internet. These are called _____.

2) When children go back to school after the long holidays there are always _____ on pencils, paper and school bags.

3) If _____ is written on the pack, you can enter the prize draw without having to buy the product.

4) For some prize draws _____ is needed to answer questions or complete a simple task.

5) _____ is a popular type of _____ as you get one free product.

Reference

Marketers and consumers are people talking about sales promotions:

1. We run a **prize draw**, or competition, every year in the summer. It's **free to enter**, so we have to label the packs with **no purchase necessary** to show that consumers don't have to buy the product to enter. This year we are thinking of changing the rules. We'd like to include **an element of skill** by asking the entrants to answer a simple question in order to take part. This way we can require **a proof of purchase**, like a receipt, from the entrants.

2. I bought this biscuits because I had a **money-off coupon**. Thirty pence off, now that's not bad. My son got it from the Internet. It's one of these new **e-coupons**. You know — an **online coupon**.

3. I always buy my shampoo when there is a **special offer**, like **three for two**. It's even better if it's **buy one get one free**, or BOGOF.

4. As the marketing manager for a breakfast cereal, I like to use **gifts with purchase** to target children. We often put a small plastic toy inside the packet.

5. My local supermarket always goes crazy in the summer with **seasonal promotions** for sun cream and leg wax. Sometimes you can't find the milk because of all the **in-store promotions**.

6. Answer the following questions briefly.

1) What are the major elements of a promotion mix?

2) How many steps are there in an effective marketing communication process? Which of the step is most critical? Why?

3) What are the major advantages of personal selling over nonpersonal selling?

4) Why do firms have established public relations department? What are the purposes of the function?

5) Which kinds of sales promotional techniques do you think are most effective for convenience goods?

6) Select three recent advertising campaigns with which you are familiar. Discuss the target audience, objectives and message executions adopted in each case.

7) Discuss the role of sponsorship in the promotional mix.

8) Discuss the role of social media as marketing tools. How is marketing on social media similar and different from traditional marketing?

9) What is meant by buzz marketing? Discuss the elements of an effective buzz marketing campaign.

10) Many companies are adopting the integrated marketing communication concept. Discuss two major problems that this marketing communication philosophy is designed to remedy.

———— Projects and teamwork ————

1. A small company that had developed an effective at-home hair-coloring system is considering using direct television. Would you recommend this medium? Why or why not?

2. Form a small group and choose three advertising media for a campaign to introduce a new line of women's personal care products under an Pechoin label.

3. In your judgment who would be the best and the worst celebrity endorsers for each of these products/services: Huawei, Florasis and the 2022 Winter Olympics.

4. With your team members, think of a nationally advertised product or service that has been running a consistent advertising message for a number of years. Search for several examples of print advertising for this brand from the back issues of the magazines.

   When you examine these ads closely, how consistent are the message content, structure and format?

   Which response(s) do you think that this campaign is seeking: awareness, knowledge, liking, preference, conviction or purchase?

   Do you think that the advertising campaign is successful in getting the desired responses? Why or why not?

─────────■ **Case study** ■─────────

Tsingtao Beer's Event Sponsorship

In August 1903, China's first brewery built with European technologies was opened in Qingdao, Shandong. After development of over a century, the brewery has turned into a world-renowned beer manufacturer—Tsingtao Beer.

I. "Passion, Dreams and Success" ("激情成就梦想") as brand value

The century-old brewery announced its new brand proposition "Passion, Dreams and Success", which caused a stir in the industry. According to the board chairman of Tsingtao Beer, the brand proposition was reflective of the brand's traditional culture of earnestness, enterprising spirits and self-improvement. It also resonated with the socialist values and added fires of passion and vitality to the brand. The proposition highlighting the importance of passion to dream and success was a strong cultural appeal to the young generation.

II. Sponsoring "China Dream" ("梦想中国")

On June 16, 2005, Tsingtao Beer announced its sponsorship of the second season of "China Dream"—a TV contest show hosted by CCTV. The show officially adopted the brand proposition "Passion, Dreams and Success" of Tsingtao Beer as the theme.

The cooperation benefited both sides. According to public statistics, the exclusive sponsorship of "China Dream" for half a year brought Tsingtao Beer handsome returns—the brand accurately, extensively spread its cultural value and shaped its brand image in the minds of consumers through the show. It is learned that product sales volume rose by at least 8% following the regional tryouts of the contest.

III. Sponsoring the 2008 Beijing Olympics

The Olympics has demanding requirements for sponsors, and, for years only globally influential enterprises had the chance to sponsor the sports event. Obtaining the sponsorship of the Beijing Olympics was reflective of Tsingtao Beer's superior product quality and sound corporate image, and this was a great chance to spread the cultural value of "Passion, Dreams and Success". Availing itself of the sponsorship, Tsingtao Beer intensified efforts in brand promotion, which reaped sound effects.

The value proposition "Passion, Dreams and Success" was in alignment with the slogan "One World, One Dream" of the 2008 Beijing Olympics. The cooperation between the brewery and the event was grounded on the alignment between Olympic spirits and the brand value.

An official of the Beijing Organizing Committee for the Olympic Games said in an address for the cooperation that hosting the Olympic Games was a century-old dream of the Chinese nation. Tsingtao Beer, as a century-aged business and a world-renowned brand, provided active support and endorsement for the games, which enhanced the Organizing Committee's confidence and determination in hosting the event. For over a hundred years, Tsingtao Beer made contributions to China-foreign exchanges. Its cultural quality centering on passion, openness and integrity would be a light spot of the Olympic culture.

Tsingtao Beer's sponsorship of the sports events is a typical case of event marketing. To conduct event marketing, enterprises should first measure the input-output ratio, because not every event marketing campaign can achieve good effects at low costs. Besides, every sponsorship should be aligned systematically with the idea of integrated marketing communications and be included into the planning of the whole event marketing. In nature, event marketing capitalizes on hot topics and events of media focus and public concerns. Playing a central role in hot topics or events increases the chances of being accepted and liked by the public.

Questions:

1. How did Tsingtao Beer become a sponsor of the sports events?

2. How did the event sponsorship benefit Tsingtao Beer?

3. Discuss the pros and cons of event sponsorship.

Chapter Ten
Marketing Planning

Objectives:

After studying this chapter, you should be able to:

- State the process of "marketing planning";
- Explain companywide strategic planning and its four steps;
- Conduct different kinds of "marketing analysis";
- Formulate "competitive strategies";
- Design strategies for the elements of "marketing mix";
- Understand the "implementation" and "control" of marketing planning.

Framework

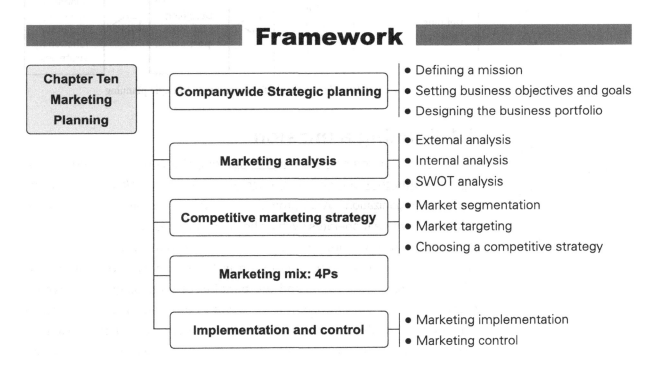

Throughout the book, we have examined the nature of marketing, the environmental context within which organizations operate, approaches to market information and market research, important decisions regarding segmentation, targeting, positioning and differentiation, and issues related to the 4Ps (product, price, place and promotion) in the marketing mix. This chapter brings all we have learned together to discuss marketing planning. Market planning is the process of organizing and defining the marketing

> ⊞ 营销策划是组织和确定公司的营销目标，发展营销战略和战术来实现营销目标的过程。

aims of a company and gathering strategies and tactics to achieve them. To begin, we look at the company's overall business portfolio. Next, we discuss how marketers conduct inside and outside environmental analyses for a company. We then examine the process of formulating competitive strategies and marketing mix. Finally, we look at the implementation and the control of marketing planning.

⊞ 公司整体战略规划是指公司建立和保持其目标和能力与不断变化的市场机会之间的战略匹配的过程。

1. Companywide strategic planning

Each company must find a suitable plan for long-run operation that makes the most sense given its specific situation, resources and opportunities. This is the focus of companywide strategic planning — the process of developing and maintaining a strategic fit between the organization's goals and capabilities and its changing marketing opportunities. The four steps of companywide strategic planning are: (1) defining a mission; (2) setting business objectives and goals; (3) designing a business portfolio; (4) planning marketing and other functional strategies (see Figure 10.1).

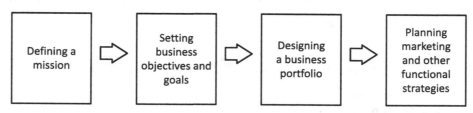

Figure 10.1 The process of companywide strategic planning

⊞ 使命陈述是关于公司在大环境下想要完成的远景目标的简要陈述。

1.1 Defining a mission

A mission statement is a short statement of a company's purpose for what it wants to accomplish in the larger environment. What is the overall goal of an organization? What product or service do we provide? Who is the customer? Where it operates? What should our business be?

A mission statement should be market-oriented and focuses on customer's need. A good illustration is Huawei's mission statement: "Huawei's mission is to expand the benefits of technology to everyone, everywhere." To achieve this, Huawei developed a digital inclusion strategy that focuses on three areas: technology, applications, and skills. Huawei believes that technology will make life better for every individual, home, and organization.

⊞ 企业短期目标和长期目标是在建立阶段性优先级别和让公司取得成功的重要组成部分。

1.2 Setting business objectives and goals

After defining a mission, the company needs to turn it into detailed objectives to support its each level of management. Each manager should be responsible for the achievement of the objectives. Business objectives and goals are an essential part of establishing priorities and setting company up for success over a set period of time. Huawei's business goal is to make itself more competitive, build trust among its customers, and survive market competition.

There is a hierarchy of objectives, including business objectives and marketing objectives. Huawei's overall objective is to build profitable customer relationships by developing advanced devices. To achieve this, more marketing objectives should be accomplished. The objectives of improving market shares, reducing selling costs and increasing profits can be important for different periods of time.

1.3 Designing the business portfolio

Guided by the company's mission statement and objectives, the company must begin to plan its business portfolio. A business portfolio is a company's set of investments, holdings, products, businesses and brands. A product portfolio is the product mix for market segments. Marketing managers attempt to make a product appeal to specific groups of people, called segments. A best portfolio can match the strengths and weaknesses to opportunities in the environment. Business portfolio planning includes two steps:

⊞ 业务组合是公司的一系列投资、控股、产品、业务和品牌的总和。

1) Analyzing its current business portfolio and deciding investments should be given to which product/business;

2) Forming the future portfolio by developing strategies for growth and downsizing.

To analyze current portfolio, the first issue is to identify and decide the key businesses of the company, which can be called the strategic business units. A strategic business unit (SBU) is a fully-functional unit of a business that has its own vision and direction. Typically, a strategic business unit operates as a separate unit, but it is also an important part of the company. Next, each SBU should be assessed to be given different supports it deserves. In this way, more resources can be given to valuable SBUs in a period of time. SBUs can also be evaluated, normally by portfolio-analysis methods on two aspects: 1) the attractiveness of the market or industry where the SBU operates; 2) the strengths of the SBU in that market or industry. The most popular approach of planning portfolio is developed by the Boston Consulting Group, a leading management consulting firm.

⊞ 战略业务单元是具有自己的愿景和方向的全功能业务单元。

Using the BCG matrix, a company analyzes all its SBUs according to the growth-share matrix. On the vertical axis, market growth rate provides a measure of market attractiveness. On the horizontal axis, relative market share serves as a measure of company strength in the market. The growth-share matrix defines four types of SBUs: stars, cash cows, question marks and dogs.

Once the company has classified its SBUs, it must determine what role each will play in the future. One of the four strategies can be applied to each

SBU. The company can invest more in the business to build its share. Or it can hold the market share of the SBU at the current level. Or it can harvest the SBU, getting short-term cash flow regardless of its long-term development. Or the company can also divest the SBU by selling it or phasing it out and using the resources elsewhere. As time passes, the positions of SBUs may change in the growth-share matrix.

田 为了抓住主要问题和重要机遇，公司有必要对营销环境、目标、战略和活动进行系统的检查。

2. Marketing analysis

<u>To identity key problems and opportunities, a systematic examination of a firm's marketing environment, objectives, strategies and activities is needed.</u> The marketing analysis is the basis on which a plan of action to improve marketing performance can be built. The marketing analysis gives answer to these questions:

- Where are we now?
- Where are we heading?
- How can we get there?

The answers to these questions depend on an analysis of the internal and external environments of a business. An external analysis focuses the forces that the company cannot control while an internal analysis concentrates on the areas and factor that are under control.

2.1 External analysis

External analysis covers the macroenvironment, the market and competition. The macroenvironment consists of board environmental issues that may impinge on the business. These include the economy, social/cultural issues, technological changes, political factors and ecological concerns.

Table 10.1 External marketing analysis checklist

Macroenvironment
Economic: inflation, interest rates, unemployment
Social/Cultural: age distribution, lifestyle changes, values, attitudes
Technological: new product and process technologies, materials
Political: monopoly control, new laws, regulations
Ecological: conservation, pollution, energy
The Market
Market: size, growth rates, trends and developments
Customers: who are they, the roles they play in the purchase decision making process, their choice criteria, how, when, where do they buy, how do they rate us vis-à-vis competition on product, promotion, price, distribution
Market segmentation: how are customers grouped, what benefits does each group seeks

Continued

Distribution: power changes, channel attractiveness, growth potential, physical distribution methods, decision-makers and influencers
Suppliers: who and where they are, their competences and shortcomings, trends affecting them, future outlook
Competition
Who are the major competitors: actual and potential
What are their objectives and strategies
What are their strengths (distinctive competences) and weaknesses (vulnerability analysis)
Market shares and size of competitors
Profitability analysis
Entry barriers
Operating results (by product, customer, geographic region)
Sales
Market share
Profit margins
Costs
Strategic issues analysis
Marketing objectives
Market segmentation
Competitive advantage
Core competences
Positioning
Portfolio analysis
Marketing operations, effectiveness
Product
Price
Promotion
Distribution
Marketing structures
Marketing organization
Marketing training
Intra-and interdepartmental communication
Marketing systems
Marketing information systems
Marketing planning system
Marketing control system

Statistical analyses

Market analysis consists of statistical analyses of market size, growth rate and trends and customer analysis. Also, distribution analysis includes important movements in power bases, channel attractiveness studies, an identification of physical distribution methods, and understanding of the role and interests of decision-makers, and influences within distributors.

Competitor analysis

Competitor analysis examines the nature of actual and potential competitors, and their objectives and strategies. It helps identify their strengths (distinctive competences), weaknesses (vulnerability analysis), market shares and size. A very popular and famous external analysis framework is <u>Porter's five forces model. Porter explored the reasons why some industries appeared to be inherently more profitable than others, and concluded the five forces that are related to industry attractiveness: the threat of new entrants; the threat of substitutes; the bargaining power of suppliers; the bargaining power of buyers; and the rivalry between existing competitors</u>. Each of these five forces, in turn, determines the strength of each force.

⊞ "波特的五力竞争模型"：解释了有些行业具有更高利润性的原因，总结出与行业吸引力相关的五大要素：新进入者的威胁、代替品的威胁、供应商的议价能力、购买者的议价能力、同业竞争者的竞争程度。

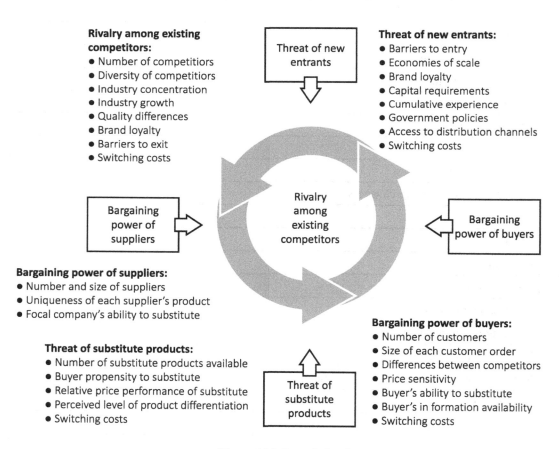

Figure 10.2 Porter's five forces model

● *The threat of new entrants*

Since new entrants can increase the level of competition in an industry, they have the potential to reduce the attractiveness. The threat of new entrants depends on the barriers to entry. Key entry barriers include:

— economies of scale

— capital requirements

— switching costs

— access to distribution channels, and

— others

● *The bargaining power of suppliers*

The cost of raw materials and components can be the largest part of costs of a company, influencing its profitability. Higher bargaining power of suppliers leads to higher costs. The bargaining power of suppliers will be high when:

— there are many buyers and few dominant suppliers

— they offer differentiated, highly valued products

— suppliers threaten to integrate forward into the industry

— buyers do not threaten to integrate backward into supply

— the industry is not a key customer group to the supplier

A firm can reduce the bargaining power of the supplier by looking for new sources of supply and designing standardized components so that many suppliers are able to produce them. A case in point is the e-book reader industry a decade ago. For a very long time, e-book readers were sold at high prices though the manufacturing process which was neither technology-intensive nor technically complicated. The reason lies in the fact that an oligopolist controlled the supply of ink needed in making e-book readers throughout the world, and it charged manufacturers of e-book readers very high price for its ink.

● *The bargaining power of buyers*

The power relationship between buyers and suppliers can affect the attractiveness of an industry. However, it should be pointed out that such relationship will change over time. The bargaining power of buyers can be greater when:

— there are few dominant buyers and many sellers

— products are standardized

— buyers threaten to integrate backward into the industry

— suppliers do not threaten to integrate forward into the buyer's industry

— the industry is not a key supplying group for buyers

● *The threat of substitutes*

Substitute products can lower industry attractiveness and profitability because they influence the price levels. The invention of e-cigarettes foreseeably casts influence on the tobacco industry. The threat of substitute products depends on:

— buyer's willingness to substitute

— the relative prices and performance of substitutes

— the costs of switching to substitutes

The threat of substitutes can be reduced by building up switching costs.

● *Rivalry among existing competitors*

The intensity of competition between competitors in an industry depends on the following factors:

— *Structure of competition*: There is more intense competition when there are a larger number of competitors or a few equally balanced competitors; there is less intense rivalry when a clear leader (at least 50% larger than the second) exists with a larger cost advantage.

— *Structure of cost*: High fixed costs encourage price cutting to fill capacity.

— *Degree of differentiation*: Highly differentiated products are difficult to copy that are associated with less rivalry.

— *Switching costs*: When a product is specialized, switching costs are high and rivalry is reduced.

— *Strategic objectives*: Competition is likely to be more intense when a company is playing hold or harvest strategies.

— *Exit barrier*: When the exit barriers are low, rivalry will be more intense.

2.2 Internal analysis

An internal analysis is the thorough examination of a company's internal components, both tangible and intangible, such as resources, assets and processes. It helps the company decision-makers accurately identify areas for growth or for rectification to form a practical business strategy or business plan. Resource analysis is a way firms understand an organization's competencies and the value of resources. Resource includes tangible and intangible resources. Human resource, financial resource, physical resource, organization resource, etc. are tangible resources and technological resource and reputation, etc. are intangible resources. A firm should identify and understand the current status of all the resources, and it has to make good use of them.

> ⊞ 资源分析是企业了解其能力和资源价值的一种方法。资源分析涵盖有形资源和无形资源。

To be competitive in the market, a firm should have its core competences. Perhaps the most important part of a core competency is that it needs to be as unique and difficult to replicate as possible. In a competitive market, competition is going to quickly recognize what it is a firm is doing that allows it to have success, and they are then going to imitate that element of the business as soon as they can. An important issue is that the core competences need to be relevant to target customers in order to make a difference to target customers at the end of the day. If the competencies don't actually have any impact on the customers, they really aren't going to help the company rise above the competition.

2.3 SWOT analysis

A structured approach to evaluating the strategic position of a business by identifying its strengths, weaknesses, opportunities and threats is known as a SWOT analysis. It provides insights into the external (opportunity and threat) and internal forces (strength and weakness) of a firm.

Some guidelines must be followed when using a SWOT analysis. <u>First, not only absolute, but also relative strengths and weaknesses should be identified</u>. Compared to competitors, relative strengths and weaknesses are identified. Strengths can be both absolute and relative, but they need to be looked at objectively as they can sometimes turn into weaknesses. Also, an absolute weakness of competitors should be identified because it can be a source of relative strength if overcome. Second, opportunities and threats should be listed as they review the performance of the trends outside the business.

⊞ 在 SWOT 分析中，分析的不仅仅是绝对优势和弱点，也需要分析相对优势和弱点。

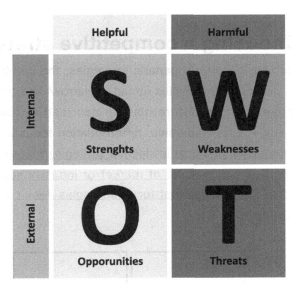

Figure 10.3 SOWT framework

SWOT analysis is a useful tool not only for making decisions in business contexts, but also for decision making in daily scenarios. An important step in SWOT analysis is to try the best to list all items under "S", "W", "O" and "T", and to measure the weight of each item.

3. Competitive marketing strategy

⊞ 营销策略明确目标市场，以及基于对最佳市场机会的分析而提出的价值主张。

<u>The marketing strategy lays out target markets and the value proposition that will be offered based on an analysis of the best market opportunities</u>. It is the logic by which the business unit hopes to achieve its goal and objectives.

3.1 Market segmentation

The company decides which customers it will serve (segmentation and targeting) and how it serves them. It identifies the total market, then divides it into smaller segments, select the most promising segments and focuses on serving and satisfying customers in the chosen segments. Through market segmentation, companies divide large, heterogeneous markets into smaller segments that can be reached more efficiently and effectively with products and services that better match their needs. Market segmentation also provides smaller businesses with an opportunity to find out and operate in niche segments.

3.2 Market targeting

After the possible market segments and opportunities have been identified, the next step is deciding which and how many segments to target. When evaluating different market segments, two factors must be considered: the segment's overall attractiveness and the company's objectives and resources. The five types of targeting decisions are: undifferentiated marketing, differentiated marketing, focused marketing, customized marketing and mass customization.

田根据"波特的一般战略"，差异化战略和成本领先战略注重在广大市场和行业领域中的竞争优势，而差异化聚焦战略和成本聚焦战略则侧重在较小的细分市场中寻求能力发展。

3.3 Choosing a competitive strategy

According to Porter's generic strategies, the combination of the scope of competitive activities (broad vs narrow) and two competitive advantages (cost vs differentiation) can lead to four strategies: differentiation, cost leadership, differentiation focus and cost focus. <u>The differentiation and cost leadership strategies focus on competitive advantage in a board range of market or industry segments, while differentiation focus and cost focus strategies seek competence in a narrow segment.</u>

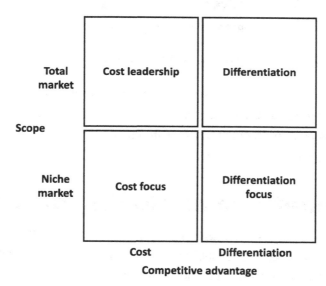

Figure 10.4 Porter's generic strategies

Differentiation

A differentiation strategy focuses on providing a product or a service with distinctive attributes, in comparison with the competition, to reach a broad market. To differentiate the offering can lead to a price premium because it gives the customers a reason to prefer one product over another. But it can also be a risky strategy. It needs high-level investments which may not necessarily guarantee successful differentiation.

Cost leadership

The cost leadership strategy aims to achieve to the lowest cost position in an industry. It is difficult to deploy the strategy because the management must constantly work on reducing cost at every level to remain cost-competitive. Although, it is highly effective in gaining market share as well as drawing the customers' attention, it is difficult to use this strategy for a long time. The management team of the company has to constantly reduce the cost of not just one product, but the entire product portfolio. Cost leadership does not mean that a company produces goods which are of inferior quality at comparatively lower prices. The strategy of sacrificing quality for price cut will ultimately lead to failure. To deploy the cost leadership strategy, a company has to produce/sell goods which are of acceptable quality and capable of satisfying specific needs of a set of customers at a price which is much lower than other competitors. A famous cost leader in China is Xiaomi. A balance of fair price and acceptable product (at the core, actual and augmented levels) leads to its popularity among young people.

Differentiation focus

Differentiation focus is an approach to competitive advantage in which a company attempts to outperform its rivals by offering a product that is perceived by consumers to be superior to that of competitors even though its price is higher; in adopting a differentiation focus strategy, the company focuses on narrow market coverage, seeking only to attract a small, specialized segment. Apple's MacBook adopts the differentiation focus strategy.

Cost focus

In the cost focus strategy, a firm seeks a cost advantage in its target segment, while in differentiation focus a firm seeks differentiation in its target segment. Both variants of the focus strategy rest on differences between a focuser's target segment and other segments in the industry. Cost focus exploits differences in cost behavior in some segments, while differentiation focus exploits the special needs of buyers in certain segments.

4. Marketing mix: 4Ps

To carry out the marketing functions, the firm needs to develop a marketing program or strategy. In 1953, Neii Borden first introduced the concept of marketing mix. The marketing mix refers to the set of actions or tactics that a company uses to promote its brand or product in the market. The 4Ps make up a typical marketing mix — price, product, promotion and place. However, nowadays, the marketing mix increasingly includes several other Ps like packaging, positioning, people and even politics as vital mix elements.

Figure 10.5 Marketing mix: 4Ps

Price

Price refers to the value that is put for a product. It depends on costs of production, value perceived by customers, segments targeted, ability of the market to pay, supply–demand relationship and a host of other direct and indirect factors. There can be several types of pricing strategies, each tied with an overall business plan. Pricing can also be used as a basis to differentiate and enhance the image of a product.

Product

In the marketing terms, product refers to both tangible and intangible offerings that can satisfy customer needs and provide value for customers. The product must deliver a minimum level of performance; otherwise even the best work on the other elements of the marketing mix won't do any good.

Place

Place refers to the point of sale and the distribution channel. In every industry, catching eyeballs of consumers and making it easy for them to buy it is the main task of a good "place" strategy. Consumers are often willing to pay premiums for accessible goods. That is why retailers pay premium rents for the right location. In fact, the mantra of a successful retail business is location.

Promotion

Promotion refers to all the activities undertaken to make the product or service known to the user and trade. The core of promotion is communication — sending the right message to the right audience in a right way. This can include advertising, word of mouth, publicity, public relations, and sales techniques like discount, incentives, commissions and awards to the trade, as well as consumer schemes, direct marketing, contests and prizes.

All the elements of the marketing mix influence each other. They make up the business plan for a company. If handled right, the marketing mix can give it great success. But handled wrong, the business could take years to recover. The marketing mix needs a lot of understanding, market research and communication with stakeholders, from users to trade to manufacturing and several others.

5. Implementation and control

In achieve marketing success, companies need to pay attention to marketing management. Managing the marketing process requires not only the analysis and planning but also the implementation and control process.

5.1 Marketing implementation

An outstanding marketing strategy counts for little if the company cannot implement it correctly. Marketing implementation is the process of applying the marketing plan and assigning team members to accomplish it, setting deadlines to complete tasks to achieve marketing goals and objectives. While marketing planning addresses what and why of marketing activities, implementation addresses the who, where, when and how.

In this stage, many managers focus on "doing things right" (implementation), instead of "doing the right things" (planning). Implementation deals with the process of bringing life to the marketing plan. The marketing plan starts to live on a daily calendar instead of living on papers. Marketing implementation translates it into action. Marketing implementation mainly involves the following 6 steps: 1) setting exact expectations for getting things done quickly; 2) determining the required resources for executing the plan; 3) documenting a marketing strategy; 4) building a workflow to execute every piece of content; 5) having a plan to manage projects; 6) measuring the results.

⊞ 营销实施是实施营销计划，分配团队成员执行计划任务，设定完成任务的期限，以实现营销目标的过程。

5.2 Marketing control

Since many accidents may happen during the implementation of marketing, managers must practice constant marketing control. Marketing control is a process where the company management or executives analyze and assess their marketing activities and programs and taking corrective actions to ensure objectives are fulfilled. In this stage, marketing goals first are set and management then measure its performance in the marketplace and evaluate the issues of any differences between expected and actual performance. According to this evaluation, management takes corrective actions to reduce deviations and steer all efforts towards the goal.

⊞ 营销控制是公司管理人员分析和评估他们的营销活动和计划，并采取纠正措施以确保目标实现的过程。

Summary

In Chapter 10 we bring what we have learned in the previous chapters together to make marketing plans. Each organization needs a strategic plan for its sustainable long-term development. There are several steps in companywide strategic planning: 1) defining a mission; 2) setting business objectives and goals; 3) designing a business portfolio; 4) planning marketing and other functional strategies. The company first has to make a mission statement—a short statement of a company's purpose for what it wants to accomplish in the larger environment. Business objectives and goals are important to business success over a period of time. For designing business portfolio, we introduced a key concept—strategic business unit (SBU), which refers to a fully-functional unit of a business that has its own vision and direction. The BCG matrix is a useful tool to classify a firm's SBUs. Whether a company is to invest, to hold, to harvest or to divest a SBU depends on whether it is a star, question mark, cash cow or dog in the BCG matrix.

Before making marketing planning, a firm

needs to make marketing analysis, both external and internal analysis. External analysis covers the macroenvironment, the market and competition. Specific elements to be examined under each category are listed. For competitor analysis, the Porter's five forces model is introduced. The model concludes five forces that are related to industry attractiveness: the threat of new entrants; the threat of substitutes; the bargaining power of suppliers; the bargaining power of buyers; and the rivalry between existing competitors. Internal analysis covers both tangible and intangible components of a company, such as resources, assets and processes. To be competitive in the market, a company must develop its core competence. SWOT analysis is a useful tool to frame favorable and unfavorable, internal and external elements relevant to decision making. SWOT analysis is widely applied in business contexts.

Another important task for companies is to develop competitive marketing strategy. There are several steps to develop a marketing strategy: segmentation (dividing up the whole market into smaller segments), targeting (choosing which segment(s) to serve), positioning (deciding the position of your offering/brand in the minds of consumers) and differentiation (deciding what marketing offerings that best serve target customers). The Porter's generic strategies classifies competitive strategies into four types according to the scope of competitive activities (broad vs narrow) and the competitive advantages (cost vs differentiation): differentiation, cost leadership, differentiation focus and cost focus. The next step is to design the marketing mix: product, price, place and promotion. The details about the designing of these four elements are provided in the previous chapters in this book.

Once a marketing plan is drawn up, the next step is to implement it and to control the implementation process. For the planning stage, what's important is "doing the right things"; for the implementation stage, companies focus on "doing things right". Marketing control is to track the implementation process, analyze and assess the marketing activities and take corrective measures where necessary.

Key terms

companywide strategic planning	SWOT analysis
mission statement	Porter's generic strategies
business portfolio	marketing implementation
strategic business unit (SBU)	marketing control
Porter's five forces model	

Exercises

Review and discussion

1. Make word combinations with "market" and "marketing" using words from the box. Then match the word combinations with the definitions below.

methods	mix	plan	segments	strategy	target

_____ 1) groups of consumers with similar needs or purchasing desires

_____ 2) the consumers, clients or customers you want to attract

_____ 3) a definition of the company, the product/service and the competition

_____ 4) detailed information about how to fulfil the marketing strategy

_____ 5) the techniques you can use to communicate with your consumers

_____ 6) the combination of different elements used to market a product or service

2. The extracts below are from a SWOT analysis. Do they describe strengths, weaknesses, opportunities or threats?

1) Competition is growing in this market, which could lead to a price war. There are now a lot of sites that offer the same service and product categories as Amazon. Amazon is a global brand but in some local markets the main competitor could be stronger and preferred by consumers.

2) Amazon has added a lot of new categories, but this may damage the brand. For example, offering automobiles may be confusing for customers. Due to increased competition, the offer is undifferentiated.

3) In 2004 Amazon moved into the Chinese market. There is hug potential here. In 2005 Amazon launched a new loyalty program, AmazonePrime, which should maximize purchases from the existing client base.

4) Amazon is a global brand, operating in over ten countries. It was one of the first online retailers and today it has an enormous customer base. It has built on early success with books, and now has product categories that include jewelry, toys and games, food and more. It has an innovative customer relationship management program.

3. Complete the table first. Then complete the sentences below using words from the table.

Verb	Noun	Adjective
		opportune
strengthen		
threaten		
weaken		

1) Currently, the company is under _____ from its main competitors.

2) In order to grow, the company will have to create new _____, not just exploit existing _____.

3) We need to minimize _____ and _____.

4) To remain ahead of the competition we will need to anticipate _____ such as increased raw material costs.

4. Match the examples (1-4) with the marketing analysis (a-d).

_____ 1) Your customer groups or segments—for example, teenagers or business people.

_____ 2) Information on the competitors and the marketplace.

_____ 3) What you sell or provide, and your unique selling point—that is, what distinguishes your product or service from others on the market.

_____ 4) The competition in the marketplace. You will also need to include information on their positioning—how they control the way the customers see the products or services.

a. Current market situation analysis

b. Competitor analysis

c. Product/Service analysis

d. Target market analysis

5. Translate the following sentences into English.

1) 企业使命反映企业的目的、特征和性质。明确企业使命，就是对本企业是干什么的、本企业应该是怎么样的两个问题进行思考和解答。

_____

_____

2) 企业高层必须对各个经营单位及其业务进行评估和分类，确认它们的发展潜力，决定投资结构。在规划投资组合方面，波士顿矩阵广为应用。

_____

_____

3) 投资组合战略决定的是哪些经营单位需要发展、扩大，哪些应当收割、舍弃。

_____

_____

4) 从广义上说，某个行业内的所有厂商都在与生产替代产品的行业进行竞争。替代产品所提供的价格越是吸引人，则对行业利润的限制越大。

_____

_____

5) 企业是在市场竞争中壮大发展的，只有在激烈的市场竞争中有效地实施正确的竞争战略，才能战胜竞争对手来发展自己。

_____

_____

6. Answer the following questions briefly.

1) Discuss some of the difficulties that can be encountered in making marketing planning work in an organization. How can these difficulties be overcome?

2) Discuss the role and limitations of the external analysis phase of marketing planning.

3) Explain companywide strategic planning and its four steps.

4) Discuss how to formulate "competitive strategies".

─────── Projects and teamwork ───────

Suppose you are a marketing manager in a mobile phone company. You have made notes while preparing a marketing plan for a product or a service. Answer the following questions in relation to this product or service.

Questions to ask

1) How can I best define my business? What kind of company are we? Are my objectives SMART?

   SMART:

   Specific—Be precise about what you are going to achieve.

   Measurable—Quantify your objectives.

   Achievable—Are you attempting too much?

   Realistic—Do you have the resources to make the objective happen (manpower, money, machines, materials, minutes)?

   Timed—When will you achieve the objective? (Within a month?)

2) Should I focus on repeat business, thereby keeping the customers we've got, or should I focus on gaining new customers?

3) Do my customers share any patterns, habits or repetitive behaviors? For example, do they all shop in the same kinds of shops?

4) Are there any market segments or groups of consumers that are underserved—not provided for enough or at all?

5) Is the product or service viable? Will it make a profit?

6) Is it accessible? Is it easy for the audience to get or start using?

7) How well did previous marketing methods work?

8) Which marketing mediums, or communication channels, are best for my audience?

9) Should I use a cross-section of media or should I just focus on one medium?

10) Can I time my marketing campaigns to coincide with seasonal sales or product launches?

11) How much is the cost compared to sales? Are we making enough money to cover our costs?

12) How can I get feedback from my audience?

Case study

OPPO's Advertising Campaign

As a global corporation, OPPO sells products to the US, Europe, Japan, South Korea and other Southeast Asian countries and regions. To better introduce its smartphones into the overseas markets, OPPO constructed a selling network that covers the whole world. It not only input large quantities of manpower and resources into product development and innovation, but also invested lots of money into brand building and product placement. The aggressive moves in terms of technology and advertising turned OPPO into a top–range electronic device brand in China.

I. Precise product positioning

Since the reform and opening–up, China's economy has been developing rapidly and the living standards of the Chinese people are on the rise. Demands for and dependence on electronic products are increasing. Under the context of the rapid economic development, smartphones have huge user base and big market potentials. The smartphone market also features fierce competition from both foreign and domestic brands. Therefore, it is important for OPPO to design differential product advantages for specific groups. In the current buyer's market, the good market performance of OPPO can be partly attributed to its segmentation, targeting and brand positioning strategies, which also laid down a solid ground for future promotion.

The music phones of the OPPO Real series launched in August 2008 were intensively advertised on its superior sound effects and elegant, fashionable styles, quickly gaining consumer likings. The Ulike series launched in December 2009 was also well received by the market. Both the series targeted young women. Though the two series targeted the same broad segment, they were differentiated from one another. Compared with OPPO Real, Ulike was priced higher and had more mature designs in appearance. OPPO Real targeted younger campus girls who liked bright colors and stylish designs, while Ulike targeted office ladies who liked classic and elegant designs. OPPO covered the young women group with the two series.

II. Product placement in TV shows

With the advancement in telecommunication and Internet technologies, OPPO put relentless efforts into R&D and innovation. The Find series was launched for young men. OPPO's advertising strategy is characterized by the use of diversified, extensive channels for information spread so that the advertised products can be noticed and remembered by the audience in the era of information explosion.

First, the extensive launch of high-quality commercials deeply implanted the brand image of OPPO in the minds of consumers. Under the context of fierce market competition, OPPO invested massively into advertisements, most of which were aired during peak hours on Zhejiang TV, Hunan TV, CCTV and other mainstream channels. In spite of high advertising costs, these TV channels boasted a large number of loyal viewers during prime time, guaranteeing sound communication effects.

Another reason for airing commercials on the mainstream TV channels lied in the high positioning of the media vehicles, which was beneficial to brand enhancement of OPPO. To achieve better promotional effects, the brand chose the interactive "online + offline" mode of advertising, creating viral word-of-mouth. Apart from intensive advertising, OPPO continued to upgrade and innovate its products to keep the brand vibrant.

Second, OPPO because the sponsor of several popular TV shows such as "Happy Camp" of Hunan TV, "If You Are the One" of Jiangsu TV and "Keep Running" of Zhejiang TV. The OPPO phones were ubiquitously present in these entertainment programs as props and prizes. As these hot TV shows are extensively watched by the young generation, advertising on them is in alignment with the brand's marketing concept of "pursuing beauty", brand positioning and target audiences. The sponsorship of the entertainment shows targeting young people helped OPPO go viral, thus building a solid market ground for brand development.

Questions:

1. What have you learned from OPPO's successful advertising strategies?

2. Try to develop a refined advertising program for OPPO.

Glossary

Chapter One The Nature of Marketing

- 市场营销（marketing）：通过为客户创造和传递价值来满足和超越客户需求，从而实现企业经营目标的过程。
- 以客户为导向（customer orientation）：一切营销活动围绕满足客户，为客户创造、沟通和传递价值。
- 需要（need）：是人类感觉到的缺乏某种东西的状态。
- 欲求（want）：是在文化和个体因素共同影响下的人类需要的表现形式。
- 需求（demand）：有购买力支撑的欲求就变成需求。
- 客户满意度（customer satisfaction）：当感知价值达到或超过客户的期望时，他们就会感到满意。
- 客户关系管理（customer relationship management）：通过为客户提供卓越的价值和使客户满意来建立和维持具有营利性的客户关系。
- 客户资产（customer equity）：是指公司所有现有顾客和潜在顾客终身所带来的价值的总和。
- 营销组合（marketing mix）：通常包括 4Ps，即产品、价格、地点和促销。
- 社会营销（societal marketing）：社会营销力求在社会（人类福祉）、客户（满意）和公司（利润）之间取得平衡。
- 关系营销（relationship marketing）：是指为了共同利益而与客户个人、供应商、员工、社区、政府机构和其他利益相关者建立起长期的、增值的、具有成本效益的关系。
- 病毒式营销（viral marketing）：是指在营销中有效利用互联网达到快速传播的效果。

Chapter Two The Global Marketing Environment

- 微观环境（microenvironment）：由公司直接环境或业务系统中的参与者组成，这些参与者影响其在所选市场中有效运营的能力。
- 宏观环境（macroenvironment）：由多种宏观力量组成，这些力量不仅影响公司，而且影响微观环境中的其他参与者。
- PEST：是代表宏观环境中四大主要力量的首字母缩写词——政治（P）、经济（E）、社会（S）和技术（T）。
- 政治环境（political environment）：由影响或限制特定社会中的组织和个人的法律、政府机构及压力团体组成。
- 税收（taxation）：政府用来调整收入分配的工具之一。
- 通货膨胀（inflation）：衡量一个经济体中的生活成本的指标。
- 人口统计学（demographics）：是对人口规模、密度、位置、年龄、性别、种族、职业和其他人口维度的研究。
- 企业社会责任（corporate social responsibility）：是指个人或组织应该对其行为影响自然环境和公众负责的伦理原则。
- 营销伦理（marketing ethics）：是影响个人或团体行为和决定的道德原则和价值观。

- 消费者运动（consumer movement）：消费者运动涉及维护消费者权益的个人、团体和组织。
- 技术环境（technological environment）：包括创造新技术的力量、创造新的产品和市场机会。
- 环境评析（environmental scanning）：营销人员需要监控和分析宏观环境和微观环境中的所有因素和行动。

Chapter Three Understanding Customer Behavior

- 发起者（initiator）：发起购买决策过程的人。
- 影响者（influencer）：试图就购买决策结果说服他人的人。
- 决策者（decider）：拥有权力和 / 或经济能力就购买做出最终决定的人。
- 购买者（buyer）：进行交易的人。
- 使用者（user）：产品的实际消费者或使用者。
- 纠缠力（pester power）：孩子们隐蔽地影响或公开地纠缠父母使其购买他们想要的产品的能力。
- 复杂型购买行为（complex buying behavior）：当消费者高度参与购买决策过程并感知到不同选择之间的巨大差异时，他们会产生复杂的购买行为。
- 和谐型购买行为（dissonance-reducing buying behavior）：当消费者高度参与购买决策过程，这种购买通常是昂贵的、不常发生的或有风险的，他们几乎看不出不同选择之间的差异时，就会产生这种购买行为。
- 多变型购买行为（variety-seeking behavior）：其特点是消费者参与程度低，但消费者能够感知到不同选择之间的显著差异。
- 习惯型购买行为（habitual buying behavior）：消费者习惯性地购买东西，参与度低，且不同选择之间几乎没有差异。
- 消费者的参与程度（consumers' level of involvement）：指他们参与购买决策过程的程度。
- 自我形象（self-image）：当购买可能影响一个人的自我形象时，消费者的参与度相对较高。
- 感知风险（perceived risk）：当感知到购买犯错所带来的风险较高时，消费者的参与度相对较高。
- 社会因素（social factor）：当个人是否被社会接受取决于其做出正确的购买选择时，消费者的参与度相对较高。
- 享乐影响（hedonistic influence）：当购买带来高度的快乐或保证未来的幸福时，消费者参与度通常较高。
- 需要抑制因素（need inhibitor）：阻止消费者从意识到需要进入购买决策过程下一个阶段的事物。
- 内部搜寻（internal search）：消费者从记忆中检索基于个人经验和营销传播所获得的信息。
- 认知集（awareness set）：一系列进入消费者认知的品牌和产品。
- 诱发集（evoked set）：供消费者认真考虑和仔细评估的候选品牌和产品清单。
- 从众心态（herd mentality）：是指人群中的个体成员放弃他们的个人意志，与感知到的大众统一意愿趋同的现象。
- 认知失调（cognitive dissonance）：购买者在购买某样商品后对所选品牌的缺点，及其他被放弃的选择的好处而感到担忧或不安。
- 动机（motive）：当需要有足够的强度时就变成了动机。
- 信仰（belief）：是个人对某事所持有的描述性想法。
- 态度（attitude）：是个人对某个事物或观点的相对稳定的评价、感觉和倾向。

- 信息处理（information processing）：人们接收、解读刺激，并将刺激存储在记忆中，随后进行检索的过程。
- 感知（perception）：是人们选择、组织和解释信息以赋予这个世界意义的过程。
- 选择性注意（selective attention）：是指人们筛选掉他们所接触到的大部分信息的倾向。
- 选择性失真（selective distortion）：是指人们倾向于用自己一贯的思维来解释信息。
- 选择性保留（selective retention）：意味着消费者很可能会记住他们喜欢的品牌的优点，而忘记竞争品牌的优点。
- 参照群体（reference group）：是指影响个人态度或行为的一群人。
- 技术标准（technical criteria）：与产品或服务的性能表现有关，例如可靠性、耐用性、性能、风格、舒适度、交付、便利性和品位。
- 经济标准（economic criteria）：涉及价格、运营成本和残值（例如汽车的以旧换新抵价）。
- 社会标准（social criteria）：关于某项购买对个人感知到的与他人关系的影响，以及社会规范对个人的影响。
- 个人标准（personal criteria）：关于产品或服务与个人心理的关联。

Chapter Four Marketing Information and Marketing Research

- 营销信息系统 （marketing information system /MIS）：涵盖及时准确地收集、整理、分析、评估和分发所需信息给营销决策者的人员、设备和程序。
- 客户关系管理（customer relationship management/CRM）系统：整合各部门信息，并提供给所有与客户打交道的员工。
- 营销情报（marketing intelligence）：涉及系统地收集和分析关于竞争对手和市场变化的公开信息。
- 营销调研（marketing research）：是指一家组织对其所面对的市场环境的相关数据进行系统的设计、收集、分析和汇报。
- 二手数据（secondary data）：是指现成的信息，该信息是他人为其他目的而开发的，作为二手信息为营销人员所获得。
- 一手数据（primary data）：是指研究人员为了当前具体情况或目的而主动收集的信息。
- 样本（sample）：是指在营销研究中被选中代表整个群体的一部分人群。
- 定性研究（qualitative research）：是指对小样本的深入研究，目的是深入了解客户行为、态度和感受等。
- 定量研究（quantitative research）：通过研究或大或小的样本，定量研究侧重于系统地收集大量可量化的数据，并得出统计结论。
- 观察法（observation）：是指不干预过程地观察人们、人们的行动和情况来收集一手数据。
- 人种学研究（ethnographic research）：包括派遣训练有素的观察员在消费者的自然生活环境中观察他们并与他们互动。
- 深度访谈（in-depth interview）：也称为单独访谈（individual interview），涉及就单一主题深入面谈单个客户，面谈可在他们的家中或办公室、街道或商场中进行。
- 小组访谈（group interview）：是由主持人（研究人员）对一组客户进行的非结构化或半结构化面谈。由于主持人通常将小组讨论聚焦在某些主题上，因此也称为焦点小组访谈（focus group interview）。
- 调研（survey）：是指通过向一组受访者询问调查问题来收集信息的定量方法。

- 简单随机抽样（simple random sampling）：样本是随机选择的，每个个体被选中的机会均等。
- 分层随机抽样（stratified random sampling）：首先将总体划分为组或类别，然后从每个组中随机抽取样本。
- 配额抽样（quota sampling）：首先将总体划分为类别，然后从每个类别中选取配额内的个体。
- 接触点（touch point）：是指客户与公司之间的每一次接触。
- 客户关系管理（customer relationship management/CRM）：是指管理详细的客户信息并细致管理客户的"接触点"，以最大限度地提高客户的忠诚度。

Chapter Five Segmentation, Targeting, Positioning and Differentiation

- 市场细分（segmentation）：将市场划分为具有特定需要、特征或行为的较小客户群体，不同的群体需要单独的产品或营销组合。
- 生活方式细分（lifestyle segmentation）：旨在根据人们的生活方式对消费者进行分类；生活方式反映在人们的日常活动、兴趣和看法中。
- 按人口统计细分（demographic segmentation）：是根据诸如年龄、性别、家庭规模、家庭所处生命周期阶段、收入、职业、教育、宗教、种族、世代、国籍等标准将市场划分为多个群体。
- 目标市场确定（targeting）：是指评估每个细分市场的吸引力并选择一个或多个细分市场进行服务的过程。
- 无差异营销/大众营销策略（undifferentiated marketing /mass marketing）：是指公司决定忽略细分市场之间的差异，以一种营销组合来应对整个市场的策略。
- 集中化营销/利基营销策略（focused/concentrated/ niche marketing）：是指公司追求单独的细分市场或利基市场的大部分市场份额。
- 定制营销/个体营销/一对一营销策略（customized marketing /individual marketing/one-to-one marketing）：是指企业与广大顾客一对一地互动，以设计出满足个人需要和偏好的产品和服务的过程。
- 形象重新定位（image repositioning）：指保持产品和目标市场相同，但是改变产品的形象。
- 产品重新定位（product repositioning）：推出不同的产品以满足同一目标群体的需求。
- 无形的重新定位（intangible repositioning）：是指保持产品不变，但是改变细分目标市场。
- 有形的重新定位（tangible repositioning）：当产品和目标市场都改变时，就是"有形的重新定位"。

Chapter Six Products, Services and Brands

- 产品（product）：在营销专业中，"产品"这个术语不仅仅指有形的物体，指的是任何具有价值且能够满足顾客需要的东西。
- 核心产品（core product）：包括人们通过购买特定产品或服务寻求满足需要或解决问题的核心好处。
- 实际产品（actual product）：由产品功能、产品设计、产品质量、品牌名称和产品包装构成。
- 外延产品（augmented product）：围绕核心产品和实际产品为消费者提供的额外好处，构成了外延产品。
- 产品线（product line）：由一组功能和提供的好处相近的产品组成。
- 产品组合（product mix/ portfolio）：一家公司的所有产品构成了它的产品组合。

- 产品线长度（the length of the product line）：是指一条产品线内的产品数量。
- 产品组合宽度（the width of the product mix）：是指公司拥有的产品线数量。
- 产品组合规划（portfolio planning）：管理好产品以保持每个产品线长度适中和产品组合宽度适中，这个过程被称为"产品组合规划"。
- 波士顿矩阵（BCG matrix）：是一种投资组合规划方法，旨在帮助公司根据市场增长率和相对市场份额做出关于产品组合和/或产品线的决策。
- 明星产品（star）：是指高增长、高市场份额的业务或产品。
- 现金牛产品（cash cow）：是指低增长市场，但公司占有高市场份额的业务或产品。
- 问题产品/问题儿童（question marks /problem child）：是指高增长市场中，公司占有市场份额低的业务或产品。
- 瘦狗产品（dog）：是指市场增长低且占有市场份额低的弱势产品。
- 产品生命周期（product life cycle/ PLC）：是指一个产品在其生命周期内，销售额和利润将经历的各个阶段。
- 引入期（introduction）：是指随着产品投入市场，销售缓慢增长的时期。
- 增长期（growth）：是指市场迅速接受、销售额和利润增长的时期。
- 成熟期（maturity）：在某个时点，产品的销售额增长将达到峰值，然后放缓，产品进入成熟期。
- 衰退期（decline）：当新技术出现，或消费者的品位或偏好发生变化时，产品就会进入衰退期，销量额下降、利润下降。
- 新产品研发过程（new product development process）：典型的新产品研发过程包括七个阶段：创意产生、创意筛选、概念测试、商业分析、产品研发、市场测试和产品商品化。
- 品牌（brand）：品牌不仅仅是名称和符号，它代表了消费者对产品及其性能的看法和感受——即产品或服务对消费者意味着的一切东西。
- 品牌领域（brand domain）：即品牌的目标市场。
- 品牌价值（brand value）：品牌的核心价值和特征。
- 品牌认同（brand reflection）：品牌与消费者自我认同的关系，即顾客如何通过购买或使用该品牌来看待自己。
- 品牌个性（brand personality）：用人、动物或物体来描述品牌的特性。
- 品牌资产（brand assets）：品牌与其他竞争品牌的区别（符号、口号、特征、图像、关系等）。
- 品牌继承（brand heritage）：品牌的背景和文化。
- 品牌延伸（brand extension）：是指在同一市场领域内，将已有的品牌名用于新产品或新产品类别。
- 品牌扩张（brand stretching）：是指在不相关的市场中使用已有的品牌。
- 品牌国际化（global branding/ standardized branding）：指在全球范围内某个品牌采用统一的营销策略。
- 品牌本土化（localized branding）：是指品牌的营销和管理决策根据当地市场的特点和具体情况而定。
- 服务（service）：被定义为行为、付出和表现，而非物体、装置或事物。
- 无形性（intangibility）：指服务在被购买和体验之前是无法被看到、感到、听到或闻到的。
- 不可分离性（inseparability）：服务的产生和消费是同时进行的，且服务不能与其提供者分开。
- 变化性（variability）：意味着服务质量取决于提供服务的人以及提供服务的时间、地点和方式。
- 易消失性（perishability）：意味着服务不能保存以供日后销售或使用；未使用的服务能力无法保留，服务本身无法存储。

- 关系营销（relationship marketing）：与顾客建立良好关系，使他们长期持续购买公司产品或服务，这个过程称为"关系营销"。

Chapter Seven Pricing

- 固定成本（fixed cost）：是指不随生产或销售量变化的成本，如物业维护费、管理人员工资、折旧、租金等。

- 可变成本（varible cost）：是指随生产或销售水平变化而变化的成本，如流水线工人的工资、材料和包装成本等。

- 基于成本定价法（cost-based pricing）：是一种典型的定价方法，根据生产、分销和销售产品所产生的所有成本加上合理的利润空间来确定价格。

- 基于价值定价法（value-based pricing）：是指基于顾客感知到的价值而非生产成本进行定价的策略。

- 超值定价法（good-value pricing）：是指以公平的价格提供质量和良好服务的合适组合。

- 附加价值定价法（value-added pricing）：是指一些公司通过提供具有附加价值的功能和服务来保持相对较高的价格，以将其产品与竞争对手区分开来，这些附加价值能支撑高价格。

- 需求的价格弹性（price elasticity of demand /PED）：是指需求量变化相对价格变化的程度，通常用百分比表示。

- 市场撇脂定价法（market skimming pricing）：是指将新产品价格定得很高，以从愿意支付高价的顾客身上攫取最大利润的策略。

- 市场渗透定价法（market-penetration pricing）：指为了新产品能够渗透市场，将其价格定得比较低，从而吸引大量购买者，占据较大的市场份额。

- 产品线定价法（product line pricing）：是指根据产品的成本差异或顾客对每个产品感知到的价值，为产品线中的不同产品设定不同的价格，以使产品线整体利润最大化。

- 价格点（price point）：是指价格尺度上的刻度点，而不是具体价格本身。

- 任选产品定价法（optional-product pricing）：可选或配套产品与主产品一起定价称为任选产品定价法。

- 附属产品定价法（captive product pricing）：附属产品是指那些需要与主要产品一起使用的产品，此类产品的定价称为附属产品定价法。

- 副产品定价法（by-product pricing）：是指设定副产品的价格以覆盖副产品存储和交付的成本，使主产品的价格更具竞争力。

- 产品捆绑定价法（product bundle pricing）：几种产品被组合捆绑在一起，以低于所有产品单独价格总和的价格出售，这就是产品捆绑定价法。

- 折扣（discount）：是购买特定商品所享受的直接降价。

- 进货折扣（purchase discount）：是企业提供给及时付款的客户，通常是分销商的折扣。

- 数量折扣（quantity discount）：是提供给购买大量商品的客户的折扣。

- 推广定价法（promotional pricing）：指产品的价格偶尔会低于正常价格甚至低于其成本，以营造一种购买的兴奋感和紧迫感。

- 顾客差别定价法（customer-segment pricing）：在顾客差别定价法中，相同的产品或服务针对不同的顾客收取不同的价格。

- 产品形式定价法（product-form pricing）：根据产品形式而非价格对不同版本的产品收取不同的价格。
- 地点定价法（location pricing）：在不同地点提供的产品定价不同，即使在不同地点销售该产品的成本相同。
- 时间定价法（time pricing）：是指在不同的季节、月份、日子甚至时间段，以不同的价格提供产品或服务。
- 心理定价法（psychological pricing）：是指考虑到价格产生的心理效应的定价策略。
- 参考价格（reference price）：是客户在考虑特定产品的价格时心目中所参考的价格。
- 地理区域定价法（geographical pricing）：是指针对不同地理区域的顾客定价不同。
- 平行进口（parallel importing）：是指将拟销往国外的货物重新进口回到国内市场，并以低于公司目标价格的价格销售。

Chapter Eight Place

- 营销渠道 / 分销渠道（marketing channel/distribution channel）：由多个独立的、帮助消费者或企业用户获得或使用产品的机构组成。
- 渠道整合（channel integration）：是指渠道成员之间进行整合的模式，既包括由独立生产商和中间商组成的传统营销渠道，也包括由一个渠道成员拥有的整个分销渠道。
- 传统的营销渠道（conventional marketing channels）：由松散连接的独立生产商、批发商和零售商组成的渠道，每个角色都以最大化自己的利润为目标。
- 垂直营销系统（vertical marketing system /VMS）：由一个渠道成员控制整个分销渠道，生产商、批发商和零售商统一行动。控制权有三个来源，即某个成员对渠道的所有权、成员之间的契约或源自大规模或庞大运营规模的经济权力。
- 合同式垂直营销系统（contractual VMS）：由个体生产商和中间商通过合同联合在一起，目的是实现规模经济。
- 管理式垂直营销系统（administered VMS）：是指一个渠道成员源于其规模或运营规模获得控制。
- 多渠道分销系统（multichannel distribution system）：当生产商使用不同的分销渠道将产品销往不同的市场时，就形成多渠道分销系统。
- 密集型分销（intensive distribution）：旨在通过向各个市场的大量经销店供应商品来扩大市场覆盖率。
- 选择性分销（selective distribution）：是指生产商在某个市场中选择有限数量的特定经销店来销售其产品。
- 独家经销（exclusive distribution）：是指生产商在某一特定市场只选择一个批发商、零售商或分销商来销售其产品。

Chapter Nine Promotion

- 整合营销传播（integrated marketing communication）：仔细整合通过不同的渠道传递的清晰的、一致的、能够体现竞争力的信息，这一过程称为"整合营销传播"。
- 理性诉求（rational appeal）：理性诉求鼓励人们的自利行为，声称产品具有某些好处或强调其在质量、性能、经济性或价值方面的独特卖点或突出特征。
- 感情诉求（emotional appeal）：感情诉求试图调动人们悲观或乐观情绪作为购买动机。

- 道德诉求（moral appeal）：针对的是人们的正义感。

- 广告（advertising）：由特定赞助商付费，进行非个人展示和推广创意、产品或服务的一种推广形式。

- 告知型广告（informative advertising）：旨在创造对产品、服务、组织、人员、地点、创意或事业等的初始需求。

- 说服型广告（persuasive advertising）：是试图增加人们对现有产品、服务、组织、人员、地点、创意或事业的需求。

- 提醒型广告（reminder advertising）：在公众面前反复提及产品、服务、组织、人员、地点、创意或事业，以增强先前推广活动的效果。

- 目标和任务匹配法（the objective and task method）：不是根据销售额、竞争对手的广告支出或公司可用的最大资源来设置广告预算，而是将预算与传播目标和实现这些目标所需的任务成本联系起来。

- 促销（sales promotion）：一种短期激励措施，旨在通过各种促销手段（例如优惠、免费礼品和折扣）来鼓励消费者购买或贸易商销售产品或服务。

- 减价优惠（money-off）：指通过降价直接为消费者提供价值。

- 优惠包装（bonus pack）：通过提供额外的产品数量但保持价格不变的形式提供附加值，通常用于饮料、洗涤剂、牙膏等。

- 优惠价（premium）：为了激励消费者购买而提供免费或低价格的产品。

- 优惠券（coupon）：是购买者在购买指定产品时获得优惠的凭证。

- 公共关系（public relations /PR）：通过积极正面地宣传、树立良好的企业形象、处理或消除对企业不利的谣言和事件，与所有利益相关者建立和管理良好关系的过程。

- 赞助（sponsorship）：旨在获得宣传、创造娱乐机会、促进与品牌或公司的积极联想、改善社区关系并创造促销机会。

- 品类独家赞助权（category exclusivity）：是在一个活动中，每个产品类别只能有一个赞助商。

- 人员推销（personal selling）：由公司的销售人员进行产品推销，以卖出产品和与顾客建立关系。

- 直接营销（direct marketing）：直接营销涉及与精心确定的目标消费者直接沟通，在沟通过程中可得到立即回应。

- 直邮营销（direct mail marketing）：是指通过邮政服务将信函、小册子、样品、CD 和 DVD 等材料寄到收件人的指定地址。

- 目录营销（catalogue marketing）：是指通过邮寄或在商店中将产品目录分发给代理商和顾客的方式来销售产品。

- 电话营销（telemarketing）：是指使用电话直接向客户销售产品。

- 直接响应电视营销（direct-response TV marketing）：包括直接响应电视广告和家庭购物频道两种形式。

- 社交媒体营销（social media marketing）：是使用社交媒体在线对顾客进行营销传播，并让他们参与这个传播过程。

- 移动营销（mobile marketing）：是指通过移动设备（包括智能手机和平板电脑）进行的营销传播。

- 产品植入广告（product placement）：是一种新的非面对面销售形式，产品和 / 或其标志被故意植入在电影、电视、歌曲和视频游戏中，通常是需要付费的。

- 展览（exhibition）：是一种在商业环境中将买家、卖家和竞争对手聚集在一起的促销工具。

- 环境广告（ambient advertising）：是指在不寻常的物品上或通常不会看到广告的不寻常的地方投放广告，例如购物袋、邮政包裹的包装纸、汽油泵喷嘴、街道人行道和公路的广告牌上。
- 游击营销（guerrilla marketing）：是指通过低成本、创造性的非常规手段，用几乎"伏击"消费者以吸引他们注意力的方式来传递促销信息。

Chapter Ten Marketing Planning

- 营销策划（marketing planning）：是组织和确定公司的营销目标，发展营销战略和战术来实现营销目标的过程。
- 公司整体战略规划（companywide strategic planning）：是指公司建立和保持其目标和能力与不断变化的市场机会之间的战略匹配的过程。
- 使命陈述（mission statement）：是关于公司在大环境下想要完成的远景目标的简要陈述。
- 业务组合（business portfolio）：是公司的一系列投资、控股、产品、业务和品牌的总和。
- 战略业务单元（strategic business unit）：是具有自己的愿景和方向的全功能业务单元。
- 波特的五力竞争模型（Porter's five forces model）：该模型解释了有些行业具有更高利润性的原因，总结出与行业吸引力相关的五大要素：新进入者的威胁、代替品的威胁、供应商的议价能力、购买者的议价能力、同业竞争者的竞争程度。
- 资源分析（resource analysis）：是企业了解其能力和资源价值的一种方法。资源分析涵盖有形资源和无形资源。
- 营销策略（marketing strategy）：营销策略明确目标市场，以及基于对最佳市场机会的分析而提出的价值主张。
- 波特的一般战略（Porter's generic strategies）：根据"波特的一般战略"，差异化战略和成本领先战略注重在广大市场和行业领域中的竞争优势，而差异化聚焦战略和成本聚焦战略则侧重在较小的细分市场中寻求能力发展。
- 营销实施（marketing implementation）：是实施营销计划，分配团队成员执行计划任务，设定完成任务的期限，以实现营销目标的过程。
- 营销控制（marketing control）：是公司管理人员分析和评估他们的营销活动和计划，并采取纠正措施以确保目标实现的过程。